Phenomenology and
the social world

International Library of Sociology

Founded by Karl Mannheim
Editor: John Rex, University of Warwick

Arbor Scientiae
Arbor Vitae

A catalogue of the books available in the **International Library of Sociology** and other series of Social Science books published by Routledge & Kegan Paul will be found at the end of this volume.

Phenomenology and the social world

The philosophy of Merleau-Ponty
and its relation to the social sciences

Laurie Spurling

Routledge & Kegan Paul
London, Henley and Boston

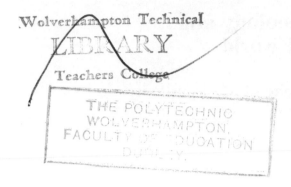
First published in 1977
by Routledge & Kegan Paul Ltd
39 Store Street,
London WC1E 7DD and
Broadway House,
Newtown Road,
Henley-on-Thames,
Oxon RG9 1EN and
9 Park Street
Boston, Mass. 02108, USA
Set in Monotype Times by
Kelly and Wright, Bradford-on-Avon, Wiltshire
and printed in Great Britain by
Lowe & Brydone

British Library Cataloguing in Publication Data

Spurling, Laurie

Phenomology and the social world. — (International library of
sociology).
1. Social sciences 2. Phenomenology
I. Title II. Series
300'.1   H91   77–30141

ISBN 0 7100 8712 8

Contents

Preface   ix

Acknowledgments   xiii

Introduction   1

1   The programme of existential phenomenology   6
    Merleau-Ponty and phenomenology   6
    Merleau-Ponty's critique of empiricism and rationalism   10
    Being-in-the-world   14
    Intentionality   16
    The body   21
    Perception   25
    Object and world   30
    The three worlds of perception   32
    The primacy of perception   34
    Space, distance, movement   35
    Time   38
    Other persons   40
    Consciousness as perceptual   42
    Consciousness as expressing   43
    A note on Merleau-Ponty's late philosophy   45

2   Speech   48
    The phenomenology of speech   48
    Speech as intersubjectivity   52
    Speech as intentionality   53
    The conceptual and gestural levels of speech   54

                                                                  v

Speech and thought   56
Sedimentation and structure   57
Speech as praxis   60
Wittgenstein: from ideal language to everyday speech   62
Ethnomethodology: the reflexivity of speech   65
The ambiguity of speech   66
Speech and the world   72
Authentic speech   73

3   Society   76

Positivism   76
Living with positivism   78
The question of meaning   81
Phenomenology and social science   84
Society as intersubjective reality   86
The concept of situation   87
The concept of structure   89

4   Marxism   94

*Existential phenomenology and Marxism: the charge of
   incompatibility*   93
The continuity between phenomenology and Marxism   98
A note on relativism and truth   103
Equivocations   105

5   Ethics   110

Description and evaluation   111
Phenomenology: the grounding of values in facts   116
Freedom   119
Freedom and responsibility   122
Freedom and moral rules   124
Authenticity   125
Self-revelation and self-deception   127
Spontaneity   130
Embodiment   132
Merleau-Ponty's humanism   134
Ambiguity and dialectic   135
An existential ethics   140

6   Philosophy   143

The reflective and the pre-reflective   143
The critique of introspection   145
Philosophy as radical reflection   146

Merleau-Ponty's conceptual revision   149
Philosophy as re-presentation   153
A note on truth and adequacy   155
Non-thematic knowledge   157
The paradox of philosophy   162

7   Conclusion
The transcendental and the descriptive   164
Phenomenology as a dialectic between the transcendental
   and the descriptive   167
Blum: the failure of the descriptive   170
Schutz and the ethnomethodologists: the failure of the
   transcendental   171
Wittgenstein: an unhappy dialectic   175
Sartre: a dialectic without synthesis   179

Notes   183

Bibliography   197
Works of Merleau-Ponty cited in the text   197
Other works cited in the text   197

Index   203

Preface

The Introduction sets the tone of this book by presenting Merleau-Ponty's existential phenomenology as a way of integrating philosophy and social science, so that a unified and coherent perspective on man in the world can be offered. This does not mean yet another philosophic system, nor a monument to pure reason, but, in fulfilment of the promise of Husserl's phenomenology, *a return to lived experience.* Phenomenology, in Merleau-Ponty's hands, is an investigation of naïve experience, that is, experience as it appears to consciousness before it has been submitted to critical or scientific reflection.

Chapter 1 gives a broad overview of Merleau-Ponty's philosophical programme. It looks at its main areas of concrete description which are presupposed in the succeeding chapters, notably the phenomenology of the body, of perception, of movement and distance, of space and time, and of other people. It also introduces us to the basic concepts of phenomenology – being-in-the-world, intentionality, embodiment, motivation, structure, expression, etc. – which define its mode of approach. These concepts aim to be grounded in naïve or lived experience and hence describe the original unity of human existence, of consciousness in-the-world, at a level more primitive (logically and phenomenologically) than that presupposed by those conceptual splits between mind/body, self/other, reason/emotion, knowledge/life, etc., which are characteristic of the thought of the natural attitude and of scientific or objective modes of thought.

Chapter 1 is, then, an introductory chapter, prior to an investigation of those areas of Merleau-Ponty's phenomenology that specifically seem to overlap the domains of conventional philosophy and social science. Chapter 2 considers the phenomenology of speech, seeking to show how the expressivity of speech, which we normally take for granted, is possible or intelligible. Linguistic meanings are taken to be a 'higher' level of meaning or significance than the primitive significance that all experience manifests in terms of its field-structure. Linguistic meanings articulate and greatly refine the primordial physiognomy of the world which is given to us by perceptual experience. Merleau-Ponty is interested in how speech is a manifestation of intentionality, of man's defining quality of transcendence, and so turns to a study of what he calls the gestural or existential level of speech, more primitive than its conceptual or intellectual level, where speech functions as a kind of praxis. The phenomenology of speech reveals another feature common to human experience: that it consists of a dialectic between sedimentation and innovation, or creativity within a structure. These themes are amplified by an excursus into Wittgensteinian philosophy and ethnomethodology and their studies of how speech actually works.

In chapters 3 and 4 we come to those areas of experience and behaviour, namely society and history, that are specifically seen as the subject matter of social science. Yet what phenomenology teaches us is that the social and historical dimensions of human existence cannot be understood in isolation from experience and behaviour as a whole.

Chapter 3 demonstrates that the dominant paradigm in social science, positivism, teaches the social scientist to treat the phenomena he studies 'objectively', to discover causal relations between empirically ascertained 'facts'. Phenomenology undercuts the whole positivist programme by looking at how 'facts' are constituted as meaningful phenomena in human experience and praxis, and hence how social experience is possible or intelligible in the first place. It reveals a core of generality or typicality inherent in all experience, and also a primitive intersubjectivity in perceptual experience, which is greatly developed and expanded in speech. Conventional social science, under the influence of positivism, investigates society as a 'thing', as a massive and inert system confronting the individual. Phenomenology puts this metaphor into perspective. It argues that the externality and objectivity of society can be understood as an extension, onto the social level, of the sedimentation and habitualization inherent in experience and existence. But this externality and objectivity, while certainly lived as real, is constituted out of human praxis and relationships sedimented over time, and has no existence apart from the experience and behaviour of those men who make it up. The objectivity of society is phenomenologically intelligible only as a sedimented intersubjectivity. We see, then, the tendency of all human existence towards the establishment of structures or *Gestalten*: on the behavioural level, where parts of the body co-ordinate to reveal a general or global functioning; and on the social level, where patterns of human interaction coalesce to form that comprehensive structure we know as society.

It is in terms of this structural patterning, as chapter 4 argues, that history is intelligible. Merleau-Ponty forges a Marxist perspective to phenomenology in order to demonstrate that history is neither a chaotic collection of accidental happenings, nor a chain of events rigidly determined by iron laws of historical development, but is an ambiguous phenomenon, an area where individual projects and praxis interact to form an overall tendency, probability, or direction to history. Thus history can be seen to have a provisional significance, or several provisional significances, as events coalesce to form structures or totalities, by means of which any individual happening is given its meaning. History, then, is comprehensible as a continual transformation of chance into pattern. The paradox of history is, like society, that man becomes estranged from these patterns, these sedimented experiences and behaviours, which are constituted out of his own praxis, and yet which, over time, become externalized and reified, so that man no longer recognizes his own projects or intentions in what he has created. This fundamental thesis of alienation, which is the basic link between phenomenology and Marxism, is rooted in lived experience, where its inescapable tendency towards habitualization and anonymity manifests a kind of primary alienation of all being-in-the-world.

The phenomenological concern with alienation puts it already into the ethical arena. Chapter 5 presents, first, a formal analysis of the relationship between philosophy and ethics, and, second, an outline of an existential ethics drawn from Merleau-Ponty's descriptions of human existence. The formal argument is, simply, that any description of being-in-the-world presupposes an implicit ethics, since there is no clear or viable distinction, in the social world, between description and evaluation. The constellation of concepts that make up an existential ethics are then elucidated: freedom, authenticity, embodiment, spontaneity, etc. They all promote a view of an *integrated* existence, a potentiality inherent in all human existence, since existence is understood phenomenologically as a series of dialectics between structures on different levels and of different kinds. It is this feature of being-in-the-world that is expressed in Merleau-Ponty's concept of ambiguity, which makes reference to the fact that any given phenomenon can be seen to belong to different structures, and hence be meaningful on different levels and in different ways.

In chapter 6 philosophy and thought, and their relation to experience, are considered. The main task of philosophic reflection, according to Merleau-Ponty, is to bring us, and help us understand unreflective experience and behaviour. But the unreflective experience of which reflection makes us aware is not pure or pristine, otherwise it would not be amenable to reflection: it is rather the unreflective-as-apprehended-by-reflection. But this is not an admission of defeat, for reflection is not cut off from the unreflective. On the contrary, all that needs to be done is to bring before our attention the pre-reflective or lived knowledge we ourselves manifest in our daily lives, for example when we say that our body knows where it has just been scratched, or that we know how to ride a bicycle or make a joke. It is such knowledge that philosophy seeks to re-activate, albeit in a certain style, by re-minding us of what we already know.

In the Conclusion, it is argued that Merleau-Ponty's phenomenology can be understood as a dialectic between a descriptive and a transcendental impulse, and it is this overall dialectical relationship that enables it to encompass, and give a coherent perspective on, being-in-the-world, and in particular those areas often considered to be the exclusive subject matter of the social sciences. It is finally suggested that this dialectic between the descriptive and the transcendental can be used to compare Merleau-Ponty's phenomenology with other versions of the relationship between philosophy and social science: that of Alan Blum, of Schutz and the ethnomethodologists, of Wittgenstein, and of Sartre.

Acknowledgments

I would like to thank, in appreciation of what I have learnt from them: my Ph.D. supervisor, Dr W. Mays, of the University of Manchester, for his help and advice; Mr P. Connerton of Gonville and Caius College, Cambridge; Peter Simons, Barry Smith and Kevin Mulligan, of the University of Manchester; Mr Jeff Coulter and Dr Ray Plant, also of the University of Manchester (and in spite of the critical remarks I have accorded them in the text); Miss Sarah-Jane Ballard, for her intellectual stimulation; my parents, for their love and continual support.

I am grateful to Mr Jules Feiffer for permission to reproduce two cartoons from the *Observer*.

Introduction

In his book *The Divided Self* (1965) R. D. Laing offers a description of a way of existing in the world known as schizophrenia. This condition is characterized by a series of deep splits: between the self and the world, between the self and others, and within the self. It is this lack of a fundamental integration in a person's experience and behaviour that Laing describes as 'being mad'. The vocabulary of current psychiatric and psychological disciplines, however, instead of attending to a diagnosis of these splits and the formulation of ways of overcoming them, tends itself to mirror and hence reinforce them:

> The words of the current technical vocabulary either refer to man in isolation from the other and the world, that is, as an entity not *essentially* 'in relation to' the other and in a world, or they refer to falsely substantialized aspects of this isolated entity. Such words are: mind and body, psyche and soma, psychological and physical, personality, the self, the organism. All these terms are abstracta. (p. 19)

It seems to me we find an analogous position in philosophy and social science today. In modern capitalist society our lives are essentially fragmented: between work and leisure, love and sex, the individual and society, 'us and them', East and West, workers and employers, and so on. These reflect, and are reflected by, those splits in terms of which we understand ourselves: mind and body, reason and emotion, masculine and feminine, etc. What is needed is a mode of understanding that can come to terms with these fragmentations and splits and offer some kind of diagnosis (=seeing-through) of our contemporary lives. We need a philosophy (in the broadest sense of the term) that will be in contact with our *experience* – at all its levels and in all its complexity – and will enable us to take a perspective on it.

1

Yet what philosophy and the social sciences have to offer us, at least in contemporary Anglo-Saxon countries, are modes of knowledge and research which are themselves fragmented and split. Philosophy and social science proceed in almost total isolation from each other. Furthermore each is cut up into various parts or subjects: philosophy into its various branches (ethics, political philosophy, modern philosophy, epistemology, metaphysics, etc.), and social science into its various subdisciplines (sociology, psychology, history, linguistics, anthropology, etc.). Neither, at present, can offer us any general understanding of ourselves and of our times.

In philosophy we still find the profound influence of positivism. For positivism philosophy – or any mode of knowledge – is conceived as the construction of an ideal logical language which has to fulfil certain methodological criteria (for example, analytical or empirical verifiability). The objects of philosophical scrutiny will be only those phenomena that can be accommodated in this special philosophical language. What is characteristic about this language is its logical precision; and hence all the obscurities, imprecision, and ambiguity of our everyday experience in the world cannot be accounted a valid subject for philosophy. Not surprisingly, the philosopher gets out of his philosophy only what he puts in: a highly formal and abstract language which can handle only those phenomena which are capable of highly formal and abstract expression. All those realms of human knowledge and experience which do not permit this treatment (for example, ethics, religion, art, sex, emotion, humour, etc., etc.) are either ignored, or re-defined in order to be put through the philosopher's mangle.

The main competitor to positivism, in Britain and America, is linguistic philosophy (otherwise known as ordinary language philosophy or conceptual analysis). In spite of the many fruitful insights of its founder, Ludwig Wittgenstein, the overall result has been a philosophy as narrowly academic as the philosophy it was intended to replace. The philosopher is now accorded the role of an intellectual plumber, to be called in when someone – professional academic or layman – gets into trouble with the workings of his language (the analogy with the Watergate Plumbers, who dealt with political rather than intellectual subversion, is perhaps not inappropriate). Linguistic philosophy concerns itself entirely with what it calls ordinary language, its uses and its misuses, and attempts to make clear how we use our words. A contemporary practitioner puts it as follows:

What specifies this book as a work of philosophy is its analytical approach to the subject, concerned to elucidate the meaning of 'community' and related concepts.

 . . . virtually no philosopher would at the present time see the

role of his activity in terms of attempts to issue directives and to formulate ideals *vis-à-vis* a pattern of activity to which he has only an external relationship. On the contrary, his role is much more second order and parasitic. He is concerned far more with the *elucidation* of concepts and ideas connected to such first order pursuits – in this particular case the idea of community. He is concerned . . . with trying to understand what the sociologist, the politically committed, the social worker and man in the street *mean* when they talk about 'community'.
(Plant, 1974, p. 2)

Now there is nothing wrong with teasing out what people mean by certain concepts or words, showing the presuppositions and system of beliefs that lie behind their choice of certain terms – indeed, this can be a very valuable exercise. But a philosophy which offers us no more than this conceptual analysis and exploration, which fails to put its findings into a more general framework so that we can see how language and its uses relate to men's behaviour, experience and whole way of living – such a philosophy can offer us very little insight into our lives. It is true that linguistic philosophers would argue that it is not their function to provide such insights, and they explicitly dissociate themselves from all attempts at constructing a 'life-philosophy'. Nevertheless, a philosophy which seeks to put forward a general philosophic understanding of man in the world, from those fundamental layers of experience such as perception and sexuality, to less primitive layers such as language and intellection, will not necessarily only result in a simplistic and naïve issue of directives and formulation of pious ideals (although *any* philosophy will secrete a certain ethical view of the world, and hence will be engaged – tacitly or otherwise – in offering directives and ideals). Indeed, it will be my argument that an overall philosophical perspective, as provided by Merleau-Ponty, will be able to locate such insights or contributions to knowledge offered by linguistic philosophers or others within a general understanding of man in the world. In short, it is my contention that Merleau-Ponty puts Wittgenstein into perspective, and not vice versa.

The situation of the contemporary social sciences is no better. Again the dominant paradigm is positivism, or some version of it, in which social science is seen as the collection of 'facts', a 'fact' being defined as that which is thrown up by the positivist methodology. Even approaches that attempt to go beyond positivism often start from positivist premises (see, for example, Pollner's (1974) critique of Becker). Furthermore, alternatives that seek to be explicitly phenomenological – such as the work of Schutz and some ethnomethodologists – and which aim to re-orient the social sciences away from the schematism and abstraction of positivism, still fail to elucidate adequately our lived experience and provide a perspective for self-understanding (see my Conclusion).

The two general approaches to the study of man in society that have offered such a comprehensive framework, namely Marxism and psychoanalysis, have been largely ignored by Anglo-Saxon academics in philosophy, and, until fairly recently, in social science. And even when they have been taken up, it has usually been in positivist versions. The hermeneutic interpretations of Marx and Freud that are commonplace on the Continent, and which are embodied in the work of the existential phenomenologists, have made little impact in Britain.

This characterization of the contemporary scene in philosophy and social science is, of course, highly schematic and over-generalized. Yet, I believe, there is a very great and pressing sense of frustration among students and academics today that reflects the malaise in contemporary knowledge, and its inability to come to terms with our experience of living in the world. It is in this light that phenomenology, and in particular the existential phenomenology of Merleau-Ponty, can be understood. Merleau-Ponty's philosophy attempts to lay the foundations for an overall perspective that can encompass the whole range of contemporary human experience and behaviour. This desire for comprehensiveness explains the marked eclecticism of Merleau-Ponty's phenomenology, which is a mix of classical phenomenology (Husserl), classical existentialism, Hegel, Heidegger, Marxism, psycho-analysis, *Gestalt* psychology, structural linguistics and Sartrean philosophy (to mention only the most clearly defined elements). Existential phenomenology is also compatible with contributions made from more recent schools of thought, such as Wittgensteinian philosophy and ethnomethodology, as will be demonstrated.

But if Merleau-Ponty's phenomenology attempts to give a general philosophic perspective, it does not result in the construction of a rigid system of concepts which can immediately categorize human experience. As Kierkegaard put it: 'in relation to their systems most systematisers are like a man who builds an enormous castle and lives in a shack close by; they do not live in their own enormous systematic buildings' (quoted in Heaton, 1972b, p. 135). The philosophy of Merleau-Ponty continues the thrust of Kierkegaard's existentialism, which centred on human existence in its concreteness and contingency rather than system-building, so that perhaps the philosopher could recognize himself in his philosophizing. Existential phenomenology 'does not propose to connect concepts, but to reveal the immanent logic of human experience in all its sectors' (*Sense and NonSense* (p. 65), hereafter cited as SNS. A list of Merleau-Ponty's works, with the abbreviations I have used, appears in the bibliography at the end of the book). This immanent logic is brought to light in a subtle and loose philosophy, one which employs concepts that are fluid and not fully determinate nor explicit. Phenomenology provides that frame, or series of frames, through which we can view our experience and being-in-the-world in order to begin to comprehend it in all its ambiguity, profundity and essential interconnectedness. Writing of Merleau-Ponty's political philosophy in words that are applicable to his whole philosophic endeavour, Sartre (1965b, p. 194) comments:

> In many archaic religions, there are holy persons who exercise the function of *lieur*. Everything must be attached and tied by them. Merleau-Ponty played their part politically. Born of union, he refused to break it and his function was to bind.

Philosophy, for Merleau-Ponty, is an attitude of wonder in the face of the world, a constant questioning and desire for understanding, not in the hope of attaining some merely intellectual solution, nor of dissolving the paradoxes and ambiguities of life, but rather in the hope of perhaps attaining some kind of directedness or orientation. The goal of philosophy is to enable each of us to rediscover his situation in the world, not in full clarity, since we are never transparent, to ourselves, but in a way that makes the world and ourselves a bit more accessible to our understanding. Philosophy has its birth in that attitude of meditation and rumination where, in our daily lives, we try to come to terms with our lives and see what we are and where we are going. It aims to incorporate itself into our lives, and to reunite knowledge with our basic interests (Habermas, 1970b). Hence the philosopher's never-ending search for meaning in everything he finds: 'true little incidents are not life's debris, but signs, emblems and appeals' (S 313).

1 The programme of existential phenomenology

Merleau-Ponty and phenomenology

To understand Merleau-Ponty's philosophy within the history of philosophy, it would be necessary, at least, to look at the philosophies of Descartes, Kant, Hegel and Heidegger, and it would be crucial to investigate, in detail, the phenomenology of Husserl. This – the relationship between Merleau-Ponty and his intellectual predecessors – would indeed demand an opus in itself, and I have neither the intention, space nor competence to consider such a task. Rather I prefer to remain silent on this topic, and urge the reader to consult other works (such as Spiegelberg, 1971), even at the risk of promoting the false impression that Merleau-Ponty's philosophy somehow arose *sui generis*, in isolation from its philosophical heritage or contemporary context. Nevertheless, in spite of these misgivings, since Merleau-Ponty's phenomenology is so profoundly indebted to Edmund Husserl, a few very brief remarks on Husserl's programme of phenomenology are called for, if only to serve as a way into a discussion of how Merleau-Ponty viewed phenomenology. Caricature cannot be avoided at the best of times.

A fundamental theme underlying Husserl's work, especially in his later years, is his concern to transcend all beliefs or doctrines which threaten to turn philosophy into the accumulation of empirical facts. Such a philosophy he termed *naturalistic*, which he defined as 'a phenomenon consequent upon the discovery of nature, which is to say, nature considered as a unity of spatio-temporal being subject to exact laws of nature' (Husserl, 1965, p. 79). Naturalist (or positivist) philosophy modelled itself after the aims and methods of the natural sciences, and conceived of the world as a collection of things, essentially independent of consciousness or of man. There was no place, in naturalistic philosophy, for an understanding of consciousness, of ourselves and our relation to the world. Nor was there a

6

place for a philosophy seeking truths or insights that were not immediately reducible to empirical fact or generalization. In short, naturalism dissociated itself from what in the history of philosophy had become known as reason. It was the rise of naturalism which Husserl, in his last writings, identified as the cause of a 'crisis' in European culture and civilization, a crisis consisting in the seeming collapse of reason and its exteriorization and absorption in naturalism. Husserl saw only two responses to this crisis:

> The crisis of European existence can end in only one of two ways: in the ruin of a Europe alienated from its rational sense of life, fallen into a barbarian hatred of spirit; or in the rebirth of Europe from the spirit of philosophy, through a heroism of reason that will definitely overcome naturalism. (1965, p. 192)

Phenomenology was the philosophy that was going to accomplish this rebirth of reason. Phenomenology was the study of 'phenomena', of that which appears to consciousness. Hence the famous slogan 'back to the things themselves', meaning the things themselves as they originally appear to consciousness. But phenomenology was not only meant to be *descriptive* of consciousness and its acts. In his later philosophy in particular Husserl argued that phenomenology is also *transcendental*, in that the world apprehended as human and meaningful was to be understood as constituted by consciousness. Rational inquiry, for Husserl, involved searching for reasons, which in this case meant revealing the ground or origin of phenomena in consciousness (see Bruzina, 1973). Phenomenology, unlike naturalism, refused to consider the world as essentially independent of consciousness; rather, the world was understood as a *correlate* of consciousness. This is expressed in the fundamental thesis of *intentionality*, according to which all consciousness is consciousness of something, that is, any act of consciousness intends its correlate in the world. For example, any perceptual act of consciousness intends a real perceived object in the world. Emotions reveal the same intentional structure: one is frightened *of*, angry *with*, etc. Consciousness, in its acts and manifestations, is essentially directed towards the world. All its acts have both a subjective pole, consciousness itself, and an objective pole, the world.

The method Husserl advanced for investigating the intentional structure of consciousness was the *phenomenological reduction*. This was an attempt by the philosopher to suspend all his beliefs about phenomena that he has accepted on scientific or common-sense grounds in order to concentrate on recording and comprehending that which cannot be further suspended or reduced, that is, what appears to consciousness after the elimination of all our preconceptions of what *ought* to appear to consciousness. Our ordinary beliefs about what exists and what is real, and the world that is taken-for-granted in our everyday lives, are 'put into brackets', and only what naïvely appears to consciousness under the phenomenological reduction is accepted as valid evidence. The *natural attitude* – of common-sense, everyday living (and of science) in which I accept the world and the objects in it as unproblematic, taken-for-granted and given independently of consciousness – is transcended and replaced by a philosophic or transcendental attitude, in which the world, as experienced and known in the natural attitude, is understood as the intentional correlate of consciousness.

One point needs to be stressed about how Husserl viewed the phenomenological reduction: it was also what he called an *eidetic reduction*, a concern to find the 'essences' or ideal meanings of the various acts and manifestations of consciousness. Phenomenology is not interested in the contingent, the merely factual or accidental – all this falls under the phenomenological reduction, which is meant to leave us with only the essential core of consciousness and its workings. Husserl writes:

> pure phenomenology as science, so long as it is pure and makes no use of the existential positing of nature, can only be essence investigation, and not at all an investigation of being-there. . . . Phenomenology can recognize with objective validity only essences and essential relations. . . . (1965, p. 116)

Merleau-Ponty in general accepted this characterization of philosophy, and attempted to carry out a broadly phenomenological programme in his work. Like Husserl, he makes the idea of reduction central to his philosophy (although not defining it in quite the same way as Husserl, as we shall see), characterizing phenomenology as an investigation of the natural attitude from a transcendental perspective:

> It is because we are through and through compounded of
> relationships with the world that for us the only way to
> become aware of the fact is to suspend the resultant activity,
> to refuse it our complicity (to look at it *ohne mitzumachen*,
> as Husserl often says), or yet again, to put it 'out of play'. Not
> because we reject the certainties of common sense and a natural
> attitude to things – they are, on the contrary, the constant theme
> of philosophy – but because, being the presupposed basis of any
> thought, they are taken for granted, and go unnoticed, and
> because in order to arouse them and bring them to view, we
> have to suspend for a moment our recognition of them. (PP xiii)

Merleau-Ponty is particularly influenced by Husserl's latest writings, where he introduced the notion of the *Lebenswelt* to refer to the world as encountered and lived in everyday life, given in direct and immediate experience independent of scientific interpretations. The *Lebenswelt* or life-world is the setting of our common-sense, daily activities; it is the world of familiar objects, routine tasks and mundane concerns. In the natural attitude we live in the life-world, and yet, under the influence of scientific presuppositions, we apprehend it as 'objective' and external to us, existing independently of our actions and interests. Husserl saw the task of philosophy as clarifying the essential structure of the life-world and showing how it presupposed the work of consciousness. This was also Merleau-Ponty's concern; phenomenology was for him a kind of archaeology, where the structure of the life-world was to be dug out from under the sedimentation of scientific knowledge and beliefs, and its intentional roots brought to light.

Yet there is a basic change of emphasis in Merleau-Ponty's phenomenology. Whereas for Husserl any reduction was an eidetic reduction, an investigation of essences, Merleau-Ponty focused instead on human *existence*, on man in the world and his concrete and contingent way of living. Phenomenology, for Merleau-Ponty, incorporated a study of what Husserl termed 'being-there', the particular and contingent form of man's existence in the world. Hence for Merleau-Ponty, as for Heidegger and Sartre, phenomenology becomes an existential phenomenology, concerned not just with the structure of the life-world, but also with man's way of existing in the life-world. Phenomenology is no longer conceived as a study of essences, but of the relation between essences and facts. Or, to put it another way, existential phenomenology is the study of phenomena, which are both factual (they exist for consciousness) and essential (they are meaningful for consciousness).

It is in this sense that Merleau-Ponty's philosophy can be termed existentialist. Like the classical existentialists, Merleau-Ponty considers a concrete analysis of existence, with particular emphasis on action, as grounding the more traditional epistemological concerns of philosophy dealing with knowledge and thought (Macquarrie, 1973). Merleau-Ponty's existentialism is thus an attempt to bring Husserl's phenomenology 'down to earth' (in Wittgenstein's sense).

This change of emphasis involves some modification in Husserl's programme as understood by Merleau-Ponty, and in particular Husserl's conception of the phenomenological reduction (how far Merleau-Ponty has correctly understood Husserl is not here at issue). Because he stresses that man is incarnated in the world, and that all thought is founded on this fact, Merleau-Ponty argues that:

> The most important lesson which the reduction teaches us is the impossibility of a complete reduction. . . . If we were absolute mind, the reduction would present no problem. But since, on

9

the contrary, we are in the world, since indeed our reflections are carried out in the temporal flux on to which we are trying to seize (since they *sich einströmen* as Husserl says), there is no thought that embraces all our thought. (PP xiv)

Similarly, Merleau-Ponty rejects the notion that consciousness *constitutes* the world in the sense of creating it. This would make the world into the simple correlate of thought, and turn philosophy into an idealism of which, in Merleau-Ponty's eyes, Husserl is some-times guilty. But the world is not created by consciousness, it is already-there. For Merleau-Ponty consciousness is in essential dialogue with the world, and all meaning is the result of this dialogue. It is in this sense only – that any reference to the world necessarily entails a reference to consciousness – that consciousness can be said to be constituting.

Merleau-Ponty's critique of empiricism and rationalism

Husserl, at least in his last writings, envisaged phenomenology as a response to the threat of naturalism (or positivism). In similar vein, Merleau-Ponty's existential phenomenology takes off from an extended critique of two schools of philosophy, empiricism and rationalism. These Merleau-Ponty regarded as naturalistic or positivist philosophies in their prejudice in favour of an 'objective' thought, which can take into account only an 'objective' world, and so are incapable of transcending the natural attitude which, indeed, they presuppose.

The critique of empiricism occupies most of *The Structure of Behaviour* and is carried over in the *Phenomenology of Perception*. Empiricism – which includes the British empiricists and behaviour-ism – is characterized by its *atomistic* approach: all experiences or behaviours of an organism are decomposed into what are considered to be a series of basic elements – such as sensations or sense-data – or basic responses – such as reflexes. All so-called psychological processes are to be reduced to such physiological simples, and all behaviour is to be understood in terms of the external and causal relations between these simples.

The empiricist account of behaviour fails, however, because its atomistic approach cannot account for the evidence of *general* or *structural* behaviours in organisms. Behaviour is not made up of the random association of countless reflexes or stimulus-response chains – this, indeed, is characteristic only of pathological behaviour which lacks any overall organization. Normal behaviour, on the other hand, exhibits a form of general co-ordination or functioning which con-trols and orders the individual reflexes. Merleau-Ponty cites as

evidence for this general functioning the following: cases of sub-
stitutions of skills in the body, such as the ability to transfer one's
handwriting from paper to a blackboard, even though a different set
of muscles are involved; examples of detours effected when a part of
the body is unable to be used and alternative routes are provided so
that the organism can continue to function; and evidence from brain
lesions which provoke structural disorders affecting the workings of
the whole body, and hence revealing a fundamental organization of
the body. None of this can be accounted for by empiricism, which
defines behaviour as the simple response to stimuli emanating from
the environment. However, it appears that in some sense an organism
chooses its own environment. This is so because the stimulations
an organism receives from its environment arise only because the
preceding movements of the organism have exposed its receptors to
those stimulations. In other words, for Merleau-Ponty behaviour is
better understood as a dialogue or dialectic between organism and its
environment, in which each patterns the other, instead of the simple
product of environmental conditioning. Behaviour is neither conditioned nor random. It is rather an expression of the *biological
meaning* of the total situation in which it occurs:

> If I catch my toe on a root while walking, the flexor muscles of
> the foot are suddenly relaxed and the organism reacts by
> accentuating this relaxation, which will liberate my foot. If, on
> the other hand, I miss my step while coming down a mountain
> and my heel strikes the ground sharply before the sole of the
> foot, the flexor muscles are once again relaxed suddenly, but the
> organism reacts instantly by a contraction. . . . Here the
> variations of responses in the presence of analogous stimuli is
> related to the *meaning* of the stimulations in which they appear and,
> inversely, it can happen that situations which appear different
> if they are analyzed in terms of physical and chemical stimuli
> provoke analogous reactions. (SB 44–5, italics added)

This inability to account for the structural and meaningful aspects
of behaviour is a result of the empiricist notion of experience.
Experience is defined simply as the recording of sensations or impressions received from the environment. This, however, is completely artificial – it is hard to find examples of pure sensations in
our actual experience except perhaps in such cases as dozing. Our
experience does not consist of a series of isolated sensations somehow joined together, but is organized in terms of a field-structure.
We never normally experience dots of sensation, but points on a
horizon, figures on a ground, so that our experiential field is primitively patterned. But this is ignored by empiricism which isolates
experience from its context. A red seen on a white ground or on a

purple ground will not be seen as the same, yet the concept of sensation skates over such differences. Empiricism postulates a simple parallel between sensations and the nervous system, but again this is not borne out. Our retina, for example, is not homogeneous, and certain parts of it are blind to blue or red, yet I do not see any discoloured areas when looking at a blue or red surface (SNS 48). Furthermore the notion of sensation levels down all experience to the passive recording of stimulation, allowing for no differentiation between kinds of experience, or between those experiences attended to and those passed over or ignored. Empiricism seems to pay no attention to the varying degrees of attention we give to our experience which influences its intensity and duration for us.

Empiricism, then, offers only an artificial and fragmented picture of experience and behaviour. It cannot, for example, account for innovation, creativity or improvisation in behaviour, since it makes it intelligible only in terms of responding to given stimuli. Learning for empiricism can only take place on an extended 'trial-and-error' basis. But then it follows that, strictly speaking, there is no learning. The atomistic and causal preconceptions of empiricism rule out in advance any appreciation of the general alteration of behaviour and the acquisition of new goals and new meanings which occur in true learning. Finally, the physiological reductionism that empiricism practises makes it totally unsuitable for understanding the human or cultural world, since it has no conception of meaning or significance which man projects around himself, but must reduce everything it sees to simple causal and physiological mechanisms.

Turning to rationalism, which would include the philosophies of Descartes, Kant, the neo-Kantians, and some elements of Husserl and Sartre, we find a kind of philosophy which at first sight appears totally opposed to empiricism. Instead of viewing the world as a collection of externally related facts, as does empiricism, for rationalism the world is the result of the constituting processes of consciousness. It is the mind that gives meaning to the world, and its mode of operation can be grasped in pure reflection. Yet, while appearing to be totally opposed to empiricism, it can be seen that in fact rationalism trades off the empiricist view of the world. Rationalism accepts the sensations, reflexes, etc., which empiricism posits as the elementary stuff of the world and which are in themselves meaningless. It merely adds that it is mind that injects these with meaning, that joins up the dots of sensation to give a picture of the world. So, in one sense, rationalism is merely a higher level built on top of empiricism. In another sense, it can be seen as the simple inverse of empiricism. To every empiricist thesis, the phrase 'consciousness of . . .' or 'thought of. . .' is added, so that the objective world is not construed as self-sufficient, but as the creation of consciousness or thought. In either case, there is the same presupposition of an objective world which is in itself meaningless.

Merleau-Ponty's specific objections to rationalism concern its view of reflection and of consciousness:

> The world is there before any possible analysis of mine, and it would be artificial to make it the outcome of a series of syntheses which link, in the first place sensations, then aspects of the object corresponding to different perspectives, when both are nothing but products of analysis, with no sort of prior reality. Analytical reflection believes that it can trace back the course followed by a prior constituting act and arrive, in the 'inner man' – to use St. Augustine's expression – at a constituting power which has always been identical with that inner self. Thus reflection itself is carried away and transplanted in an impregnable subjectivity, as yet untouched by being and time. (PP x)

Rationalism isolates consciousness from the world, and splits the self into an outer self – in contact with the world – and an inner self – which is beyond the world. Furthermore, rationalist reflection loses sight of its own beginnings and ground in the pre-reflective or un-reflective life of man. Most of our everyday activities are not carried out in full reflective clarity: taking a walk, catching a bus, eating, smoking, watching television, etc., are unreflectively engaged in. In Ryle's (1949) terminology, 'knowing how' is more fundamental than 'knowing that'. Rationalism also forgets that reflection entails a change in the structure of consciousness, in which consciousness turns back from the world onto itself, but in so doing inaugurates a division between the consciousness that is reflecting, and the consciousness-reflected-on, hence engineering a split within con-sciousness. In short, in identifying consciousness *tout court* with reflection, rationalism cannot allow for any dialectic between the reflective and the pre-reflective levels of consciousness. Thus, like empiricism, it levels consciousness down. Instead of conceiving consciousness as the blind receptacle of stimulation from outside, it moves to the other extreme and turns consciousness into a wholly constituting and explicit enterprise, operating on the world in full self-awareness. The actual diversity and variety of types of con-sciousness – morbid, primitive, child-like, etc. – as well as cases where consciousness fails to be even potentially transparent to itself, such as insanity, self-deception, dreaming, forgetfulness, slips of the tongue and so on, are not taken seriously, and are often accredited as simple perversions of the will.

And so, in spite of their apparent differences, empiricism and rationalism converge to present a remarkably similar picture of the

13

world. Both suffer from what Merleau-Ponty terms a 'prejudice in favour of the world'. Empiricism stops there; it has no concept of consciousness or subjectivity, but only of an objective world. Rationalism conceives of consciousness as occupying some place above and beyond the objective world, which somehow endows the inherently senseless physical world with significance. For empiricism, there is no subjectivity. For rationalism, subjectivity occupies some ethereal realm where it operates on the world from a distance. Neither can conceive of any living dialogue or dialectic between the subject and the world. Both are inherently dualistic, relying on the rigid distinction between subject and object, physiology and psychology. Both are also atomistic, decomposing experience into little bits, to be joined together either by random association, or through explicit and conscious acts of *Sinngebung*. Merleau-Ponty sets himself the task of transcending both in terms of a phenomenology of existence.

Being-in-the-world

In *The Structure of Behaviour* Merleau-Ponty had already introduced the notion of *Gestalt* (synonymous with form or structure) which went beyond the analyses offered by either empiricism or rationalism, and in particular transcended the dichotomy of consciousness and nature which each presupposed. The notion of *Gestalt* refers to the ability of an organism to function in a global, structured way, exhibiting a general co-ordination of its parts oriented towards the achievement of certain goals or intentions. As such, *Gestalten* are neither empirical things (being relations between parts) nor forms of consciousness (since they are not the product of thought, and exist in organisms which do not display self-consciousness) (SB 127–8). Neither behaviour nor experience is reducible to the sum of its parts, but manifests a primitive structure. And this is amenable neither to the causal explanation of empiricism, which can conceive of only external relations between discrete entities, nor to the rationalist assumption of a pure, reflective and transparent consciousness, since the structure of behaviour and experience are normally opaque to it. In a similar way, Merleau-Ponty's focus on behaviour, on the organism in action as it meets and organizes its environment around it, achieves a transcendence of the consciousness/thing dichotomy. Behaviour is the projection and enactment of possibilities and intentions of the organism outside of itself, and expresses a certain integration of the organism with its environment:

> The gestures of behaviour, the intentions which it traces in the space around the animal, are not directed to the true world or pure being, but to being-for-the-animal, that is, to a certain

milieu characteristic of the species; they do not allow the showing
through of a consciousness, that is, a being whose whole
essence is to know, but rather a certain manner of treating the
world, of 'being-in-the-world', or of existing. (SB 125)

Existential phenomenology starts not from the assumption of an
'objective' world in-itself, nor from a pure, constituting consciousness, but from their union, or rather their transcendence in its
investigation of how organisms, and especially human organisms,
are in-the-world.

The concept of being-in-the-world is further elaborated in *Phenomenology of Perception* in Merleau-Ponty's discussion of the phenomenon of the phantom limb. This is manifested, for example, in the case
of a man who has lost his leg and who feels a phantom or imaginary
limb when he has a stimulus applied to the path from the stump to
the brain. Anaesthetics with cocaine do not do away with it, and
there are cases of phantom limbs without amputation arising as a
result of brain injury. Now the problem of understanding this
phenomenon is quite simple. There are *psychological* factors involved,
since an emotion or circumstance which recalls those in which the
initial disability happened creates a phantom limb in a subject who
had none before. But there is also need of a *physiological* explanation,
since the severance of the nerves to the brain abolishes the phantom
limb. What needs to be comprehended, then, is how the psychological
and physiological factors relate to each other (PP 77). This can only
be done by an analysis which centres on the whole mode of existence
of the subject in question, on the way he projects an environment
around himself, that is, on the way he is in-the-world. The phantom
limb is not a purely physiological phenomenon, operating below the
level of consciousness, since the subject has only to look to see he in
fact has no limb. But neither is the phantom limb purely psychological
in the rationalist sense in which the subject must 'really' know he has
no real limb. Here we are trapped in a dichotomy between ignorance
and knowledge, between absence and presence. But the subject is
neither ignorant nor knowledgeable, but only pre-reflectively and
implicitly aware of his limb. The limb is neither absent nor present
but *ambivalently* present. The phantom limb expresses an ambivalent
mode of being-in-the-world, in which the subject, through his injury,
must change his world, and yet cannot accept this:

What it is in us which refuses mutilations and disablement is an
I committed towards a certain physical and inter-human world,
who continues to tend towards his world despite handicaps and
amputations and who, to this extent, does not recognize them
de jure. The refusal of this deficiency is only the obverse of our
inherence in a world, the implicit negation of what runs counter

15

to the natural momentum which throws us our tasks, our cares, our situation, our familiar horizon. (PP 81)

The phantom limb is the expression of only one mode of being-in-the-world; in different subjects it can take different forms. Some subjects, for example, come near to blindness without fundamentally changing their world; they collide with objects, but refuse to wear glasses or acknowledge to themselves that their visual senses are seriously deficient. Other subjects, at the slightest disability, lose their world and make themselves into premature invalids (PP 79–80). In the same way, there are those people who project themselves passionately into their world, and its stability is dependent on the intensity and duration of their relationships with other people. Others, more cautious, protect their world from too close contact with possible dangers, and are content to live their lives in an ordered and measured manner.

It must be stressed that these modes of being-in-the-world are not engaged in or lived in conscious or explicit reflection. The refusal of recognition of the phantom limb, which is a refusal to reconstitute one's world, to identify oneself as a cripple and no longer to see objects as grasp-able or kick-able – this is not a *deliberate* or conscious refusal, but rather takes place at the level of pre-reflective awareness. It is the mistake of rationalist philosophies to consider our lives as made up of explicit and deliberate choices and decisions, whereas in fact our life is directed on a pre-conscious level, so that conscious deliberation often has the form of *post factum* rationalization.

There is, then, a certain consistency in our 'world', relatively independent of stimuli, which refuses to allow us to treat being-in-the-world as a collection of reflexes – a certain energy in the pulsation of existence, relatively independent of our voluntary thoughts, which prevents us from treating it as an *act* of consciousness. It is because it is a preobjective view that being-in-the-world can be distinguished from every third person process, from every modality of the *res extensa*, as from every *cogitatio*, from every first person form of knowledge – and that it can effect the union of the 'psychic' and the 'physiological'. (PP 80)

Intentionality

The notion of being-in-the-world is broadly synonymous with a number of other terms which appear in Merleau-Ponty's writings, and which he employs to define human reality; *existence*, which has the connotation of standing out or emerging (ex-isting); *transcendence*, which expresses man's defining capacity for being constantly engaged in transcending or surpassing the given; *praxis*, which Merleau-Ponty defines as 'the ensemble of activities by which man transforms physical and living nature' (SB 162); *style*, which is the 'preconceptual generality' (PW 44) or pre-thematic unity of any series of activities; and, finally, *intentionality*, that crucial concept of Husserl's which Merleau-Ponty takes up, but with a changed emphasis.

Intentionality means that all consciousness is consciousness of something, that it is in original and primitive contact with the world, and is oriented towards that world. As there are different ways for consciousness to be in-the-world, so there are different ways for consciousness to intend its object. Some intentions are clear to themselves; some, on the other hand, are 'lived' rather than known. For example, we may have an impression of something not quite right or out of place in a room we have just entered, without being able to say exactly why. It is only later that we discover the reason for our impression: the asymmetrical position of a picture frame (SB 173). In a similar way, we can build up a remarkably accurate picture of someone from the way he dresses, or the room in which he lives, without being able to spell out the exact logic of our deductions, or indeed enumerate all the details of his clothes or furniture (for example, the colour of his shirt or bedspread). In an attempt to do justice to these different levels of intentionality, Merleau-Ponty, claiming support from Husserl, makes a basic and crucial distinction between two kinds of intentionality; *intentionality of acts*, which is that of our judgments and express volitions when we consciously and voluntarily take up a position; and *operative or fungierende intentionality*, which is only brought to light through the phenomenological reduction, and which Merleau-Ponty characterizes as:

> that which produces the natural and ante-predicative unity of the world and of our life, being apparent in our desires, our evaluations and in the landscape we see, more clearly than in objective knowledge, and furnishing the text which our knowledge tries to translate into precise language. (PP xviii)

It is this notion of operative intentionality which Merleau-Ponty sees as the most profound sense of intentionality, and which phenomenology seeks to elucidate (so that when Merleau-Ponty refers to intentions, he will mean operative intentions rather than express or conscious intentions, unless he indicates otherwise).[1]

Operative intentionality is that intentionality by which consciousness projects a human setting around itself, a setting in which it lives. What distinguishes it from intentionality of acts, from posited intentions, is that operative intentionality is ante-predicative, non-thematic, in fact the ground of any explicit and voluntary acts of intentionality, as well as all acts of judgment and discursive reasoning.

17

It is a relationship of being rather than of knowing: 'the unity of the world, before being posited by knowledge in a specific act of identification, is "lived" as ready-made or already-there' (PP xvii). It is evident in, for example, the fact that the choices we make in our lives are for the most part existential or pre-thematic, resting on deep-seated existential patterns which are expressed in our acts and decisions like the theme of a play. The 'will' – that often convenient fiction of philosophers and moralists – is in fact usually invoked when we consciously try to go against some deeper movement, as when we *try* to relax when we are tense, or *try* to go to sleep when there are 'things on our mind'. In a similar way, we have express intentions, for example a plan to climb a particular mountain, which might not even be explicitly formulated to ourselves or to others, and in terms of which I will evaluate my environment, for example in seeing this mountain as climbable and that mountain as too steep or high. But it is a more profound operative intentionality which in general evaluates the potentialities of my whole environment, so that objects appear as graspable or out of reach, inviting or threatening, as obstacles or aids (PP 440). Again, our sexual or affective life is not explicable either in terms of blind, involuntary impulses, nor as explicit acts carried out in full self-awareness, but as a kind of pre-thematic patterning of the world. In the natural attitude, before we explicitly attend to them, objects and people have a certain sexual physiognomy for us, and are experienced as having a certain emotional or erotic colour or style. Whether we like it or not, certain faces are attractive or unattractive to us, certain people arouse us sexually and others do not, certain actions and objects carry erotic connotations while others leave us cold.

Because operative intentionality is pre-thematic, and is the ground of all our explicit acts of reflection or intention, it is extremely difficult to catch it at work, for it is 'concealed behind the objective world which it helps to build up' (PP 138, n. 2). One method of describing it is to attend to our pre-reflective or naïve experience as closely as possible, in an attempt to reveal, or at least catch a glimpse of its intentional ground. This is illustrated in the descriptions of our naïve experience of the body, of perception, space, time, movement, etc., which occupy much of *Phenomenology of Perception* and which are briefly explicated in this chapter. All of these examples of lived experience express the same theme, of consciousness intentionally patterning a world around itself. But since it makes no sense to speak of consciousness in isolation from the world, or the world apart from consciousness, Merleau-Ponty conceives of intentionality as a two-way process, in which both consciousness and the world are patterned through their intercourse. Thus, although it might appear surprising, Merleau-Ponty ascribes intentionality to phenomena in the world:

'The sensation of blue . . . is doubtless intentional, that is to say, it does not rest in itself like a thing, that it aims towards and signifies outside of itself' (quoted in Zaner, 1971, p. 183).

But there is another method for apprehending operative intentionality, which Merleau-Ponty also uses for elucidating the notion of being-in-the-world, namely the method of describing cases of its breakdown which would throw into relief its normal functioning. The workings of operative intentionality can be read off from what fails to appear when it breaks down – not in the sense, however, of a simple subtraction of parts from the normal to the pathological, as though the difference was quantitative, but in the sense of understanding the qualitative change of behaviour from the normal to the pathological, a change in the level of the overall significance of the behaviour. Merleau-Ponty considers at some length the case of a patient called Schneider, whose brain was initially damaged by a shell, and whose general behaviour manifests a persistent and structural form of pathology. For example, if he is ordered to perform an abstract movement with his eyes shut, Schneider has to go through a whole series of preparatory operations in order to 'find' the operative limb and the direction, pace and correct plane of the movement.

> If, for instance, he is ordered to move his arm, with no detail
> as to how, he is first of all perplexed. Then he moves his whole
> body and after a time his movements are confined to the arm,
> which the subject eventually 'finds'. (PP 109)

The patient seems to experience his body as an amorphous mass into which actual movement itself introduces divisions and links. There is no general impairment of movement – the patient can move his body as requested – nor of thought – the order is understood and eventually correctly executed. It is not even the capacity for abstract thought that is lacking, for Schneider can carry out quite complex abstract operations by the laborious method of working out hypotheses and then putting them into operation. What is lacking is something more profound, what Merleau-Ponty terms *motor intentionality*, that form of operative intentionality upon which any successful movement or thought is grounded, and which enables the normal subject to 'home in' on the essentials of any command and carry it out spontaneously. In normal subjects the body is an expressive and lived unity of its parts, so that all movements are undertaken and enacted intuitively and as a whole from beginning to end, without any kind of thematic intellection or working out. Schneider, however, is unable to pattern his actions; he evolves either an ideal formula for the action or launches himself into a series of blind efforts in an attempt to perform it. He lacks what is presupposed in any normal action: the background of its envisaged

19

completion, so that the whole movement is oriented and directed from the start (see C. Smith, 1964a, p. 120 onwards). Schneider experiences his body not as an intentional unity, but as a series of isolated parts, so that he has to think through his actions instead of living in them (it should be noted that the case of Schneider fits the rationalist view of being in-the-world remarkably well, in which all activity has an explicit and thematic intellectual component to it; rationalism, like empiricism, seems more suited to describing pathological existence than normal functioning).

Because he experiences no expressive unity in his body, Schneider finds none in the world. The world has lost its physiognomy for him: it no longer calls forth emotional responses from him, or only blunted ones, nor can he experience it as the receptacle of his own projects. He lives in a world levelled down, in an alien world. His behaviour is stereotyped and rigid. He never sings or whistles of his own accord. He never takes any sexual initiative and sees women as neither attractive nor unattractive. He does not go out on walks, but only on errands. He rarely speaks spontaneously, but only in accord with a plan drawn up in advance. He can understand questions relating to his here-and-now situation, but cannot make sense of hypothetical or negative questions. He cannot play act by putting himself in an imaginary situation. Schneider illustrates a basic disturbance of operative intentionality and reveals how normal being-in-the-world can be understood as a projection of what Merleau-Ponty calls an *intentional arc*:

> the life of consciousness – cognitive life, the life of desire or perceptual life – is subtended by an 'intentional arc', which projects round about us our past, our future, our human setting, our physical, ideological and moral situation, or rather which results in our being situated in all these respects. It is this intentional arc which brings about the unity of the senses, of intelligence, of sensibility and motility. And it is this which 'goes limp' in illness. (PP 136)

In its extreme form, a breakdown of operative intentionality, the failure to project an intentional arc, results in insanity. The world is no longer experienced as a living, meaningful unity, but as fragmented and alien. A schizophrenic says:

> A bird is twittering in the garden. I can hear the bird and I know that it is twittering, but that it is a bird and that it is twittering, the two things seem so remote from each other. . . . There is a gulf between them, as if the bird and the twittering had nothing to do with each other. (PP 282)

With the collapse of intentionality and the fragmentation of the

20

world comes a breakdown in the experience of space, in the replacement of perceptions by hallucinations, and of time, illustrated in the freezing of the present and the death of the future exhibited in schizophrenia.

The body

We have already made mention, in the discussions of being-in-the-world and intentionality, of the role of the body, which is that by means of which consciousness is situated in the world. Merleau-Ponty rejects the conception of a pure, spectator consciousness, and turns instead to the evidence of experience, which reveals consciousness as *embodied* or incarnated in a situation. Thus, for Merleau-Ponty, the study of consciousness in the world is a study of consciousness as embodied, and hence a study of the body as experienced, or what Merleau-Ponty sometimes calls the lived body or body proper.

Empiricism and rationalism could only acknowledge an *objective body*, the body considered as a physical object in the world, made up of flesh, bone and blood. The body as objective is the body we find in the accounts of anatomy and physiology, the body as an object for medicine. But, while the body is in one sense an object, if we look at our lived experience of the body we realize that it is not like other objects in the world. Whereas I move external objects by means of my body, which shifts them from one place to another, I do not move my body in this way. Instead I move my body directly, or, to put it another way, my body moves itself, since it is always with me. I do not find my body at one point in space and transfer it to another, since I have no need to look for it (PP 94). It is by means of my body that I can observe objects and situate myself in relation to them. But I cannot observe my body in the same way, there is no perspective I can gain on the whole of my body, since it is my body which enables me to have a perspective, as it is my body that enables me to move. Now rationalism was not unaware of these facts; but since it could only move from the notion of object to that of pure thought, it could not conceive of any synthesis between these two notions, which meant it had to somehow relate a physical, objective body to a pure, non-physical mind. This resulted in the doctrine of the 'ghost in the machine', where the body was considered to be the physical container of an ethereal mind. This left, however, the insoluble problem of how mind, which occupies no place in physical space or time, could in any way be related to the physical body (see also Ryle, 1949).

Merleau-Ponty overcomes this dilemma by refusing to start from the opposition between a physical body and a pure, non-physical

21

mind. He grounds them both onto the more primitive (in a logical or phenomenological sense) level of being-in-the-world, of which the lived body is the intentional expression. There is, for example, a kind of latent knowledge (in the sense of knowing how) manifested by my body, an awareness of itself which is not explicable as the work of a non-corporeal mind somehow operating on the body. In describing the body as it appears to our naïve experience, we are brought to acknowledge the existence of a *body image* which functions below the level of our conscious reflection:

> If my arm is resting on the table I should never think of saying that it is *beside* the ash-tray in the way in which the ash-tray is beside the telephone. The outline of my body is a frontier which ordinary spatial relations do not cross. This is because its parts are inter-related in a peculiar way: they are not spread out side by side, but enveloped in each other . . . my whole body for me is not an assemblage of organs juxtaposed in space. I am in undivided possession of it and I know where each of my limbs is through a *body image* in which all are included. (PP 98)

The body image reveals a *phenomenal body*, which enables us to know, for example, where we have just been stung by a mosquito without having to search for the spot in objective space, or where the parts of our body are that are hidden from view. When we reach for an object, we look at the object, not at our hand, since the co-ordination of our body is not something we have to consciously attend to, but is pre-reflectively apprehended in terms of the functional values of its various parts in terms of our particular project at hand. So, for example:

> If I am sitting at my table and I want to reach the telephone, the movement of my hand towards it, the straightening of the upper part of the body, the tautening of the leg muscles are super-imposed on each other. I desire a certain result and the relevant tasks are spontaneously distributed amongst the appropriate segments. (PP 149)

The phenomenal body is to be understood as an 'expressive unity', a 'synergic system', to be compared not to a physical object but to a work of art. It is the seat of intentionality, so that in projecting itself onto the world, it makes the world the arena for my intentions. My body is also able to extend its hold on the world through the use of instruments or tools. A blind man's stick, for example, is no longer an external object for him, but an extension of his own (phenomenal) body in which he is able to feel the pavement through his stick, as the key-bank of a typewriter, or the controls of a car, are incorporated into the body of an experienced typist or driver.

22

The unity and synergy of the body are not things that need to be constantly achieved, but tend towards *sedimentation*, so that the skills and habits acquired by my body in its movements and use of instruments become permanently available for future use. The formation of habits and skills expresses 'our power of dilating our being in the world, or changing our existence by appropriating fresh instruments' (PP 143). This sedimentation or acquisition of behaviours which then function quasi-automatically, serve as a ground for my being-in-the-world, freeing the energy and attention of the body and allowing it to evolve novel ways of acting and relating. This dialectic between sedimentation and innovation in fact defines the way my body is in-the-world.

The study of the body as experienced can be seen to raise two kinds of problems. The first concerns the relation between mind and body, the second the relation between the objective and phenomenal body. With regard to the first problem, it has been objected by some commentators that Merleau-Ponty's thesis of embodiment, the unity of mind and body, manages in fact to liquidate all cases where mind can be distinguished from the body, and instead of exploring their interrelation Merleau-Ponty simply dissolves mind into the body.[2] However, it is not true that Merleau-Ponty assimilates consciousness or mind into the body. He argues instead that the relationship between mind and body is ambiguous, since in one sense consciousness cannot be conceived except as embodied (cf. 'I am my body'), and yet in another sense there are times when we can identify consciousness as distinct from, although still related to, the body (cf. 'I have a body'). The relation between mind and body is understood phenomenologically in terms of the notions of *integration* and *Gestalt*. The terms consciousness (or mind) and body are, if you like, ideal-types, neither of which can exist in isolation from the other, and both of which function as two subordinate structures which can be integrated in different ways and to different degrees. There is dualism, a distinction between consciousness and the body, when, for example, my body is ill, and I experience it as an impediment to my projects, or when hunger, thirst or sexual desire prevent my thoughts or emotions from surfacing. Again, there are times, in timidity or embarrassment for example, where I do not experience my body as the spontaneous expression of my intentions, but as a barrier or mask separating 'myself' from the world. There are also times when, in 'flights' of imagination or fantasy, I experience myself as no longer 'in' my body. There is, then, a 'truth of dualism' (SB 209). But this dualism can only be partial and provisional, since if consciousness should be totally loosened from its anchorage in the body, it would have no means of expression, of actualizing itself, and so would literally cease to be. Similarly, my body, if it is no longer 'animated'

23

and ceases to be the expression of the intentionality of consciousness, would no longer be a living body, but would fall back into the state of a physical-chemical mass. In the same way, there are times of almost total integration between consciousness and body, in those moments when we are truely 'at home' in our bodies (such as, perhaps, sexual intercourse) and experience our body, not as a screen between us and the world, but as our opening onto the world. Nevertheless, this integration is never absolute and it always fails, since it depends on the interrelation of distinct structures (SB 210). Integration between mind and body, even if always partial and provisional, always occurs, however, since both structures are grounded on a level even more fundamental, namely our whole mode of being-in-the-world or existence. And so:

> Man taken as a concrete being is not a psyche joined to an organism, but the movement to and fro of existence which at one time allows itself to take corporeal form and at others moves towards personal acts. Psychological motives and bodily occasions may overlap because there is not a single impulse in a living body which is entirely fortuitous in relation to psychic intentions, not a single mental act which has not found at least its germ or its general outline in physiological tendencies. (PP 88, italics added)

In the same way the question of the relation between the objective and phenomenal body (which de Waehlens (1970) raises as a possible area of difficulty for some commentators) can be understood in terms of each representing two layers or structures which in actual functioning are integrated to a varying extent. The objective body can be understood as the depository of those automatic physiological processes that make up a large part of our relationship with the world, making my body always vulnerable to physical disease or injury. Indeed, the rhythms of sleep, hunger, thirst, sex, etc., provide a constant background and overall style to all our activities. The distinction between the objective and phenomenal body is one between two layers, or two significations: the body as physiological organism, and as the expression and real-ization of my intentions, projects and desires. In any concrete case we find different degrees of integration or non-integration between them. For example, the distortions of El Greco's paintings are not simply the result of some physical anomaly of vision, but are an expression of the interplay between this physiological fact and its integration into El Greco's whole mode of being-in-the-world:

> When irremedial bodily peculiarities are integrated with the whole of our experience, they cease to have the dignity of a

cause in us. A visual anomaly can receive a universal signification by the mediation of the artist and become for him the
occasion of perceiving one of the 'profiles' of human existence.
The accidents of our bodily constitution can always play this
revealing role on the condition that they become a means of
extending our knowledge by the consciousness which we have
of them, instead of being submitted to as pure facts which
dominate us. Ultimately, El Greco's supposed visual disorder
was conquered by him and so profoundly integrated into his
manner of thinking and being that it appears finally as the
necessary expression of his being much more than as a peculi-
arity imposed from the outside. (SB 203)

Perception

It is in terms of a phenomenological description of perceptual
experience that Merleau-Ponty considers that the relations between
consciousness and the world are most clearly and profoundly
evident. Once again, his descriptions take off from a critique of the
accounts of perception offered by empiricism and rationalism. For
empiricism, perception is a passive recording of sense-data received from the environment, which then become associated to
form distinct objects. Rationalism introduces thought or judgment
as that which interprets these inherently meaningless impressions of
the outside world received by consciousness. What we are offered is
perception either as a blind, undirected, mechanical process, or as
the same process but with acts of intellection superimposed on them.
In both cases there is presumed to be a basic dichotomy between
subject and object, inside and outside, and the assumption of a
physical world determinate and explicit in itself, which is simply
recorded by consciousness. Both empiricism and rationalism trade
off the *constancy hypothesis*, which asserts that, the objective world
being given, it passes onto our sense-organs messages which are
registered and then deciphered so as to reproduce the original text.
There is then considered to be a point-by-point correspondence and
causal relation between the stimulations or sense-data from the
environment and our elementary perceptions (PP 7).

A brief consultation of our naïve perceptual experience, however,
reveals that the constancy hypothesis is not a *description* of how we
perceive, but a *construction* or 'scientific' idealization positing, in
accord with 'scientific' presuppositions about valid knowledge,
how we *ought to* perceive. Our actual perceptual experience bears
witness to a primitive patterning of our perceptions into visual fields,
with horizons of indeterminacy and points of clear vision. That is,
all perception has the form of a figure/ground structure, and all

perceptual objects are perceived in terms of their context (ground, horizon). Furthermore, what happens to be the figure and what the ground in any perception depends on how we focus our gaze, on our interests at hand, as much as on the perceptual object(s). Perception itself, through its primitive patterning, *causes there to be* figures and grounds, determinate objects with their indeterminate horizons, so that 'normal functioning must be understood as a process of integration in which the text of the external world is not so much copied as composed' (PP 9). Perception *structures* the perceived world; it is not so much the passive recording of sense-data as an expression of our perceptual intent. This is illustrated by the fact of perceptual gaps, where, for example, a face may be perceived as familiar without the colour of the eyes being registered. Perceptual gaps are not simple failures to perceive but evidence that we perceive in accord with our interests and purposes at hand. Neither does perception depend on specific acts of interpretation by consciousness. In the natural attitude we 'live' in perception, apprehending perceptual subjects as charged with emotion or significance, as having an immanent sense which is prior to any explicit acts of intellection on our part. For example, a football player does not perceive the football field as an 'object', but as an area demarcated from the crowd of spectators, cut up into lines of force (the goals, the touch lines, etc.), which motivate, call forth and direct his actions, and enable him to participate in the game without the player bringing any of this to his explicit attention. 'The field itself is not given to him, but is present as the immanent term of his practical intentions' (SB 169). In short, the perceived world, as it appears to perceptual consciousness, does not consist of a vast number of spatiotemporally distinct objects which it is the task of perception to record and reproduce, but rather of a system of interlocking visual fields, grounds and figures, allowing distinct and individuated objects to emerge only from a background of unclarity, and making perception synonymous with a primitive patterning of the perceived world. For perception, 'there are no things, only physiognomies' (SB 168).

Whereas empiricism made perception into a simple automatic process, like the working of a camera, rationalism, while trading off this view at a basic level, superimposed upon it acts of judgment or intellection. For empiricism, perception is purely physiological, for rationalism it consists in two distinct layers, the physiological (recording sense-data) and the psychological (acts of interpretation). Phenomenology shows, however, that perception is neither purely physiological and automatic, nor purely psychological and reflective, nor even a mixture of these which preserves the distinction, but is a *pre-reflective* (pre-conscious, non-thematic) intercourse with the world which, like all manifestations of being-in-the-world, blurs the distinction between the physiological and psychological. Perception is a primitive openness to the world: indeed, it has something anonymous or impersonal about it, in that perception entails a certain sensitivity to colours, forms, outlines, etc., which never reach the level of reflection. I do not perceive the blue of the sky in the same way I decide to read a book or become a lawyer, since these are expressly personal acts which create a situation for me, whereas my perception of blue is a pre-personal opening of my body to the sensation of blue. 'So, if I wanted to render precisely the perceptual experience, I ought to say that *one* perceives in me, and not that I perceive' (PP 215).

Nevertheless rationalism is not entirely wrong in making perception a series of explicit acts of intellection, since perception is not wholly an impersonal affair, but incorporates a whole range of experiences from the explicitly reflective to the totally unreflective and impersonal. For example, if I am looking at some sheets of white paper and do not analyse my perception, the sheets look equally white. If, however, I focus on them, the sheets change their appearance, and some now appear grey. That is, by focusing, by turning critically and judgmentally towards what I am seeing, I separate the region under scrutiny from its ground, and thus interrupt the visual field which had assigned to each part its determinate colouration. In other words, the whiteness of the paper does not lend itself to precise classification within the white – black range in my unanalysed perception. It is only by explicitly focusing, by asking myself what it is that I see, that I have turned the greyness of the sheets of paper into a *quality* of that paper (PP 226). There are, then, explicit acts of perception, in cases of focusing in order to make out what it is we see, or in cases of ambiguous perception where we are not sure what we do see. In these cases we interrupt our uncritical and total absorption in the visual spectacle in order to interpretatively put together the elements of perception to give meaning to what we see and assign it its particular features and qualities. Nevertheless these represent only a relatively small class of perceptions, and presuppose that spontaneous vision which puts me in direct contact with the world, and which I unreflectively live in. 'Perception is not a science of the world, it is not even an act, a deliberate taking up of a position; it is the background from which all acts stand out, and is presupposed by them' (PP x – xi).

Perception is not the operation of pure mind or thought – which is not to deny that perception contains elements of thought – but is *embodied*. I perceive with my body, since the position and movement of my body both enables me to see and determines what is accessible to my vision. The theory of the body is already a theory

27

of perception. The anonymity which is there when I open myself entirely to my perceptual field functions as the ground or base layer of all perceptions, in the same way that my objective body is a layer presupposed in all the operations of my phenomenal body. Indeed, my visual field, since it is animated and patterned by my phenomenal body which is oriented towards its tasks and interests at hand and engaged in marking out possible areas of activity in the world, is also a phenomenal field.[3] Now the fact that my perception is embodied means that it is *perspectival*. If I attend to my actual perceptual experience, I will become aware that I only see 'profiles' of any object, that is, I see it at any given moment from one side at a time. Now, of course, subsequent perceptions can 'fill out' the perceived object as I move round it and view it from different sides and angles – nevertheless, at any given moment, I can see no more than my perspective allows. Objects in perceptual experience, therefore, never appear in full determinacy, since I can never see an object from all sides at once.

In the natural attitude, however, I am unaware of perspective, and believe my perception reaches the things themselves. Here we seem to have a contradiction: on the one hand, we critically experience perception as perspectival; on the other hand, we naïvely experience perception as direct access to the real world so that we see not 'profiles' of objects but the objects themselves. The contradiction is only apparent, however. Perspective is not a limitation on perception, but the condition on which the real world appears to us. It means that while perception brings me the real world, I can never apprehend it all at once, or from all sides. Perspective, that is, is simply the mark of my incarnation and embodiment in the world. But it does bring to light two essential aspects of perception: first, that it is *temporal*, which means that any given perception is informed by its predecessors and successors, and that the perceived object achieves its unity only in time; second, that perception confounds the *subject/object* distinction, since what might be seen as its subjective component (perspective) and its objective component (access to the real world) are only two sides of the same coin, and are fused in any given perception.

This second aspect of perception can be further elucidated. In one sense perception can be seen as motivated by the subject, since it depends on the body's placement and direction, on our present interests and concerns, and on our ability to focus and hold parts of the visual field under scrutiny. But perception is also motivated by the perceptual object, as *Gestalt* psychology has demonstrated. It requires, for example, considerable effort on my part to take the spaces between trees on an avenue as figures and the trees as the background, since we naturally and spontaneously see the trees emerging

from an indistinct and empty ground. Again, the following group-
ing of dots:

. .   . .

are always perceived as six pairs of dots, revealing an immanent
logic behind our perception. We see our visual world in terms of
meaningful *Gestalten* or structures which we are generally not at
liberty to disrupt. It is my visual field as a whole that directs my gaze,
assigning value and significance to each part of my field in terms of
an overall pattern. Our perception of colours, for example, depends
on the structure of my visual field as articulated by the level and degree
of lighting (PP 304–17). In short, perception manifests a structure
which is more primitive than the subject/object distinction. Perception
expresses operative intentionality, as Merleau-Ponty indicates:

> This subject-object dialogue, this drawing together, by the sub-
> ject, of the meaning diffused through the object, and, by the
> object, of the subject's intentions – a process which is physio-
> gnomic perception – arranges round the subject a world which
> speaks to him of himself, and gives his own thoughts their
> place in the world. (PP 132)

Perception, then, is intentional, and expresses the intentional
unity of the body in concord with the world. This is illustrated by
the phenomenon of binocular vision. The passage from double,
blurred, unfocused vision to the convergence of our gaze upon a
single object is not explicable in terms of an inspection of the mind,
but as the synergic expression of the body's intending a single perceptual object. To this end, the eyes cease to function as separate
organs, but co-ordinate in order to allow the body to pull itself
together, synthesize its parts, and enable it to real-ize the intention
that animates it. The establishment of single and focused vision is
an achievement of the (phenomenal) body as it projects a visible
and intentional setting round about itself (PP 232). In this projection of a setting, perception reveals a primitive significance or sense
of the perceived world. The sense of a perceived object depends on
the subject's orientation, the direction of his vision (neatly expressed
in the French by the ambiguity of the word *sens* which means
both sense and direction). So, for example, a face seen 'upside-down'
and a face seen 'the right way up' are not the same, for the upside-
down face is perceived as distorted and grotesque.

> To invert an object is to deprive it of its significance. Its being
> as an object is, therefore, not a being-for-the-thinking-subject,
> but a being-for-the-gaze, which meets it at a certain angle, and
> otherwise fails to recognize it. (PP 253)

29

A phenomenology of perception leads us to acknowledge that phenomena have a primitive significance for us, that sticks to them, prior to any act of reflective interpretation on our part.

Object and world

The theory of perception enables us to see how a phenomenological understanding of the concepts of object and world is possible. Perceptual objects (or, indeed, the objects of any mode of experience) are not experienced as spatio-temporal individuals, but as a pre-reflective unity intended by perceptual consciousness in terms of its perceptual syntheses of spatial and temporal perspectives. Objects are not determinate and external to the perceiver, but physiognomic, the embodiment of perceptual intentions, and hence serve to draw consciousness together and effect its unity (PP 71). The unity of the object and the unity of perceptual consciousness presuppose each other and are dialectically interdependent. Hence, as has been noted before, the objects of perception are themselves intentional:

> The sentient and the sensible do not stand in relation to each other as two mutually exclusive terms. . . . It is my gaze which subtends colour, and the movement of my hand which subtends the object's form, or rather my gaze pairs off with colour, and my hand with hardness and softness, and in this transaction between the subject of sensation and the sensible it cannot be held that one acts while the other suffers the action, or that one confers significance on the other (PP. 214)

Perceptual objects share a system of interlocking horizons, they form a system in which each relates to the others. Now the fact of my embodiment means that I can occupy only a given point in space and time, and hence only perceive objects from my point of view. And it happens that objects get in each other's way and restrict my vision. Yet because objects are not passive and inert receptacles of my gaze, but are intentional unities, my look becomes a form of habitation of the object, and it is in terms of this habitation that I can perceive aspects of other objects hidden to me.

> Thus every object is the mirror of all others. When I look at the lamp on my table, I attribute to it not only the qualities visible from where I am, but also those which the chimney, the walls, the table can 'see'; the back of the lamp is nothing but the face which it 'shows' to the chimney. I can therefore see an object in so far as objects form a system or a world, and in so far as each one guarantees the permanence of those aspects by their presence. (PP 68)

Hence we do not perceive discrete objects, but chains of objects linking up with each other and subject to the overall patterning of my visual field. This systematic interrelatedness of objects helps us understand perceptual illusions. The fact that our senses can be deceived has often been cited as evidence that we cannot trust our senses, which therefore need to be 'corrected' by our 'scientific' knowledge. But these illusions can be explained in terms of the descriptions of perception and object that have been given. It has been argued, for example, that our senses are deceptive because large things seen at a distance look small, and round pennies seen from an angle appear elliptical. But this merely expresses the fact that all perception is perception from somewhere, and each perception can only offer us one perspective on the perceived object. Each perspective is informed by previous and later perspectives, which together make up the object-for-us. Hence when we get to see the object close up, or the penny face on, we will perceive the object within a far clearer field, and see its 'true' size or shape. Similarly, the fact that a stick half immersed in water looks bent is explicable in terms of perspective. Since objects often get in each other's way, it can be seen that making the stick look bent is water's way of getting in the way of our perception of that bit of the stick that is under water. It is the visual field as a whole, and the articulation of objects within it, that determines which parts of it are clear to our vision and which parts are indeterminate or ambiguous, and hence possibly subject to illusion.

Illusions are possible only because there are veridical perceptions, so that any present mis-perception is always open to future correction when my perceptual grip on the object is firmer. Perception is *incomplete* – I can never see an object from all sides or angles at once, so that its fullness always eludes me, and hence it is subject to endless exploration – but not *insufficient*, since although the world of objects outruns me, I am directly open to it, and it is potentially accessible to my gaze. It is the horizon – the systematic interrelatedness of perceptual objects – that guarantees their unity and their realness. Hence all objects presuppose the *world*, that which is made up of all possible objects and their interrelations. The world is the 'horizon of all horizons', 'the style of all possible styles' (PP 330), the field incorporating all potential fields, the indeterminacy which is the ground of all determinacy, in short 'that which guarantees for my experiences a given, not a willed, unity underlying all the disruptions of my personal and historical life' (PP 330). There is then the absolute certainty of the world in general, although not of any one thing in particular (PP 297). All my perception presupposes a 'perceptual faith', a primordial belief (*Urglaube*) in the realness of my perception and of the world, a faith that is never questioned in

31

natural perception. That is not to say that it is not immune from doubt; it is, after all, still a faith, and there are cases of almost total insanity where the perceptual faith collapses. Nevertheless, all questioning of the world presupposes that there is something to question, and all doubt assumes there is some form of certainty, if only the certainty that I do in fact doubt, and that it is myself who is doubting. All human activity is a form of commerce with the world, which is present as the background to all possible experiences. 'I may well close my eyes, and stop up my ears, I shall nevertheless not cease to see, if it is only the blackness before my eyes, or to hear, if only silence' (PP 395).

The three worlds of perception

In an important article Dreyfus and Todes (1962) argue that Merleau-Ponty's theory of perception is based on the distinction between three levels of perception, constituting three perceptual worlds (where the term 'worlds' refers to a degree of generality at a level below that of *the* world). The first they call the *pre-objective world* proper, where consciousness moves freely from figure to ground, or from ground to figure, without establishing permanent figures or grounds. Perception tends to be of visual fields, which distribute an overall sense to each segment, rather than of sharply distinguished figures and grounds. Perception at this level is simple openness to the world, and is pre-personal. Corresponding to the pre-thematic and lived unity of the world is the primordial unity of the senses, which intercommunicate and interpenetrate (PP 229).

The second world is the *Lebenswelt*, where the primordial figure – ground structure is supplemented by a 'virtual figure', the definite expectation of a figure emerging from a ground. Here we have a stabilization of perceptual experience and the formation of determinate perspectives based on recollection and recognition. Perception becomes fully intersubjective, interpenetrating with language, so that my perceptions share in commonly held assumptions and expectations about the perceptual world. Finally we arrive at the *scientific world*, which is in fact not a perceptual world at all, but the apprehension of fully determinate figures in isolation from their perceptual ground, and where the characteristics of figures are deduced from scientific premises.

Dreyfus and Todes note that these three worlds of perception are not clearly distinguished in Merleau-Ponty's writings. For example, Merleau-Ponty often uses the term 'pre-objective world' to refer to what are for Dreyfus and Todes the first *two* worlds (the pre-objective and *Lebenswelt*), whereas the term 'pre-personal world' refers only to the first world. However, this is not simple carelessness on Merleau-Ponty's part (although he could perhaps be clearer) for, as Dreyfus and Todes acknowledge, the three worlds are idealizations, they implicate each other and are frequently mixed in actual perceptions. The *Lebenswelt* (the second world) is particularly ambiguous, since it partakes of features of the original pre-objective world – in that it is pre-reflective and endows the objects of perception with affective and motor significance in terms of its interests at hand – and of the scientific world – in that it allows for permanent and stable perceptual objects tending towards the scientific ideal of objects purged of all ambiguity and indeterminacy. The natural attitude can be characterized as this latter mixture of features of the *Lebenswelt* and the scientific world. We may note, in addition, that any given perception may be seen to belong to more than one world, in so far as any perception lies on a continuum between comprehensive vision (characteristic of the pre-objective world) and critical focusing (characteristic of the *Lebenswelt* or scientific world).

There is one point which should be noted about the concept of a pre-objective world and pre-objective experience, which is simply that if it is pre-objective, how is it to be comprehended or elucidated? I consider this problem in detail in chapter 6. For the moment, the simple answer is that pre-objective experience, although not reflective, is by no means *unconscious*, and is at least potentially able to be brought to awareness, and spill over into our more conscious experience. Dreams, for example, operate at the pre-objective level, yet the primordial symbolism they manifest implicates many of our waking perceptions. This is also true of mystical experiences or experience under certain drugs. [4] But it is art in particular which takes the birth of meaning in the pre-objective world as its theme. Cézanne, for example, makes a basic distinction between the spontaneous organization of the things we naïvely perceive and the human organization of ideas and sciences which influence all our perceptions (SNS 13). He wished to return to this primordial, pre-objective world before it is invested with humanity, which is not absent even in photographs of a landscape which constantly suggest man's presence. In ordinary perception we perceive in terms of our pragmatic interests, in terms of financial value, usability, the place of objects in our particular schemes. Now art seeks to get away from this – not by reaching the things-in-themselves, since there can be no perception free of subjectivity or presuppositions, and since perception does not record the external world, but structures it – but by making the return to the pre-objective world the actual project of art. Hence art involves a 'distortion of a distortion' (Park, 1970, p. 123), the artificial distortion of the already pragmatically distorted perception in the natural attitude, in an attempt to rid the object of its human pretensions and associations and return to the level of pre-objective

33

perception. One thing should be noted about all these attempts to return to the pre-objective world, however, and that is that they are all indirect. One goes *through* dreams, drugs or art, and then tries to interpret the experiences that one can grasp. The pre-objective world, by its very nature, cannot be apprehended in full clarity.

The primacy of perception

Merleau-Ponty's major work, *Phenomenology of Perception*, and many of his later writings concentrate on perceptual experience, since perception is regarded as a primary and primitive level of experience, on which 'higher' levels – thought, discursive reasoning, understanding – are built. This thesis is known as the primacy of perception, by which Merleau-Ponty means 'that the experience of perception is our presence at the moment when things, truths, values are constituted for us' (PM 25); or again: 'The perceived world is the always presupposed foundation of all rationality, all value and all existence. This thesis does not destroy either rationality or the absolute. It only tries to bring them down to earth' (PM 13). The relationship between perception and thought, as between all pre-reflective and reflective experience, is understood in terms of the notion of *Fundierung*. The *founding* term – perception, the pre-reflective – is primary or primitive in the sense that it is the ground of the *founded* term – thought, the reflective – and in the sense that the founded are presented as determinate or explicit forms of the founding. Nevertheless, the primacy of perception or the pre-reflective does not mean that thought or the reflective are absorbed into them, since it is only through thought that we apprehend perception, and through reflection that we can grasp the pre-reflective. Neither are perception or the pre-reflective primary in any empiricist or historical sense, but only logically or phenomenologically (PP 394).

Rationality is then not understood as the operation of pure thought in isolation from more primitive layers of experience, but in terms of its ground in perceptual experience. Perception discloses an immanent meaning or Logos in experience and the world, and it is this that founds the experience of rationality. 'To say that there exists rationality is to say that perspectives blend, perceptions confirm each other, a meaning emerges' (PP xix). That is, phenomenology looks to the birth of rationality in the emergence of an intersubjective significance in our experience. Yet this can never be taken as given or non-problematic, for around every area of meaning lies a horizon or zone of non-meaning. Rationality or reason must be understood in terms of its relation to non-reason, since it is precisely this inter-relation which marks the emergence of sense from non-sense (SNS 3–5). Reason can never be presupposed, but must be viewed as a presumptive unity on the horizon of time, where any present *Gestalt* or meaningful configuration can be broken up, only to be re-formed at a later date.

Similarly with *truth*, a concept which – phenomenologically – is closely related to rationality. We base all our notions of truth, not on some supposed absolute or self-evident operations of mind, but on the reality of our perception of the world. All truth is grounded on perceptual truth (PP xvi). Experience gives us coherent perceptions, immediately self-evident experiences, and these are the foundation of all ideas of truth.

Finally the *self* or *I*, as we have seen, is not to be considered as primitive, but founded on pre-reflective or impersonal experience. There are experiences when we are aware of a self 'behind' experience, but also experiences when there appears no consciousness of a self or an 'I', but just a flow of experiences:

> We have the experience of an *I* not in the sense of an absolute subjectivity, but indivisibly demolished and remade by the course of time. The unity of either the subject or the object is not a real unity, but a presumptive unity on the horizon of experience. (PP 219)

Subjectivity is understood, then, as a 'presumptive unity', as a form of self-recovery in which consciousness draws itself together, as a centre of meaning when experiences blend and the possibility of rationality or truth emerges. There is, indeed, evidence that the self is non-primitive by its relatively late development in children, who seem to start by living in direct contact with things, and only later develop a sense of perspective, of separation from the world, and hence of self (PM 150). Strictly speaking, in terms of the ground of all experience in the pre-objective, we cannot talk of a self. Rather:

> I am a field, an experience. One day, once and for all, something was set in motion which, even during sleep, can no longer cease to see or not to see, to feel or not to feel, to suffer or be happy, to think or rest from thinking, in a word to 'have it out' with the world. There then arose . . . a fresh *possibility of situations*. (PP 406–7)[5]

Space, distance, movement

We can briefly consider how an existential phenomenological analysis deals with other modalities of existence, for example, space, distance and movement. In the same way as he distinguished between the objective and phenomenal body, Merleau-Ponty distinguishes *objective space* from *existential* (lived, phenomenal, virtual) *space*.

35

Objective space is the space of rulers and tape-measures, the space dealt with by science, a space in-itself which is 'there' prior to any spatial subject. This is the only space one meets in empiricism and rationalism. For empiricism, objects occupy pure positions, and have a kind of spatial orientation in-themselves apart from a subject. Rationalism – since the only space it allows is objective space – conceives of the subject as disembodied, a pure intellect without inherent directedness, though able, in thought, to trace out all possible directions in space. Both ignore lived or existential space, our actual experience of being oriented in the world and situated in relation to objects. This is spatiality of *situation* (or relation) rather than of pure *position* (or space in-itself). Spatial terms like 'top', 'bottom', 'near', 'far', etc., derive their significance from my lived space, which is my spontaneous evaluation of my environment in terms of my projects at hand.

This pre-thematic hold of my body on the world is expressed in the concept of *spatial level*, which is 'a certain possession of the world by my body, a certain gearing of my body to the world' (PP 250). My body unfolds spatial relations so that it can inhabit or be at home in its environment. If, for example, a subject is placed in a room in which he can only see the room through a mirror which reflects it at an angle of 45 degrees to the vertical, he first of all sees the room 'slantwise', so that another man walking in the room seems to lean to one side. But after a few minutes, through a redistribution of the points of top and bottom, the same man is seen as walking upright. In short, during the experiment the spatial level has been spontaneously changed as the subject projects a new spatial orientation around himself so that he can comfortably inhabit his new setting. A given spatial orientation or level, then, is the result of a dialogue between bodily orientation and the spatial orientation of my given environment, which extends to the whole spatial field (see McCurdy, 1972).

Different kinds of existential spatialities exist in relation to different modalities of being-in-the-world. For example, there is (1) *the space of night-time*: when the world of clear and articulate objects is abolished and we evolve a kind of spatiality without things; (2) *the space of dreams or myths*: in which events and objects become embedded in their vital and sexual significance and the events of objective space (and time) are distorted; (3) *the space of dancing*: an aimless and unoriented space, where the movements of the body are an end in themselves and have an emblematic value; (4) *hallucinatory space*: where the boundaries normally drawn between the body and the world collapse, and objects, instead of keeping their distance, become rooted in our body, or our body extends to the world. In these different modalities of existential space, it can be seen that the meaning of objects and of the world changes depending on the form of our spatial hold on the world: objects can become indistinct and sinister, or charged with symbolism, or totally alien. We see here, once again, operative intentionality at work carving out a primitive significance in the world.

Spatiality, in so far as it makes possible and expresses our implantation in the world, is co-extensive with existence. All existence is spatial, and space is a kind of pre-personal horizon to all our experience. The constitution of a new spatial level always takes for granted a level already given. And because we are in a world of real objects, a world not created by consciousness for its own purposes, all modalities of existential space are related in some way to physical or objective space, that space necessary for the practical utilization of objects in the world. Objective space lies on the horizon of every existential space, so that, for example, the space peculiar to dreaming must still work on and refer to the spatially distinct objects of the real world. Indeed, the loosening of existential space from its anchorage in physical space is the defining characteristic of hallucinations.

Distance can also be understood phenomenologically, in terms of our naïve experience. We decide whether an object is near or far, big or small, not in terms of a comparison with another object – for which object is to be taken as the standard? – nor even by comparing it with the size of my own body (although that is one factor), but in terms of my whole visual and spatial field, which patterns my vision and so defines what is near or far, big or small. In other words, distance, in its existential sense, is defined in terms of my perceptual grip on an object, on whether we can comfortably situate ourselves in relation to it, and hence judge its 'true' size, or whether our grip is loose or approximate, so that we have no clear evidence as to the size or distance of an object. Hence the distance from me to an object is not a space which increases or decreases, but is rather a 'tension which fluctuates round a norm' (PP 302), that norm being the adequacy and clarity of my perception.

In the natural attitude, distance is not so much determined by physical space as by availability and access as laid down by my guiding interests and concerns. I can experience myself as 'centred' – where my given setting coincides with my real interests – or as 'decentred' – where I experience myself as 'somewhere else', for example as in relation to a person who is not physically with me. This illustrates the fact that my lived space is cut up and patterned in terms of my projects. For example, the centre of my space is usually my home or dwelling, in terms of which I orient myself in the lived world. Space is cut up into paths, pavements, roads, etc., which determine the availability of different parts of the lived world.

It may indeed happen that a point very near to me in terms of physical distance is experienced as far away in terms of accessibility. For example, the physical distance between two points on either side of a wall separating two houses is very small; yet in terms of its accessibility – the fact that I have to go out of my house, knock on my neighbour's door, ask his permission to go into his house if he is in, and so on – the actual distance may be very great (see Bollnow, 1967).

Movement displays in striking fashion how our body inhabits space (and time). It reveals, behind our objective ideas about how movement occurs in terms of a change in physical space, the pre-objective experience on which it is grounded, where movement is linked to the subject and his field, and expresses a variation of his hold on the world. We must leave behind our objective prejudices about phenomena being essentially stable with static properties. The experience of movement reveals a world made up not only of things, but also of 'pure transitions', of objects defined in terms of their behaviour as they appear in my visual field – 'the bird which flies across the garden is, during the time that it is moving, merely a greyish power of flight' (PP 275). It is my whole visual field which determines what I see as at rest and what as moving. If, for example, I see a stone falling through the air, this means that my gaze is anchored in the garden, so that it is in terms of the garden that the stone is seen as moving. It is my *anchorage* in my visual field, like my spatial level, which patterns my perceptions, so that the church steeple begins to move only when I leave the sky and clouds in the margin of my vision (PP 279). It is only in cases of ambiguous perceptions, those perceptions cut off from their present context and past perceptions, that I can voluntarily choose my anchorage, as in the case of my train moving off from the station where I can either see my train as moving and the next one as stationary, or vice versa.

Time

In all our discussions of experience, we have made mention of its inescapably temporal structure. For example, we have seen above how spatial perspectives are unfolded by the body. Spatial perspectives and syntheses, however, are also inherently temporal: relations of distance, of near and far, are determined just as much by the subject's temporal situation as his spatial one – indeed, the two are inseparable. The very notion of spatiality implicates temporality: 'things co-exist in space because they are *present* to the same perceiving subject and enveloped in one and the same temporal wave' (PP 275).

Perception is also through and through a temporal as well as a spatial affair. The unity of the perceptual object is achieved through a dual temporal process of protention and retention. There is, first, *prospective* focusing, the bringing together of the confused mass of colours and reflections which flood my consciousness as I open myself to the perceived world and direct myself towards the expectation of a determinate object, so that it can be maintained that 'the object is the final stage of my process of focusing' (PP 239). There is also a process of *retrospective* apprehension of the perceptual object, since it presents itself as real and determinate prior to my act of focusing, and hence as the prime mover and stimulus to all my perceptions.

We have seen, finally, in our discussions of the relations between mind and body, the objective and phenomenal body, objective and lived space, etc., that experience tends towards integration, the fusion of subordinate structures, without ever achieving total union or assimilation. All integration is *temporal*, which is the clue to how it is achieved in the first place – since it is the thrust of my projects and intentions towards the future that link up discrete instants into a temporal pattern or *sens* (direction and significance) – and also demonstrates how integration is always precarious, since what can be patterned or structured can also be broken up as new patterns come into existence. We see, then, the phenomenon of time implicated in all our experiences.

How, then, phenomenologically are we to understand time? Time presupposes a human attitude towards time, and expresses my relationship to the world. In the objective world in-itself – if such a thing could be conceived, since my very conception is already a relation between myself and the world, and hence a world-for-my-imagination – there would be no time and no change, no 'before' and 'after', since it takes a human observer to introduce such distinctions. To say, for example, that 'the water flowing past me was yesterday at its source' is to establish my perspective on events as a vantage point, an anchorage by which to link up the water yesterday and the water now. Indeed, the very concept of an *event* in nature is the result of the human programme of cutting nature up to make it intelligible. Hence, prior to, and at a level more primitive than that of objective time, the time of clocks, we find a pre-thematic, existential experience of time as a network of operative intentionalities binding us to the world. Time is, metaphorically, not a line, moving in one direction through only one real point, the present. Neither is it a stream or river, making us believe that the past pushes the present into view, which in turn pushes the future – the problem with all spatial metaphors is that they are based on motion, which itself presupposes time. Time is rather to be understood as a flux, a pattern of intentionalities (see Spicker, 1973).

Hence existential or lived time is not a present linked to a future and to a past, or a succession of discrete instants, as it is at the objective level, but a single movement or thrust by which human projects carve out relations of 'before' and 'after' in the world. It is my field of presence, the arena of my projects and actions in the world, which is the 'primary experience' in which time and its dimensions is most clearly revealed. The future and the past are experienced as the horizons of my living present. The future is that towards which my tasks and projects are directed (pro-jected), and hence is that which makes sense of my present since it defines the orientation (*sens*), or at least the style, of my present actions. The past is an ever-receding platform to my present situation, yet which is subject to continual re-interpretation in the light of my present and future projects. Future and past are not points on a line, but intentionalities that anchor me to my environment.

In short, we find presupposed in all experience not a central *I* or self, but temporality, so that, phenomenologically, subjectivity *is* temporality ('I am . . . one single temporality which is engaged, from birth, in making itself progressively explicit', PP 407). Here we are at a level more primitive than that of subject and object, where in fact the very notions of subject and object come into being. We find 'subject and object as two abstract "moments" of a unique structure which is *presence*' (PP 430).

Yet, like the objective and phenomenal body, or objective and existential space, my lived experience of time is intimately related to an objective time which takes shape on the horizon of all modalities of existential time, to which all my experience is linked in some way, and which makes hours, days, months, years, etc., arise as fixed points. There is not a natural time, a time without subjectivity, but a *generalized time*, 'the perpetual reiteration of the sequence of past, present and future' (PP 453), the cyclic time of our bodily functions and of nature, upon which all existence is founded.

Other persons

For empiricism and rationalism, the existence of other persons has posed certain philosophical problems. It is true that for empiricism the problem of other persons does not in a sense arise, since the self is pictured as a mindless machine, so for empiricism there are no persons at all, never mind about *other* persons. What empiricism always comes up against, however, is how to relate its 'scientific' descriptions (or constructions) of human organisms to our lived experience of being-in-the-world. For rationalism, on the other hand, the problem of other persons is acute, for to recognize the other is to recognize that I am not the sole constituting agent of the world. For a philosophy which starts from the *cogito*, from the sovereignty of the self, the jump from the self to the recognition of other people is essentially problematic. Rationalism makes our apprehension of others a fundamentally intellectual affair, in which I 'read off' the existence of the other's mind by noting the similarities of our bodies, and hence reasoning by analogy that since my body is inhabited by a mind, so must the other's body contain a mind.

The rationalist account is unconvincing, however. Not only does this reasoning by analogy never seem to happen (unless we have read too much rationalist philosophy), but it presupposes what it is meant to explain, namely, the *experience* of other people. Now this is precisely where existential phenomenology starts, from how, existentially, we concretely experience other people, or, more accurately, experience takes on an intersubjective significance. Merleau-Ponty starts, not from the perspective of the objective world, nor from that of a sovereign and constituting *cogito*, but from being-in-the-world. What is given as primary is not a self – we have seen how the self is founded on pre-reflective experience – but a field of experience, a phenomenal field. Our conceptions of both the self and of others are derived from this field of experience, which is *potentially* intersubjective. This is not to deny that there is something private about my own field of experience, since it is indeed *my* experience which no one else can have. There is in some sense what Merleau-Ponty terms a 'living solipsism'. Nevertheless, as soon as we apprehend our field of experience as meaningful or structured, we are at the birth of the intersubjective significance in experience which is potentially communicable.[6]

It is my field of experience, and behind that the world as the permanent horizon to all experience, that grounds the experience of myself and of other persons. There is intersubjectivity because all experience opens onto a common world. Experience, understood phenomenologically, is essentially *open*: it blends with other experiences of mine to create structures and patterns, and blends with the experiences of other persons to create intersubjective meanings, and to found communication. We share perceptions of the same objects, we share a generalized time and space, and the same natural and human worlds as the backdrops to our lives. My body and the bodies of other people form a system, not through any reasoning by analogy, but because our phenomenal bodies gear into each other as we perform our tasks in concert, or in competition, in the lived world. The actions of two tennis players, for example, flow into one single, rhythmic pattern as one player's stroke motivates his opponent's return, and so on. The child finds around him natural and cultural objects which he learns to use 'because the body image ensures the immediate correspondence of what he sees done and what he himself does' (PP 354). Other people are a permanent horizon to my own existence, like a constant double at my side. It is the fact that my existence is constantly de-centred, since it is an interplay between generality and individuality, between anonymity and reflection, that I find the experience of the other as a 'generalized I' (PW 138), a potential in all my experiences.

Consciousness as perceptual

The thrust of this chapter, in so far as it concerns the nature of consciousness, has been to demonstrate Merleau-Ponty's rejection of the notion of a sovereign or spontaneous constituting consciousness in favour of a characterization of consciousness as essentially *perceptual*. Perceptual consciousness is fundamentally temporal. Nevertheless, although it can be maintained that consciousness, in so far as it intends a world and pro-jects itself towards a future through its actions in the world, actually unfolds temporality, this does not mean that temporal relations are simply laid down by consciousness in whatever way it pleases. Instead, temporality is in a sense what consciousness has to submit to, since, once thrown into the world, consciousness has no more power to step out of time than throw off its physical body. In short, time is a 'spontaneity' acquired once and for all (PP 427). Hence there is a form of passivity at the heart of perceptual consciousness, as is clearly evident in those experiences when we surrender ourselves to bodily or natural phenomena over which we have little or no control, as in sleep, sexual orgasm, urination, etc. (see TL, chapter 6). There are also experiences in perceptual consciousness that border on the unconscious. For example, sexuality, diffused through much of our activity and thought, gives a colour to being-in-the-world which is inherently ambiguous, since it is of its essence to be never explicit. Sexuality, especially in dreams, bears witness to

> that ever slumbering part of ourselves which we feel to be anterior to our representations, to that individual haze through which we perceive the world. There are here blurred outlines, distinctive relationships . . . having reference to sexuality without specifically calling it to mind. (PP 168)

Perceptual consciousness, then, is not sovereign or constituting because it is a dialectic between spontaneity and passivity and between the reflective and the unreflective, all of which refer to its basic feature of being *embodied* or incarnated in the world.

By denying that consciousness is constituting, however, Merleau-Ponty does not mean to suggest that it is constituted. His opposition to the term 'constituting' is that it implies consciousness *creates* the world, turning phenomenology into naïve idealism. But consciousness can be seen as constituting in the sense that the very upsurge of consciousness is synonymous with the bringing of significance to the world, as in perceptual experience which discloses an immanent pattern to experience, a layer of primordial meaning (see p. 10 of this chapter). In order to indicate that he wishes to retain this sense of constitution, Merleau-Ponty sometimes prefers to use the term 'instituting' to refer to consciousness (TL 40); implying that consciousness is not a perceptual creation *ex nihilo* but an intentionality which presupposes a body of sedimented and already constituted operations.[7]

Consciousness as expressing

Perceptual consciousness is not a substance, an object in the world, nor is it a collection of 'psychic facts' contingently and externally related to each other; rather, it can be designated as a power of signifying or expressing. Consciousness has no content, there is nothing 'in' consciousness for any causality to work on, since it is intentional and transcendent, in direct relation with the world. The relations between the various modalities of consciousness (perception, imagination, phantasy, etc.), or between different acts of consciousness, or between its acts and the sedimented and already constituted operations that each act presupposes – these relationships are not causal but *motivational* or implicatory, in which one phenomenon releases another in terms of its significance, disclosing a kind of 'operative reason' (PP 50) at work. They are linked together like the parts of a play, as the expression of a guiding theme or intention.

We have seen how consciousness founds a primitive level of meaning, for example in perceptual experience. This primordial significance is not a simple signification or designation, where there is a one-to-one relation between the sign and what it signifies. This mode of signifying belongs to the 'higher' level of speech. Here there is no real separation between what signifies and what is signified; consciousness realizes a 'symbolical "pregnancy" of form in content' (PP 291). Meaning or significance in this primitive sense is that which *makes a difference*, or that which emerges from a ground. For example,

a perceived object ... is a certain *variation* in relation to a norm or to a spatial, temporal or coloured level, it is a certain distortion, a certain 'coherent deformation' of the permanent links which unite us to sensorial fields and to a world. (AD 198)

In the same way, my tasks and projects are presented to consciousness, not as determinate objects or ends, but 'as reliefs and configurations, that is to say, in the landscape of praxis' (AD 199).

Meaning, in this primitive sense, takes place in an experiential field, which is born of the relationship between consciousness and the world, between subject and object. Meaning *is* this interrelationship of consciousness intending a world. There is meaning in all being-in-the-world even when we are not explicitly aware of it, or even if we do not consciously aim to signify anything; because every action, every gesture, makes a *difference* and effects a change in terms of a given level of conduct or in terms of my present setting:

> I may have been under the impression that I lapsed into silence
> through weariness, or some minister may have thought he had
> uttered merely an appropriate platitude, yet my silence or his
> words immediately take on a significance, because my fatigue or
> his falling back upon a ready-made formula are not accidents,
> for they *express* a certain lack of interest, and hence some
> degree of adoption of a definite position in relation to the
> situation. (PP xviii; italics added)

There is no existence which does not express something for, phenomenologically, existence is synonymous with expression. We are 'condemned to meaning', and this is our fate.

It is the recognition and disclosure of this primordial layer of significance and symbolism that Merleau-Ponty considers to be the most profound insight of Freud. At this level we find

> the idea of a symbolism which is primordial, originary,
> the idea of a 'non-conventional thought' (Politzer) enclosed in a
> 'world for us', which is the source of our dreams and more
> generally of the elaboration of our life. (TL 49)

This level of symbolism is not an unconscious, in the sense of being a subject behind a subject – justly criticized by Sartre (1969a, pp. 50–4) – or a reality beneath appearances, but an originary level of significance, on top of which are built other layers, making consciousness into a plurality of interrelated levels of significance. Hence the essential *ambiguity* of being-in-the-world, in that it is always open to several interpretations in terms of different layers of meaning. It follows also that it is difficult to maintain a rigid distinction between the real and the imaginary, since any given level of meaning implicates in some way all the others:

> our waking relations with objects and others especially have an
> oneiric character as a matter of principle: others are present to
> us in the way that dreams are, the way myths are, and this is
> enough to question the cleavage between the real and the
> imaginary. (TL 48)[8]

We have seen how the body has been defined by Merleau-Ponty as an 'expressive unity', in which causal and intentional structures are integrated to a greater or lesser degree. The body is the medium in which this dialectic between causality and intentionality is accomplished. For example, if I wish to go to sleep, I lie down in bed, close my eyes, breathe slowly and *play act* going to sleep. There finally arrives a moment when sleep 'comes', and I am taken over by a process over which I have little direct control (PP 163-4). Hence the body's role is one which 'transforms ideas into things, and my mimicry of sleep into real sleep. The body can symbolize existence because it brings it into being and actualizes it' (PP 164). The body (as embodied consciousness) is inherently symbolic or expressive. My actions and gestures are not signs that stand for some inner activities or states, but are expressive only of themselves; my bodily gestures are 'filled with' their significance, they are what they signify. The loss of speech of a girl whose mother has forbidden her to see the man she loves *expresses* a refusal of coexistence, a withdrawal into herself (PP 160-1). In other words, the concept of expression designates an interplay between different levels of significance, so that what on one level is a simple loss of speech becomes at a deeper level charged with a more symbolic meaning.

Experience, then, is through and through symbolic and expressive; the brain 'is actively translating experiences into symbols' (Langer, 1948, p. 33). Consciousness, or the body as embodied consciousness, can thus be characterized as expressing, which has the sense not only of being in a continual process of symbolizing and signifying as it intends a world, but also of real-izing and actualizing itself as significance. Consciousness ex-presses itself, that is it presses itself out into determinacy (Park, 1970, p. 112), it transcends itself by being in-the-world, and so is a field of expression that brings a whole world with it.

A note on Merleau-Ponty's late philosophy

This chapter has offered a very brief and schematic outline of Merleau-Ponty's programme of existential phenomenology, its aims, methodology, and some of its substantive analyses. It is in the light of this general programme that the more specific concerns of the following chapters – speech (chapter 2), society (chapter 3), Marxism and history (chapter 4), ethics (chapter 5) and philosophy (chapter 6) – are to be viewed. However, little or no reference has been made to Merleau-Ponty's last writings, *Eye and Mind* (in PM) and *The Visible and the Invisible*, which attempt to extend and deepen some of the themes of his earlier philosophy. I will conclude this chapter, then,

45

THE PROGRAMME OF EXISTENTIAL PHENOMENOLOGY

with a very brief note on the final development of Merleau-Ponty's philosophy.

His concerns in his last writings are in further elucidating the relationship between the body and the world, which had been his aim in his earlier works. However, in spite of his exploration of the dialectical interrelation between body and world in *Phenomenology of Perception* and other works, Merleau-Ponty in his last writings accuses himself of not having fully transcended the Cartesian and rationalist perspective which he had set out to challenge. In particular, in *Phenomenology of Perception*, Merleau-Ponty still speaks of a 'cogito', and a 'tacit *cogito*' in the sense of a pre-reflective contact of the subject with itself, and which therefore implies some kind of subject/object split. Merleau-Ponty now wants to overthrow totally any traces of Cartesianism in his philosophy. He argues that the very notion of a *cogito* presupposes thought and language, and these find their place in the more inclusive and more primitive definition of consciousness as a field of signification or expression. He had realized this, apparently, in the chapter on the body as expression and speech (PP, chapter 6 of part one), but not in his chapter on the *cogito* (PP, chapter 1 of part three), which therefore continued to perpetrate a division between subject and object (see VI 170–1, and also Kwant, 1966, pp. 22–31).

'Nature is on the inside', said Cézanne (PM 164). Phenomenology now becomes an ontology (VI 167), an elaboration of those concepts which would express the fusion of body and world and the complete transcendence of the dualism of subject and object. Such concepts would be, for example, the *flesh* of the body and of the visible, 'the coiling over of the visible upon the seeing body, of the tangible upon the touching body, which is attested in particular when the body sees itself, touches itself seeing and touching the things' (VI 146). In other words, the body is *reversible*, we can touch ourselves as we touch things, see ourselves touching, hence making the body 'a being of two leaves, from one side a thing among things, and otherwise what sees them and touches them' (VI 137). The body and the world belong to the same flesh or element (used in the old Greek sense of air, fire, water and land). The perceived world, then, is not an object, but 'the ensemble of my body's routes' (VI 247). The world and the body are an *intertwining* of routes and levels which refer from one to the other. There are spatial levels, temporal levels, colour levels, lighting levels, etc., etc., which are the lines of force uniting the flesh of the body with the flesh of the world. 'Quality, light, colour, depth, which are there before us, are there only because they awaken an echo in our body and because the body welcomes them' (PM 164).

Phenomenology is now overtly ontological in that philosophy is defined as a search for being – which is made up of the system body/

world. Being is not a substance, but is a relationship between body and world, a relationship which encompasses both terms. Being is, in a sense, to be characterized as expressing, as that which forms meaning (Park, 1970). Hence Merleau-Ponty's existential phenomenology culminates in an attempt to disclose being, in a search for the 'mirrors of Being' (TL 112).

2 Speech

The phenomenology of speech

> We live in a world where speech is an *institution* . . . language
> and the understanding of language apparently raise no problems.
> The linguistic and inter-subjective world no longer surprises us,
> we no longer distinguish it from the world itself, and it is within
> a world already spoken and speaking that we think. We become
> unaware of the contingent element in expression and communi-
> cation, whether it be in the child learning to speak, or in the
> writer saying and thinking something for the first time, in
> short, in all who transform a certain kind of silence into speech.
> It is, however, quite clear that constituted speech, as it operates
> in daily life, assumes that the decisive step of expression has
> been taken. Our view of man will remain superficial so long
> as we fail to go back to that origin, so long as we fail to find,
> beneath the chatter of words, the primordial silence, and as
> long as we do not describe the action which breaks this silence.
> (PP 184)

Here we have a succinct definition of the phenomenology of speech,
the reduction and putting into brackets of the taken-for-grantedness
and facticity of speech in order to investigate and bring to light the
birth of meaning in that silence that surrounds speech. Phenomenology searches for the movement of speech from its origin in
'primordial silence' to its existence in the natural attitude as an institution, as something already constituted. Phenomenology also seeks to
trace out the process whereby 'the world itself' becomes identified
tout court with 'the linguistic and inter-subjective world'. In normal
perception we see things as independent of our perception, and are
not aware of the perspectivism of each and every perception. And
so with speech – we live within speech and language as though they

had always existed. The names we give to phenomena are so in-grained, so 'natural', that it seems as if the name is part of the thing itself. And, again like perception, speech effaces itself: when we listen to someone speaking, we feel we are listening to *him* through the medium of his words; when we read a book the words bring us ideas, things and people, in short, a whole world.

A phenomenology of speech, as we might expect, involves a care-ful consideration of and attention to everyday speech, how it is achieved and understood. This consideration is blinkered as little as possible by prejudices concerning how we ought to investigate speech. The aim is not to explain it, decompose it, deduce it or operate on it, since this would give us only speech-as-explained, speech-as-decomposed, speech-as-operated-on, etc., and we would be no nearer understanding speech as we use it unreflectively and spontaneously in our explanations, deductions and operations. Again, the philosopher is not trying to clarify speech with a light which is not its own, to dispel the mystery of the act of expression:

> There is no analysis capable of making language crystal clear
> and arraying it before us as if it were an object. The act of
> speech is clear only for the person who is actually speaking
> or listening; it becomes obscure as soon as we try to bring
> explicitly to light those reasons which have led us to under-
> stand thus and not otherwise. We can say of it what we have
> said of perception . . . we have the same miracle of an immedi-
> ately apprehended clarity, which vanishes as soon as we try
> to break it down to what we believe to be its component
> elements. (PP 391)

Phenomenology wants instead just to *listen to* speech,[1] to see what it can teach us, without pretending to constitute its object by laying down in advance what is to count as valid evidence and what is not.

> People speak to me and I understand. . . . When expression
> is successful, it seems to me that my thought is yonder, at
> the top of its voice, in those words that I have not spoken.
> Nothing is more convincing than this experience, and there is
> no need to look anywhere else than in it itself for what makes
> it evident, no need to replace the work of speech by some pure
> operation of spirit. (PW 117)

And hence:

> All that is needed – and this is the whole of philosophy – is to
> cash in on this evidence. . . . We need only reinstate this
> experience in its dignity as evidence, which it lost through the
> very use of language and because communication seems to us
> unproblematic. (ibid.)

49

Now, to reinstate the experience of communication and comprehension as evidence, is precisely to do philosophy, and to do philosophy is to employ certain concepts and assumptions, some of which have been explicated in the previous chapter. What distinguishes the philosophic tools of phenomenology, however, is that they are designed solely to bring us the phenomenon of speech, to dig up what is buried in our everyday, unthinking and pre-reflective experience, rather than presenting to us what we have put there ourselves as a result of our operations on the phenomenon.

Empiricism and rationalism are attempts to decompose speech into its supposed elements, to explain the phenomenon of expression in terms of something else in order to give it a pseudo-clarity. Empiricism can conceptualize speech only as a series of physical sounds set alongside each other, which become associated with meanings through stimulus-response mechanisms. In behaviourism, for example, meaningful utterances are built out of the association of sounds, each sound being the response to the stimulus of the previous word. Now this view ignores the fact that utterances are meaningful wholes, manifesting their own internal structure, so that if I say, for example, 'the man who was here owes me some money', the sense of the word 'who' is not determined by the words that precede it, but by the meaning of the whole utterance. Furthermore, empiricism turns speech into an automatic and dumb operation; 'there is no speaker, there is a flow of words set in motion independently of any intention to speak' (PP 175). For empiricism, there is nobody who speaks. Rationalism does allow words to have a meaning, but makes of speaking solely an intellectual process, where the word becomes an empty container into which a pure consciousness injects significance. The word is merely an external sign of our internal thought, which alone has meaning. In short, for rationalism words as physical sounds are the body-matter of speech, while the psychological meanings of words are the mind of speech – how they relate to each other in actual speaking remains a mystery (see Ihde, 1973). Once again there is nobody who speaks, only a thinking subject. The return to the phenomenon of speech and the speaking subject, which is phenomenology, means that 'we refute both intellectualism [i.e. rationalism] and empiricism by simply saying that *the word has a meaning*' (PP 177).

To say that 'the word has a meaning' is to say that meaning is *embodied* in words and in speech, in the same way as it is embodied in behaviour and perception. Words *express* meaning in the way the body expresses intentions and behaviour expresses projects, that is, by symbolizing them and hence real-izing them (see pp. 43–5). An angry gesture or word does not make me think of anger, they do not refer to 'psychic facts' hidden somewhere in my consciousness, they *are* anger (PP 184). Speech partakes of the expressivity of all human experience. In fact it trades off the primitive levels of expression and meaning that are found in experience, and which have been indicated in the previous chapter, particularly with reference to perception. Linguistic meanings represent the institution of a new and 'higher' level of meaning. Certain actions or phenomena, for example, come to be invested with a *figurative meaning*. Thus the knitting of the brows which, according to Darwin, was originally intended to protect the eyes from the glare of the sun, or the narrowing of the eyes in order to focus more sharply, have taken on the figurative sense of meditation or thoughtfulness (PP 194). Or again, certain natural materials, when put together in a certain way, take on a new meaning as a house, and certain rhythmic movements of the body become dancing.

Hence the movement from silence to speech is not a movement from nothing to something, from non-meaning to meaning. The silence that precedes and surrounds speech is not a void, but a silence with a promise of speech, a silence pregnant with meaning, like a pause in a conversation, or the gap between each ring of the telephone. Speech is a progression to a linguistic meaning from the more primitive field-structure of experience, which is itself already a primordial level of significance with a potential for more complex layers of meaning to be constructed on top of it. Hence the essential movement of speech is from the implicit (the primitive field-structure) to the explicit, from the latent to the overt, in the same way as a perceptual figure emerges from its vaguely apprehended ground. Phenomenology shows that speech manifests the same figure/ horizon structure as perception. Every explicit linguistic meaning carries its horizon of implicit and latent significance. In other words, the *signification* of a word – its denotation, designation, overt or explicit meaning – can be distinguished from its *sense* – its connotation, its horizontal, implicit or latent meaning. Every signification emerges from a ground of possible or latent senses.

As a consequence of this we can point to two features of speech which further highlight the structural similarity between speech and perception. Perception, we have said (p. 31), is incomplete, because its perspectival character means that the fullness of the object and the world must always elude us. Speech is also *incomplete* because the possible senses of an utterance can never be exhausted. There can never be a complete utterance or language, encapsulating everything that can be said, for the simple reason that the ground of implicit sense is always larger than the explicit significations of words. Language is not countable: it is impossible to count the total number of words and all their senses, to make a complete inventory of all possible meanings. Speech is also fundamentally *allusive* or

51

indirect, since every explicit signification makes reference to its horizon of possible senses, to say nothing of those layers of more primitive meaning which ground all linguistic meanings.

Speech as intersubjectivity

Reference has already been made to the potential core of inter-subjectivity in experience (pp. 41–2). Thus perception manifests a certain typicality of structure, and partakes of levels of lighting, colour, spatiality, etc., which are present to all embodied subjects. Perception, as physiognomic, stylizes objects and people in ways that are intersubjectively available (cf. PW 59–6). Experiences blend and implicate each other. I understand an individual colour, for example, in terms of the whole system of colours, so that my recognition of a colour as red is made in terms of its not being blue, orange, etc. Meaning is a *relation* between two or more phenomena – for example, between a figure and a field, or a colour and all other colours – it is a bridge between them. Hence meaningful experiences cannot be closed in on themselves, but coalesce to form configurations and patterns of significance. Experience is open to other experiences, which includes the experiences of other people.

But it is speech, above all, which develops, expands and puts flesh on the seed of intersubjectivity latent in all experience. In speaking, we participate in a cultural object, language, which is not of our own, individual making and into which we are immersed from birth. We cannot choose the significations or senses of the words we utter, nor can we change them at will. In speech we share a common, public language which brings us a common, public, linguistic and cultural world. Speech also has a unique potential for reciprocity in that through speaking and listening to someone else speak we are able to take the role of the other, to understand things from his point of view. There is a crude kind of role-taking in perception, for example when two people are looking at an object from different angles, so that my apprehension of the object will include the other person's perspective. But speech can bring us the other as he sees himself and understands himself, and hence, to some degree, as he is. Furthermore, perception, in the challenge of conflicting perspectives, can sometimes lead a person to assert himself against another. Sartre (1969a) has shown, for example, that two persons gazing at each other can become a duel to see who will lower his gaze, and become the one-looked-at (the object), and who will hold his gaze, and hence be the looker (the subject). This conflict, however, can be interrupted and broken if speech intervenes, laying down a common ground of words and thoughts between the participants, and hence founding intersubjectivity where before there was conflict (S 16).

Speech can be seen to manifest intersubjectivity for another reason. Linguistic meanings are constituted by the application of *rules*. These rules tell us, for instance, how to express experiences or phenomena in speech, which experiences and phenomena can be linguistically compared or distinguished, in short how speech or language are to function. The ascription of meanings cannot be arbitrary. We cannot decide one day to call a table a 'table', and then the next day a 'horse', because then chaos would result, and instead of one public language there would be a multitude of private and mutually incomprehensible languages. To make meaning ascription consistent, orderly and predictable, it must be rule-guided. And rules, like language, are intersubjective by their very nature – for rules to exist there must be public and commonly available criteria which lay down when a rule is being followed and when it is being broken (see Wittgenstein, 1968, and Winch, 1958, chapters 1 and 2). Not that the use of rules defines speech. Rules belong to already constituted speech, to speech as sedimented, whereas there is also the contingent and innovative side to speech, which phenomenology emphasizes. Speech is rule-guided, not rule-governed. But although rules are not sufficient to account for speech, they are a necessary component of all languages, since there must be at some level a common system of meanings and conventions.

Speech as intentionality

Phenomenology, we have said, is a return to the speaking subject as he institutes a linguistic world around himself. It is speech that above all brings us the cultural world. Speech gives us access to a vast multitude of phenomena which exist only in language: for example, excuses, promises, counterparts, interruptions, results, conversations, temptations, digressions, failures, mistakes, appointments, arguments, poker, insults, etc. Such cultural phenomena make up an important part of our social world, and would not be available to those who could not participate in speech even to a small degree. Speech is also a way of cutting up and patterning the world into categories and concepts, so making it potentially intelligible to us (cf. Lévi-Strauss, 1966). In other words, speech manifests that operative intentionality that projects a human world around us, a world where our intentions find responses, and where we respond to its demands upon us. Speech brings us a world in which we can live.

This is most dramatically illustrated in cases where this intentionality breaks down, where a subject no longer feels at home in his speech and hence in the world. We have already come across the patient Schneider (pp. 19–20), whose case reveals a general pathology which throws the normal into relief. Words, like objects, have lost their physiognomy for Schneider, they have become something alien to him, something he can apprehend intellectually, by explicit acts of interpretation, but not existentially by pre-reflectively and non-discursively living in his speech. If, for example, a story is told to the patient, it is observed that he cannot grasp it as a whole, with its characteristic rhythm and style, its climaxes and digressions, but only as a linear succession of equally colourless facts or events. He can comprehend no theme, no overall pattern to the story, but can only re-tell the story by reconstituting it part by part. The words are merely the occasion for a mechanical interpretation, which is not, to be sure, devoid of intellectual content, but without allowing him to live in the words, so that they fail to transport him beyond his intellectual apprehension of the signification of each word. On the other hand, the normal subject has the power to live through the events described in words, the story is 'real' for him because words can real-ize a world through expressing it. For the normal person, words bring him events and worlds that he can live through and inhabit. Words can produce images like the waving of a magic wand (PP 133).

It is also noticed that Schneider rarely feels the need to speak. There is no spontaneous expression and realization of his intentions in speech. The normal subject, on the other hand, is a speaking subject. For him, speech is able to bring the cultural and human world, the present, past and future, the real, the possible and the imaginary, it brings him himself as he understands himself, and other people as he relates to them through talk. In speech man finds himself and real-izes himself.

The conceptual and gestural levels of speech

This consideration of the intentionality of speech as more fundamental than the conceptual or interpretive understanding of words is expressed in a basic distinction between the *gestural level* of speech and its *conceptual level*. In understanding the speech of another, for instance, the conceptual meaning of his words, their intellectual content, is 'deduced' from their gestural meaning (PP 179). That is, I grasp the other's speech as a behaviour directed towards myself or the world, as the expression of certain intentions or desires on his part. I 'feel myself into' what the other means by his words, I assimilate the style of what he says in the way I grasp the meaning of his gestures, or in the way that I learn the words of a foreign language by seeing their place in a context of action and by taking part in a communal life. All this is the ground on which I understand speech conceptually. In other words, the gestural or existential level of speech enables us to specify the horizon of senses or connotations which allow a clear conceptual signification to emerge. It is the inter-play between the gestural and conceptual levels of speech that gives much of the flavour to ordinary speech. For example, the simple sentence: 'Would you pass the meat, please', can be understood gesturally or behaviourally in a number of different ways: as a command, a question, a joke (at a dinner party with vegetarians), a chatting-up ploy (if said to the attractive blonde sitting opposite), a complaint (if said to someone who has just helped himself to the last portion of meat), and so on.

This gestural or existential level of speech is both phenomenologically and chronologically primitive. It is phenomenologically primitive in that the gestural level is a manifestation of intentionality, which grounds all conceptual comprehension. At this level, the world is disclosed as charged with significance, and words themselves are seen to have an emotional content, as can be seen particularly in poetry.

> It would then be found that the words, vowels and phonemes
> are so many ways of 'singing' the world, and that their function
> is to represent things, not, as the naïve onomatopoeic theory
> had it, by reason of an objective resemblance, but because they
> extract, and literally express, their emotional essence. (PP 187)

The gestural level is chronologically primitive because speech starts off as the babbling of babies, where they orchestrate a kind of melody of words, of intonations, a vast array of musical sounds from which must be selected the particular sounds of one language which the baby will gradually learn. In this sense the learning of a particular language represents a kind of impoverishment of this ability to play with sounds.

This gestural/conceptual distinction allows Merleau-Ponty to criticize Piaget for his one-sided emphasis on the conceptual aspect of speech in his theory of the development of language in children. Piaget – according to Merleau-Ponty – characterizes the child's speech as 'egocentric', by which he means it is a phenomenon of self-expression rather than discursive communication or representation. Hence the child's speech is seen as deficient in terms of adult speech, where egocentricity is transcended, and language is used as a means of arriving at 'objective truths' about the world. But, as Merleau-Ponty points out (for example, CL 30), this self-expressive and vital aspect is just as much part of all language – child and adult – as its conceptual and discursive aspects. 'Piaget eliminates from adult language all that is self-expression and appeal to other people' (CL 56). However, even the power of a writer resides more in his style, in his manner of presentation and his interlacing of words, than in the communication of 'objective truths'. This is not to say that the style of a mature writer is the same as the egocentricity of a child's speech. But it has the same roots in language as gesture. The child must certainly learn to use language as a conceptual tool, as a means of intellectual argument and thinking. But the transcendence of his egocentricity is only partial, and the gestural level remains as a permanent ground to all speech.

It is this rediscovery of the existential level of speech, of speech as a gesture, that ties our understanding of speech to our understanding of the expressivity of the body. Indeed, Merleau-Ponty compares the reflexivity of speech, in that it can refer to itself or to the speaker, to the reversibility of the body, so that my left hand can touch my right hand as my right hand is touching something else, or I can hear my own voice. As Merleau-Ponty notes, my body can give significance to words, so that subjects to whom a word is shown too quickly for them to read report a kind of experience of warmth when shown the word 'warm', or a stiffening of the back and the neck when shown the word 'hard'. Evidence from experiments with subliminal perception, particularly of words with sexual connotations, tends to support this. And so, the word 'before becoming the symbol of a concept [it] is first of all an event which grips my body' (PP 235). Words possess a motor presence, a behavioural style. Meanings are *embodied* in words as in gestures.

Speech and thought

The concept of embodiment will enable us to understand the relation between speech and thought. On the rationalist model, words are a simple translation of thoughts; it is thoughts alone which have meaning, and they fill words with meaning in the same way that we fill an empty jug with water. On this view speech has no productivity of its own, but is an external sign of concepts and ideas in the mind. But speech does have a power to bring us events and worlds through the medium of words. Speech throws up images, ideas and thoughts in its wake. Speech does not translate thought, but accomplishes it. The orator, unless his discourse is merely mechanical, does not have his words already 'in his head' before he begins, but finds that the flow of words propel themselves forwards, bringing fresh words out of his mouth when he needs them. Words have the expressive power to produce new thoughts and new words in us, as we experience in stimulating dialogue with another, where the other's speech suddenly makes us aware of things we never thought of previously, or enables us to find words for ideas we have never expressed before.

> Operative language makes us think, and living thought
> magically finds its words. . . . It is when we do not understand
> that we say, 'Those are words there', and that our own

discourses, in return, are pure thought for us. There is an inarticulate thought (the psychologist's 'Aha-Erlebnis') and an accomplished thought, which suddenly and unaware discovers itself surrounded by words. Expressive operations take place between thinking language and speaking thought; not, as we thoughtlessly say, between thought and language. It is not because they are parallel that we speak; it is because we speak that they are parallel. (S 18)

It may be objected that this analysis of speech as the embodiment of thought tends to downgrade the importance of thinking (Kwant, 1963, pp. 225–6). This is not Merleau-Ponty's aim, however, but rather to indicate how thought is interwoven with speech, and how both are grounded on, and are expressions of operative intentionality. Thought is not assimilated into speech. Thought and speech can be understood phenomenologically as two subordinate structures, which interrelate in a way analogous to that of mind and body (see pp. 23–5). When speech and thought are integrated, words accomplish thought, so that there is a kind of *thought-in-speech*, an almost total embodiment of thought in words. But when thought and speech fail to be integrated, and function instead as partially independent structures – for example when I fail to understand, in the gestural or existential sense, what someone means, or when I feel that 'I can't put my thoughts into words' – then words tend to lose their productivity and are animated more by the thoughts which they translate. Actual speech and thought move between these two poles of integration and non-integration.

Sedimentation and structure

We have seen how a phenomenological understanding of speech is modelled on our understanding of experience in general, and in particular that of perception and behaviour. Now such experience has a general tendency towards *sedimentation*, the accumulation of acquired responses and patterns. Sedimentation does not prevent novel responses; indeed, it is the necessary presupposition in that it frees attention from the numerous quasi-automatic patterns of experience and behaviour and allows consciousness to engage in creative work in relation to its environment. We find the same process in speech, which can be understood as a dialectic between sedimentation and innovation. Speech is sedimented into a vast number of acquired or already constituted meanings, an always available depository of expressions which have settled into the fabric of language. This ability of language to become sedimented distinguishes it from all other expressive processes, such as music or painting. Music can indeed be written down, and paintings are preserved on canvas, yet every composer or painter feels himself to be starting at the beginning, creating a new world of expression, and able to break free of his contemporary genres or styles, whereas the writer is already immersed in a language he uses all the time, even when he is not writing. Speech enables us to find ourselves, its deposits are always available, and it is possible to speak about speech, whereas it is impossible to paint about painting (PP 190).

It is the movement between sedimentation and innovation that defines speech.

> Available meanings, in other words former acts of expression,
> establish between speaking subjects a common world, to
> which the words being actually uttered in their novelty refer
> as does the gesture to the perceptible world. And the meaning of
> speech is nothing other than the way in which it handles this
> linguistic world or in which it plays modulations on the
> keyboard of acquired meanings. (PP 186)

In other words, every *word in the speaking*, each contingent speech-act, refers to the *spoken word*, the whole sedimented body of already constituted speech and speech-acts. It follows that the time-honoured distinction between language (*la langue*) and speech (*la parole*), where speech is conceived as what one actually says, and language as the storehouse of possibilities on which the speaking subject draws, is artificial and abstract. Every act of speech, however novel or creative, alludes at the same time to language as a totality (CL 99–100). There is no speech without language, or language without speech.

In *Phenomenology of Perception* the stress is on this dialectic between sedimentation and innovation, on the physiognomic nature of speech, modelled on the phenomenology of gestural expression and the motricity of the body. Speech is understood as a refinement of pre-linguistic meanings, to which the gestural level of speech constantly refers. But there is a change after *Phenomenology of Perception* as Merleau-Ponty read de Saussure and assimilated, albeit after his own fashion, some of the elements of structural linguistics. Merleau-Ponty moved towards a view of speech as more of an autonomous system, and to this end employed the concept of *structure*.

> This characterization of speech as a structure means that
> a language is not made up of *words*, each of which is endowed
> with one or several meanings. Each word has a meaning only
> inasmuch as it is sustained in this signification by all the
> others. . . . The only reality is the *Gestalt* of language. (CL 92)

And hence meaning is *diacritic*, lying not 'in' words, but 'between' them, made up of the interrelationships of words and their place in the overall *Gestalt*. Words are conceived as values, like coins or chess pieces, rather than as pure significations. They function together in a system, so that the most exact characterization of a word is that it is what the others are not. In *Phenomenology of Perception* Merleau-Ponty went beyond the rationalist view of speech, in which it is consciousness that bestows meaning upon each word, and words are the simple translation of thought, by pointing to the productivity and intentionality of speech, and the embodiment of thought in speech. Here the transcendence of rationalism is even more radical, since meaning is construed as having nothing to do with consciousness or thought, but as solely a structural phenomenon. The concept of structure leaves behind the subject/object dichotomy on which rationalism (like empiricism) is based.

Yet we may wonder how much has really changed since *Phenomenology of Perception*. His analysis of speech in that work, in terms of the sedimentation/innovation dialectic, has been criticized as too 'psychologistic', relying too much on the notion of sediment or habit, and ignoring the structural element of language (Ricoeur, 1967, especially pp. 12–13 and 23). Now it is true that Merleau-Ponty abandons the notion of sedimentation in favour of structure after *Phenomenology of Perception*. And he also abandons the concept of the 'tacit *cogito*', a concept which could be construed as evidence of psychologism. This tacit *cogito* was defined as a kind of pre-reflective and inarticulate sense of belonging to myself, a form of consciousness of the way in which words take on expressive form and meaning (PP 402–6). Yet the notion of speech as structure makes this concept redundant, for it is the internal logic of speech, its cohesion as a *Gestalt*, which brings about expression and meaning, and this takes place within speech itself. There is not a tacit or silent *cogito*, but simply a speaking subject (see Gillan, 1973, pp. 43–6, and p. 46 of this work).

Nevertheless, the changeover from sediment to structure represents more of a change in emphasis than a radical break. The concept of structure, or *Gestalt*, is not new for Merleau-Ponty. It is, indeed, as the title of his first work illustrates, a fundamental concept for understanding being-in-the-world. Merleau-Ponty tailors de Saussure's structural linguistics very much to his own purposes, and, indeed, as has been pointed out, manages to misrepresent structuralism in the process.[2] De Saussure intended structuralism as a 'science' of linguistics, whereas Merleau-Ponty's phenomenology is always primarily concerned with the speaking subject, the subject's living relationship with himself and the world through speech. Merleau-Ponty intends the concept of structure as a *dynamic* concept, in

59

which words can combine creatively to produce novel utterances and senses, which would be impossible in a conception of structure as a static or deterministic system. Nor, in Merleau-Ponty's usage, is the concept of structure incompatible with a phenomenological analysis of consciousness, since it is consciousness which institutes structures, which then function in a quasi-independent manner.

The notion of structure, and the nature of words as diacritic, stress the essential allusiveness of speech, the fact that it signifies indirectly, a central theme of Merleau-Ponty's phenomenology of speech. But whereas, in his earlier analysis, this allusiveness is a result of the interplay between the gestural and conceptual levels of speech, or between the horizons of senses and the explicit significations of words, it is now seen as a consequence of the diacritic nature of meaning. If words are defined in terms of their surrounding words, 'it seems that *language never says anything*' (PW 32). Similarly, in a novel, 'the desire to kill is nowhere *in* the words. It is between them, in the hollows of space, time, and the significations they delimit, the way movement in the film is between the immobile images that follow one another' (PW 88). In both cases, in the earlier and later analyses, meaning is not defined as a sum of significations, but as an overall style of structure of an utterance or series of utterances. Meaning, understood phenomenologically, is a structural phenomenon, whether this structure is conceived as the result of the interplay between levels of speech, or as a consequence of the way words are put together in a given utterance.

Speech as praxis

Whether conceptualized in terms of the interplay between sedimentation and innovation, or in terms of structure, a phenomenological analysis of speech discloses speech as intentionality and as praxis. Speech brings us objects themselves:

> The denomination of objects does not follow upon recognition; it is itself recognition. When I fix my eyes on an object in the half-light, and say: 'It is a brush', there is not in my mind the concept of a brush, under which I subsume the object, and which moreover is linked by frequent association with the word 'brush', but the words bear the meaning, and, by imposing it on the object, I am conscious of reaching that object. (PP 177)

Speech is characterized by its productivity in instituting a cultural world for us. Speech, particularly in the form of ordinary, everyday, casual conversation establishes and consolidates the taken-for-grantedness of the common-sense world by the very fact that conversation can afford to be ordinary and casual. It is in and through ordinary, everyday conversation – in chit-chat, argument, dialogue, interrogation, issuing and carrying out orders, asking questions and giving answers, etc. – that we relate to other people, and so construct the particular form of our shared, intersubjective world (see Berger and Luckmann, 1966, and Berger and Kellner, 1964). The constant flow of words, of small talk, establishes the massive reality of the common-sense world. Our talk never starts from scratch and never finishes, it is always in a process of being underway. It expresses our never-ending dialogue with the world. This 'naturalness' of ordinary speech throws into relief those kinds of speech that are 'unnatural'. At one extreme there is the aphasiac, who, in order to carry on a conversation, needs 'resting points' chosen in advance, and who, in order to write on a blank page, needs a line or spot to indicate where he should begin. At the other extreme there is Mallarmé, who is fascinated by the empty page and writes nothing because he wants to say everything. In both cases the intentionality of speech, its ability to real-ize intentions and hence oneself, is lost.

This demonstration of speech as praxis shows that the representative function of speech, its capacity to designate phenomena in the world, defines only one part of speech. As the notions of speech as gesture or as structure have indicated, words cannot simply be the carriers of pure significations or meanings which would refer directly to objects in the world. Although in certain cases speech *can* function in this way, words are in fact more accurately described as tools. In words that could have been written by Wittgenstein, Merleau-Ponty writes:

The word is like a *tool defined by a certain usage*, even though we are unable to give an exact conceptual formula to this usage (CL 86)

As for the meaning of the word, I learn it as I learn to use a tool, by seeing it used in the context of a certain situation (PP 403)

Speech, then, like our body, is an instrument for intending a world.

Nevertheless, this theme of speech as praxis is not generally considered to be the area of Merleau-Ponty's phenomenology of speech that warrants development. Commentators have tended to suggest that the marriage of phenomenology with a more structural, syntactical or grammatical approach to language would be more productive.[3] Yet these have always been marginal concerns for Merleau-Ponty in his attempt to understand the intentionality of speech, the birth of meaning, and the speaking subject. In my opinion, it is the deepening and amplifying of the theme of speech as praxis that points the way forward for a phenomenology of speech. To this end, I will look briefly at the development of Wittgenstein's approach to speech, and at ethnomethodology, a recent advance that marks an interesting combination of a Wittgensteinian and phenomenological perspective, in order to suggest how Merleau-Ponty's own analyses and ideas can be refined.

Wittgenstein: from ideal language to everyday speech

In the *Tractatus Logico-Philosophicus* (1961) Wittgenstein attempted to construct an ideal language with which to describe the world. He argued that the world consists of a multitude of empirical facts and states of affairs, and that it is the function of language to copy, mirror or represent these facts and states of affairs, in the same way that a picture or photograph represents something in the world. But everyday speech is full of ambiguities and vagueness, and so must be purified if an ideal logical language, governed by logical grammar and syntax, is to be constructed (3.325). This logical language was to consist primarily of elementary propositions, or names, which assert the nature of things or states of affairs. These elementary propositions derive their sense or meaning not from other elementary propositions, since that would lead us into a vicious circle, but by 'hooking onto' reality. So for any language or mode of discourse to meet Wittgenstein's criteria of adequacy, it must consist of elementary propositions, or of complex propositions that can be decomposed into elementary propositions. Any modes of discourse that could not be expressed in terms of this logical language – such as ethics, mysticism, metaphysics or questions about life – were to be eliminated from philosophy since, philosophically speaking, they were meaningless. As Wittgenstein says in his preface: 'The whole sense of the book might be summed up in the following words: what can be said at all can be said clearly, and what we cannot talk about we must pass over in silence' (p. 3).

The result is a strange work. Wittgenstein himself was uncomfortably aware of the poverty of his philosophical programme. Although he believed that he had finally solved all the essential philosophical problems – by showing that if they did not make sense in terms of his logical language, then they must be meaningless, and hence cannot be problems – so that he could say that 'the *truth* of the thoughts that are here communicated seems to me unassailable and definitive', he then goes on to add that 'the second thing in which the value of this book consists is that it shows how little is achieved when these problems are solved' (p. 5). His positivist programme of identifying philosophy with the construction of a purified language heralds, as he himself points out, the dissolution of philosophy as anything apart from a commentary on the workings of natural science. 'The correct method in philosophy', he wrote at the end of his book, would be 'to say nothing except what can be said, i.e. propositions of natural science – i.e. something that has nothing to do with philosophy' (6. 53).

This view of philosophy as the construction of an ideal logical language is inimical to any phenomenology of speech. Merleau-Ponty refers to 'the spectre of a pure language' as a revolt against language in its existing state (PW 5). This pure language is based upon 'the myth of a language of things' (PW 7), where the word is seen as a pure sign standing for objects in the world, and hence devoid of any power of its own. Wittgenstein himself argues in similar terms (although, of course, independently of Merleau-Ponty) in his writings after the *Tractatus*, especially the *Philosophical Investigations* (1968). He criticizes his former view that language consists of elementary propositions, or names, which mirror the elementary facts of the world, or 'simples', by asking:

> But what are the simple constituent parts of which reality is composed? – What are the simple constituent parts of a chair? – The bits of wood of which it is made? Or the molecules, or the atoms? – 'Simple' means: not composite. And here the point is: in what sense 'composite'? It makes no sense at all to speak absolutely of the 'simple parts of a chair'. (1968, paragraph 47)

This rejection of an 'absolute' answer to the question 'what is the sense of simple or composite?' finds expression in Wittgenstein's introduction of a crucial concept: that of *language-games*. There is no unitary function or structure to language, no essence to it, as the *Tractatus* had suggested. Instead, Wittgenstein now argues, language is to be seen as a variety of criss-crossing parts or games, which function in partial independence of each other. Hence Wittgenstein's famous comparison of language with a toolbox.

> I have often compared language to a tool chest, containing a hammer, chisel, nails, screws, glue. It is not by chance that all these things have been put together – but there are important differences between the different tools – they are used in a family of ways – though nothing could be more different than glue and a chisel. There is constant surprise at the new tricks language plays on us when we get into a new field. (1966, p. 1)

It is in terms of this view of language as a multitude of different language-games that the name – object theory of language of the *Tractatus*, where words were held to name or represent objects in the world, is now characterized as just one language-game among others. Language is not only used to represent but has many other uses: to command, remind, speculate, make jokes, curse, greet, etc.

Meaning is not correspondence with the world, as the *Tractatus* maintained – although this can be true for certain language-games, for example naming tools on a building-site. So, for example, if Mr N dies, it is not the meaning of Mr N that dies – as the correspondence theory would have it – but the bearer of the name (1968, paragraph 40). And so: 'For a *large* class of cases – though not for all – in which we employ the word "meaning" it can be defined thus: the meaning of a word is its use in the language' (paragraph 43).

For the Wittgenstein of the *Philosophical Investigations* words are not so much names as tools, functioning like chess pieces which have their value in terms of the game as a whole. Words can also be characterized as signals (Pitkin, 1972), so that the utterance 'I am in pain' is a speech-act, a kind of pain behaviour, not a report of my 'inner state'. Words do not mirror objects in the world, but are the frame through which we see them: 'grammar tells what kind of object anything is' (paragraph 373).[4] Speech, in short, is praxis: 'words can be wrung from us, – like a cry. Words can be *hard* to say: such, for example, as are used to effect a renunciation, or to confess a weakness. (Words are also deeds)' (paragraph 546).

We see here a striking convergence with Merleau-Ponty's phenomenology of speech – in Wittgenstein's stress on meaning as use in context, his analogy between words and tools, his rejection of meaning as an internal, mental activity, to say nothing of his definition of understanding in existential rather than conceptual terms, as the mastery of a technique, involving the ability to carry out what is grasped intellectually. Wittgenstein's rejection of the logical language of the *Tractatus* entails, in Merleau-Ponty's terms, a return to the speaking subject, or as Wittgenstein says: 'What *we* do is to bring words back from their metaphysical to their everyday use' (1968, paragraph 115). Now, to be sure, Wittgenstein's concerns are not the same as Merleau-Ponty's; he is not interested in a phenomenology of speech, but in describing how everyday language is actually used. Nevertheless, in one sense Wittgenstein's analyses can be seen as a refinement of Merleau-Ponty's phenomenology, namely, in his notion of language-games, his view of language as a variety of interlocking parts. Merleau-Ponty's concepts of sedimentation or structure, in spite of their dynamic intent so as to be compatible with creativity and innovation in speech, tend to obscure this feature of speech and give a too unified view. Merleau-Ponty focuses on creative speech, which gives birth to new expressions and which 'rattle[s] the chain of language' to make the sedimented or structural unity of speech always provisional, liable to be broken up and then remoulded. The Wittgensteinian concept of language-games points to a different, if lesser, kind of creativity: the dynamic interplay which can occur between different language-games, where each language-game embodies a different 'form of life' or view of the world. It is this interrelation between different language-games that gives speech its characteristic ambiguity and capacity for implication, irony, etc: 'When someone says "I hope he'll come" – is this a *report* about his state of mind, or a *manifestation* of his hope?' (Wittgenstein, 1968, paragraph 585).[5]

Ethnomethodology: the reflexivity of speech

Wittgenstein stresses the diversity of speech, the multitude of ways in which it can be used. Ethnomethodology, while endorsing this view, pays particular attention to a feature of speech that phenomenology has made evident: its capacity for establishing and maintaining the reality of the everyday world. Ethnomethodology amplifies this, and gives it a radical twist in its central concept of the *reflexivity* of speech. Hence Garfinkel, in *Studies in Ethnomethodogy* (1967), asserts that the central recommendation of ethnomethodology 'is that activities whereby members produce and manage settings for organized everyday affairs are identical with members' procedures for making these settings "account-able"' (p. 1).

This can be explicated as follows (see Filmer *et al.*, 1972, pp. 208–16). Garfinkel is suggesting that what we take to be the objective features of speech, and of social life in general, are objective only because we express them in objective terms, that is in terms of their common or intersubjective properties, rather than in terms of their unique or context-specific features. In other words, it is a feature of all explanations, accounts or renditions that they want to render unique and specific events or objects in terms of their generality or typicality. Hence the objectivity of speech and of social settings is to be seen as *produced* in and through talk. In so far as everyday speech makes features and settings in the social world 'account-able', that is explicable, intelligible, systematic, etc., it can be seen as *constituting* the accountability, explicability, intelligibility and systematization of the features and social settings.

The concept of reflexivity implies a radical extension of Austin's notion of performatives, of 'doing things with words'. Austin (1965) isolated a class of utterances that could be understood as actions: for example, promising something to someone, naming a ship, or marrying a man and woman. For ethnomethodologists, however, *all* utterances can be understood as performatives, as social activities (Turner, 1974, chapter 16). This is so, not just because there is a large number of social actions that are only accomplished in and through talk (reporting, complaining, insulting, forgiving, etc.) or with the help of talk (practically everything), but, more fundamentally, because talk reflexively produces social order.

In order to illustrate this, ethnomethodologists look at how accounts are produced in ordinary talk. One well-trodden path of research in the social sciences is that of mental illness. An ethnomethodological approach will investigate how the phenomenon 'mental illness' comes to be seen as existing, as a fact, through the various accounting procedures of persons perceived as relevant, both lay and medical. Ethnomethodology will look at how ordinary members 'make sense of' a given person's actions, what procedures they employ in order to 'see' that person's actions as rational, i.e. carried out according-to-a-rule, or, indeed, as irrational (mentally ill). The phenomenon of mental illness is thus produced, at least in ethnomethodological terms, in these accounting procedures (D. Smith, 1974). Garfinkel's (1967) study of decision-making of jurors also looks to accounting procedures. He centres his attention on the occasioned, contingent and pragmatically motivated decisions that jurors are obliged by their situation to come to, and is led to comment: 'When the outcome was in hand they went back to find the "why", the things that led up to the outcome, and that in order to give their decisions some order, which, namely, is the "officialness" of the decision' (p. 114). That is, what makes a decision 'official' (or rational) is a function of *how* it is arrived at and seen to be arrived at, it is something that does not exist independently of the methods used for producing and presenting that decision.

Ethnomethodology demonstrates that actions (linguistic or non-linguistic) are rational in the everyday world not because they are carried out in conformity to a pre-existing set of rules or instructions, but because they are enacted, and seen to be enacted, as oriented-to-a-rule, or rule-guided. Rules exist only in the practices (linguistic or non-linguistic) that embody them, and are used by members to display the rationality of their own talk or to detect the rationality in the talk of others. This display or detection of rationality is not a self-conscious, explicit or reflective process, but is pre-reflectively carried out by any competent member (i.e. speaker). Socialization for the ethnomethodologist is thus learning to reflexively produce and manage social settings through talk and behaviour.[6]

The ambiguity of speech

Our excursus into Wittgensteinian philosophy and ethnomethodology has put more flesh on the phenomenological theme of speech as praxis. I want now to suggest that this excursus can also allow us to deepen another theme of Merleau-Ponty's analysis, that of the *ambiguity* of speech. On Merleau-Ponty's account, we might point to four ways in which speech could be considered an ambiguous phenomenon. (1) There is the fact that speech is neither thing nor mind, subject nor object, but a manifestation of intersubjectivity, a *Gestalt* or structure. (2) There is the essential allusiveness and incompleteness of speech, its interplay between different levels of meaning or significance, the diacritic nature of its signs. (3) There is its existentiality, making it part of human praxis, which is understood as neither what man does to the world, nor what the world does to him, but as a dialectic between these two aspects. (4) There is finally the transcendence of speech, where speech is seen as an expression of intentionality, as that which is instituted by consciousness, yet where it is also always already constituted, an objective, external phenomenon predating the existence of any individual speaker. Now ethnomethodology can disclose a further dimension to the ambiguity of speech, and at the same time suggest a revision of one aspect of Merleau-Ponty's approach, namely, the notion of 'already-constituted meanings'.

For Merleau-Ponty the sedimentation of speech results in the steady accumulation of 'already-constituted meanings':

> We live in a world where speech is an *institution*. For all these many commonplace utterances, we possess within ourselves ready-made meanings. They arouse in us only second order thoughts; these in turn are translated into other words which demand from us no real effort of expression and will demand from our hearers no effort of comprehension. (PP 184)

For Merleau-Ponty the process of exchanging 'ready-made' meanings or thoughts is quasi-automatic or mechanical, requiring no real effort or work on the part of the speaker or hearer(s), and involving no special skill. Unlike creative or novel utterances, which accomplish thought, sedimented or already constituted speech only translates 'second-order thought' (which is aroused by ready-made meanings). This conception of sedimentation and already constituted meanings is incorporated into Merleau-Ponty's later notion of structure, which appears in his later writings. For example:

> In expressions already habitual, there is a direct meaning which corresponds point by point to the established phrases, forms, and words. Precisely because these expressions are habitual, the gaps and element of silence are obliterated. (PW 46)

Yet it is doubtful if ordinary, everyday speech, which is not creative in the sense of producing new means of expression in the style of novelists or philosophers, can be understood on this model of a point-by-point correspondence between meaning and habitual forms or phrases. Of course everyday talk is replete with clichés and well-worn phrases. Yet what is remarkable about all speech, ordinary or otherwise, is that a finite number of words or phrases can produce an infinite number of actual utterances, so that in any conversation there is a good chance that one or more particular utterances is new in that it has never been uttered in quite the same form before. Merleau-Ponty is not unaware of this kind of creativity present in all speech: 'Language is a system of a limited number of unities serving to express an unlimited number of things' (CL 29), and, therefore, 'the totality of meaning is never fully rendered: there is an immense mass of implications, even in the most explicit of languages' (*ibid.*). The problem is that Merleau-Ponty's proposal that ordinary speech or institutionalized speech be understood in terms of sedimentation, of ready-made meanings and established phrases, demanding no real work or skill on our part, does less than justice to this creativity present in all speech, and threatens to turn everyday speakers into puppets speaking their well-rehearsed lines, or 'judgemental dopes' as Garfinkel puts it, who speak in conformity to well-established rules and already constituted utterances. It also obscures *how* these already constituted meanings are put together; for example, which are seen as relevant to the particular speech situation, in what order they should be expressed, for what purposes they are to be brought in, and so on.

Ethnomethodology, in its investigation of the creativity or artfulness of everyday speech, pays particular attention to a phenomenon displayed in all conversation known as *glossing*. Merleau-Ponty himself makes reference to this phenomenon in ordinary talk. He writes, for example:

When I chat with a friend whom I know well, each of his remarks and each of mine contains, in addition to the meaning it carries for everybody else, a host of references to the main dimensions of his character and mine, without our needing to recall previous conversations with each other. (PP 130)

That is, in a chat between friends, the fact that we are friends, that we have had previous conversations together, have shared experiences or adventures, know certain things about each other, and so on, are *glossed* in the chat, they are never made explicit, but are the presupposed, taken-for-granted and unnoticed background of the conversation. If we were to make all of these features explicit, the conversation would probably never get started, since *every* conversation presupposes glossing of some kind. There are always things that it never makes sense to question within ordinary speech:

The act of speech is clear only for the person who is actually speaking or listening; it becomes obscure as soon as we try to bring explicitly to light those reasons which have led us to understand thus and not otherwise. . . . I may say that 'I have been waiting for a long time', or that someone is 'dead', and I think I know what I am saying. Yet if I question myself on time or the experience of death, which were implied in my words, there is nothing clear in my mind. (PP 391)

In other words, in order to make ordinary conversation possible at all, we have to agree, *for all practical purposes* (this phrase is, if you like, the ethos of the natural attitude), to accept certain meanings or assumptions as taken-for granted or valid until further notice. Indeed the natural attitude is characterized by the decision not to question what there is no need for all practical purposes to question, to doubt only what it is necessary to doubt in order to make daily living possible and viable. But *which* features or assumptions are taken-for-granted by any given speakers at the start of any given conversation cannot be presupposed or laid down by the theorist. What is distinctive about the ethnomethodological approach to the study of ordinary talk is that it sees members to be engaged in *interpretive work*, all through the conversation, in order to decide what is being glossed, what is being assumed or taken-for-granted by the other speaker (or by themselves), so that an intelligible background to the speech can be built up, and sense made of the conversation as it progresses. This interpretive work is, of course, pre-reflectively carried out, and is part of 'knowing how' to speak. In short, the phenomenon of glossing – the fact that members routinely refer to only a narrow part of the scene, because to fill in the whole scene or background would never allow the conversation to get underway – means that the assumption of conversation as the simple exchange of already constituted meanings or conventional expressions, or as based upon a series of 'common understandings' which are assumed by each speaker to exist prior to and independent of their conversation, must be cast into doubt, or phenomenologically 'reduced', in order to see the praxis and interpretive work carried out in each and every conversation.

Garfinkel illustrates this in the following experiment (1967, pp. 24–31). He instructed his students to report any common conversation by writing on the left-hand side of their paper what the parties actually said, and on the right-hand side what they (the students) and the parties to the conversation understood they were in fact talking about. Garfinkel quotes a report of one such conversation, which I reproduce in full:

| Husband: | Dana succeeded in putting a penny in a parking-meter today without being picked up. | This afternoon as I was bringing home Dana, our 4-year-old son, from the nursery school, he succeeded in reaching high enough to put a penny in a parking meter when we parked in |

69

	a meter zone, whereas before he had always had to be picked up to reach that high.
Wife: Did you take him to the record store?	Since he put a penny in a meter that means that you stopped while he was with you. I know that you stopped at the record store either on the way to get him or on the way back. Was it on the way back, so that he was with you or did you stop there on the way to get him and somewhere else on the way back?
Husband: No, to the shoe repair shop.	No, I stopped at the record store on the way to get him, and stopped at the shoe repair shop on the way home when he was with me.
Wife: What for?	I know one reason why you might have stopped at the shoe repair shop. Why did you in fact?
Husband: I got some new shoe laces for my shoes.	As you will remember I broke a shoe lace on one of my brown Oxfords the other day so I stopped to get some new laces.
Wife: Your loafers need new heels badly.	Something else you could have gotten that I was thinking of. You could have taken in your black loafers which need heels badly. You'd better get them taken care of pretty soon.

Garfinkel notes that his students found the right-hand side increasingly difficult to fill up, and when he demanded accuracy and clarity. they said they found it impossible. Now Garfinkel claims that to assume that his students were invoking knowledge of a community of understandings, a background of shared and conventional meanings, to understand what the parties were talking about does not explain why they found it impossible to fill in the right-hand side. Instead, the repair of the ambiguities or glossing of the conversation, which Garfinkel had demanded of his students, became impossible to carry out because their attempt to fill out the conversation and fill in what was glossed produced new ambiguities and new glossings in their own accounts. Garfinkel comments:

> I had asked my students to take on the impossible task of 'repairing' the essential incompleteness of *any* set of instructions no matter how carefully or elaborately written they might be. I had required them to formulate the method that the parties had used in speaking as rule or procedure to follow in order to say what the parties said, rules that would withstand every exigency of situation, imagination, and development. . . . To recognize *what* is said *means* to recognize how a person is speaking, for example to recognize that the wife in saying 'your shoes need heels badly' was speaking narratively, or metaphorically, or euphemistically, or double-talking. (1967, pp. 29–30)

This *indexicality* of speech – the fact that rules, practices, procedures that members follow in making sense of their talk are essentially situated and occasioned by the particular context or scene – means that to analyse any conversation in terms of a commonly accepted background of common understandings or already constituted meanings held in common, misses the constant interpretive work going on. It misses the fact that each partner, throughout the conversation, must take into account what is being glossed by his speech, and by the speech of his partner, and what each assumes the other assumes is being glossed. Sense and intelligibility are *achieved*, they are worked for, and cannot be assumed to be present from the start. Whatever the speakers have in common will be made procedurally relevant over the course of their conversation.

This is not to deny that there exist common understandings and assumptions and shared meanings. Of course there do – there could be no speech without them. But their invocation is not enough to explain how speech occurs and how it is understood. Ordinary talk does not just consist of the swapping of chunks of already constituted meanings or habitual expressions. We also need to take into account the interpretive work that members engage in in order to 'see' which habitual expressions or common understandings are relevant to which context, what they entail, how they are followed, applied, invoked, enforced, and seen to be followed, applied, invoked and enforced. We must not blind ourselves, in Garfinkel's words, to the 'discovering character' of ordinary speech. [7]

In short, we have deepened the meaning of the ambiguity of speech. Through its concept of reflexivity, ethnomethodology investigates the paradox of speech, that talking about something rationally is to make it rational, that managing everyday settings is identical with making them account-able. The concept of indexicality points to a similar conclusion: *what* parties say in a conversation cannot be separated from *how* they talk about it. Finally the notion of glossing shows that making sense of speech is an ongoing process requiring considerable skill and competence on the part of members.

Speech and the world

I have so far endorsed Wittgenstein and ethnomethodology as amplifying and expanding some of the main themes of a phenomenology of speech (even though Wittgensteinians or ethnomethodologists would not see their own work in such a light). Nevertheless I have been selective in what I regard as the parts of Wittgenstein or ethnomethodology that can be married with phenomenology. There are indeed some parts of these two approaches which are not compatible with phenomenology, and of which phenomenology would be very critical. In particular there is a tendency in Wittgenstein (which is carried over into ethnomethodology) to treat language as an independent system to be analysed in isolation from an understanding of the world and of human experience as a whole. It is true that Wittgenstein stressed that speech is praxis, that meaning is use, and that therefore all utterances must be understood in their context. Hence to understand speech is to understand something of the world. Nevertheless in practice a Wittgensteinian analysis of speech is carried out in isolation from other forms of human experience and behaviour, so that it is cut off from its ground in being-in-the-world. Speech is held to be a form of behaviour, but there is no analysis of other forms of behaviour, or of behaviour in general. Wittgenstein leaves us hanging in the air when we wish to link up his often brilliant insights into speech with an overall understanding of man. In some ordinary language philosophy, this latent tendency becomes a central concern. Speech is studied as a totally autonomous system. 'Ordinary language' is investigated in minute detail in order to note the multiplicity of ways in which ordinary words are used, with little or no regard to the essential relatedness of speech to the world (Gellner, 1959). 'Ordinary usage' is regarded as the standard by which all questions of sense and intelligibility are to be judged, and hence a philosophical position can be 'refuted' if it fails to accord with what is judged to be this 'ordinary usage'.[8]

This segregation of speech from being-in-the-world is alien to phenomenology. The productivity and power of speech means that speech not only represents things in the world (although, as we have seen, this is not all that it does) but brings us things, makes them manifest to us:

Language is a life, is our life and the life of the things. . . .
It is the error of the semantic philosophies to close up language

as if it spoke only of itself: language lives only from silence . . .
because he has experienced within himself the need to speak,
the birth of speech as bubbling up at the bottom of his mute
experience, the philosopher knows better than anyone that what
is lived is lived-spoken, that, born at this depth, language is
not a mask over Being, but – if one knows how to grasp it
with all its roots and all its foliation – the most valuable
witness to Being, that it does not interrupt an immediation
that would be perfect without it, that the vision itself, the
thought itself are, as has been said, 'structured as a language'
(Jacques Lacan). (VI 125–6)

Language is not coincidence with things, not copies or mirrors of
them – that is the error of positivism. Nor does language break a
kind of mute 'immediation' we might have with the world, as if
words somehow got in the way. Words can, of course, be a hindrance
to our observation and commerce with things in the world, if we
allow language to give us only the familiar and the typical in the
objects and events we see and participate in (and also, in some
sense, construct), as is characteristic of the natural attitude. But
speech and language, built on layers of primitive meanings which
make the world a human world, a world-for-consciousness, can
also call forth the phenomena of the world in their primordial
significance for us. 'What is lived is lived-spoken', says Merleau-
Ponty; 'the whole landscape is overrun with words as with an
invasion', he says elsewhere (VI 155). Because being-in-the-world
is inherently charged with meaning, it can be reached by speech,
albeit in a mediated fashion.

Authentic speech

I have suggested that Merleau-Ponty's phenomenology of speech
does less than justice to the skill of ordinary, everyday talk. In a
sense this is an unfair criticism, since Merleau-Ponty is not so much
concerned with ordinary conversation, the empirical run of everyday words, of spoken words, as he puts it, but with tracing the
movement of the birth of speech, of new expressions, new ways of
speaking. In other words, Merleau-Ponty wants to study the word
in the speaking, or what he terms *authentic speech* (PP 178, n. 1,
and 179, n. 1). Authentic speech 'formulates for the first time', it is
'first-hand speech', and examples would be a child uttering its first
word, a lover revealing his feelings, or a writer or philosopher who
attempts to fashion a language adequate for expressing and awaken-
ing primordial experience. Now this creativity or novelty of authentic speech makes it a comparatively rare phenomenon in ordinary

73

speech, which accounts for Merleau-Ponty's investigations of literature and philosophy as exemplifications of authentic speech. Everyday speech, although artful and skilful, is not creative in this sense. Nevertheless, authentic speech is not absent from everyday talk. A child speaking for his first time, two people declaring their feelings for each other without sentimentality or romanticization, or similar experiences of creativity or communion are part of many people's experience. Furthermore Merleau-Ponty's point is that all speech, however trivial or commonplace, is built on top of these novel or creative expressions which, at some point in time, were uttered, brought into being, and then slowly became sedimented and available for everyday use. Language progresses by taking words or expressions and then finding new figurative or metaphorical meanings for them, thus enlarging the expressive potential of words or phrases. Edie makes this clear:

> A word which primarily designates a perceptual phenomenon,
> for example the perception of light, once constituted, is available *for a new purpose* and can be used with a new intention,
> for example, to denote the process of intellectual understanding,
> and we speak of (mental) illumination. Once established, the
> metaphorical use of the original word is no longer noticed;
> its essential ambiguity tends to fall below the level of awareness from the moment that it is taken as designating another,
> now distinguishable, experience. (1962, p.5)

All Merleau-Ponty's basic points about speech – its intimate relationship with thought, its productivity, its opening onto being – are meant to refer primarily to authentic speech, the word in the speaking, although all actual empirical speech, since it is built up of deposits of speech once authentic, can be seen to possess the same qualities, even if to a far lesser degree. Merleau-Ponty's discussions of communication or dialogue, for example, have authentic speech in mind:

> The communication or comprehension of gestures comes about
> through the reciprocity of my intentions and the gestures of
> others, of my gestures and intentions discernible in the conduct
> of other people. It is as if the other person's intention inhabited
> my body and mine his. . . . The gesture presents itself to me
> as a question, bringing certain perceptible bits of the world to
> my notice, and inviting my concurrence in them. Communication is achieved when my conduct identifies this path with its
> own. There is mutual confirmation between myself and others.
> (PP 185)

This account, which is meant to hold good for all gestures, linguistic or otherwise, is not adequate, as I have argued, to deal with ordinary conversation and the methods used in making sense of speech. But Merleau-Ponty is speaking here of authentic communication, where two (or more) persons seek to open themselves to each other in order to learn and exchange something about themselves and the world. There is 'mutual confirmation' and genuine reciprocity. It is such experiences that allow man to feel at home in speech, where his intentions are embodied and real-ized, and he is thrown out into the world and into relationships with others. In the authentic experience of dialogue, I participate in speech that I have not constructed, yet is not alien to me, but a product both of institutionalization and the ways I and my partner have moulded that institutionalized speech in order to express ourselves. 'There is said to be a wall between us and others, but it is a wall we build together, each putting his stone in the niche left by the other' (S 18). And so speech has the power both to separate and isolate us from others and the world, by functioning as a screen between my experiences and the experiences of others, and to bring us together with others by participating in a common linguistic and interhuman world.

There is much talk of a crisis in language today. Sartre (1967 and 1968, chapter 11) speaks of the sickness of words, how they are used to mask instead of disclose reality. Habermas (1970a) employs the concept of 'systematically distorted communication' to refer to speech which is not conspicuously pathological, but consists of rigid and compulsive speech patterns which engender pseudo-communication. Wittgenstein's whole philosophy can be understood an attempt to bring speech back home, to regain contact with those as areas of our language which have become cut off from us and have led us into confusion: 'A *picture* held us captive. And we could not get outside it, for it lay in our language and language seemed to repeat it to us inexorably' (1968, paragraph 115). He speaks of language going on holiday, or idling, when it is no longer embodied in praxis but is cut off from concrete being-in-the-world and used purely in the abstract, as is the case in much traditional philosophy. It is in the light of such diagnoses of the estrangement of contemporary man in his speech that Merleau-Ponty's notion of authentic speech becomes compelling. His whole phenomenology of speech can be read as an appeal to us to rediscover our roots in our speech, its ground in our pre-reflective life, its capacity for creativity and innovation, its power to bring us the world and things in the world, and its potential for genuine communication. Speech, in its most authentic sense, is, like all experience, openness to the world and to ourselves. In authentic speech I ex-press myself and embody myself in the world, and so authentic speech is also committed speech (Blum, *et al.*, 1974).

3 Society

Positivism

Sociology, in its attempt to understand society and the human world, has been dominated since its inception by a positivist paradigm. The dramatic success of the methodology of the natural sciences by the beginning of the twentieth century, as well as the concern of the young sociology to make itself academically respectable, have been factors in its embracing of the method of the natural sciences, most strikingly expressed in Durkheim's famous directive to 'treat social facts as things'. Positivism – the desire for one scientific method to cover all branches of human knowledge – in one version or another is still the dominant paradigm in contemporary sociology and the social sciences in general. It is necessary first to understand positivism and its problems when attempting to understand society before we can come to terms with existential phenomenology as a viable alternative.

Positivism is essentially a certain view of what is to count as valid knowledge of the world. Its basic premiss is the *unity of the scientific method*, the belief that the form and methods of acquiring knowledge are essentially the same in all spheres of inquiry. In practice, this means advocating the hypothetico-deductive method, or some version of it, for sociology. Kolakowski, in his book *Positivist Philosophy: from Hume to the Vienna Circle* (1972), identifies three other basic postulates of positivism, which most writers working under the umbrella of positivism would accept. These are: (1) *the rule of phenomenalism*, the belief that there is no real difference between 'essence' and 'phenomena', so that positivists believe 'we are entitled to record only that which is actually manifested in experience; opinions concerning occult entities of which experienced things are supposedly the manifestations are untrustworthy' (p. 11). (2) *The rule of nominalism*, which maintains that 'we may not assume that any insight formulated in general terms can have any real referents other than individual concrete objects' (p. 13). From this it follows that 'the world we know is a collection of individual observable facts. Science aims at ordering these facts . . .' (p. 15). (3) Finally, as a consequence of phenomenalism and nominalism, there is the rule that maintains an essential difference between descriptive and evaluative or normative statements, and refuses to call evaluative or normative statements knowledge.

To understand positivism, we need to understand what Wittgenstein calls its form of life. This form of life entails both a view of language – in which all knowledge is embodied – and a view of the world. We have already seen how Merleau-Ponty trenchantly and devastatingly criticizes the positivist view of the world as expressed in empiricism. He shows that what are called above the rules of phenomenalism and nominalism result in an atomistic picture of the world, of perception and of behaviour, unable to account for the evidence of general principles of co-ordination, or the systematic interrelatedness of perception and behaviour with the world. The phenomenalist premiss, that there is no real difference between 'essence' and 'phenomena', which sounds as though it might be similar to Merleau-Ponty's critique of Husserl's essentialism, is in fact very different. This is because what positivists accept as that which is manifested in experience, which is what defines phenomena, is extremely narrow, and hence what are to be considered as 'occult entities' extremely wide. Positivists define experience in the narrow empiricist sense of that which is recorded by the organism as stimulation in response to its environment. Experience becomes synonymous with sensations or sense-data. The crucial phenomenological concepts of *Gestalt* or structure would not pass the test of either phenomenalism or nominalism.

The positivist view of language – which we have also seen in the last chapter, and especially in the discussion of Wittgenstein's *Tractatus* (pp. 62–4) – aims to construct an ideal mode of discourse which will faithfully mirror the world of atomic facts. This ideal language should be free of the 'impurities' of normal speech, its ambiguity, its mixture of descriptive and evaluative statements, its indexicality, glossing and general imprecision. Positivism has a notion of adequate speech as impersonal, de-authored speech, free from individual bias and commitment, speech which copies nature rather than serving to reflect the speaker. Adequate speech is speech that can emanate from anyone, speech that is purely descriptive, with no traces of evaluation or normative input (Blum *et al.*, 1974, especially chapters 3 and 4).

In the social sciences, positivism has generally taken two directions. The first is what C. W. Mills (1970) has called 'abstracted empiricism', the blind and obsessive collecting of 'empirical data' (i.e.

what is thrown up by the positivist machine of an ideal, logical language) in the hope that, one day, a pattern or meaning to this vast accumulation of 'facts' will emerge. The other direction is what Mills calls 'grand theory', the construction of ideal systems or models of society in accord with the canons of adequate speech. The work of Talcott Parsons in sociology can serve as a paradigmatic example of this. He aims to construct a model of the 'social system', a framework consisting of shared values and norms, into which individuals are inserted as actors or role-players. These actors are gradually socialized into accepting these shared values and norms and so become integrated into the system. If they should happen to deviate, sanctions are brought to bear by the system in order to bring them back into line. Now this model of the social system fulfils the canons of natural scientific logic and rationality. The problem is that it operates at such a vast level of theoretical abstraction that it becomes a serious question to ask what is gained by the construction of such ideal models, as they hold only a tenuous relationship to actual lived experience in society (cf. Schutz, 1970b).

Living with positivism

The question I want to pose is simply this: given this brief and schematic account of positivism, what kind of account of society and social experience can it provide? It is not in dispute that positivism *can* provide social theories – there are very many examples of positivist or neo-positivist accounts of society. The important question is: what do we gain, or lose, by seeing society through positivist eyes? The positivist belief in the unity of the scientific method ties it in practice to a form of hypothetico-deductive theorizing, where phenomena are causally explained by subsuming them under general laws. These laws aim to order the empirical facts the theorist observes in the social world, and to show how these facts are causally interrelated. Where this gets us is elegantly demonstrated by Alan Blum (1971), where he discusses one such positivist account which attempts to subsume the action of Bill's taking and eating chicken from the refrigerator under a general, covering law. The general law put forward is to the effect that it is probable that Bill, when hungry and in the house, will eat something which he will first have to remove from the place where food is normally kept. That is, Bill's action of eating chicken is *explained* by this formulation of a general law (p. 130). Blum goes on to comment:

> We must note that 'edible food' is not 'chicken', and that the proposed explanation does not preserve what we might take to be the grammar of the action for Bill (his action of eating

chicken). The particular situation has meaning for Bill in his disposal of the chicken, and the description of his action as 'eating edible food' seems like a limp reproduction of this action. The point of all this is that while the deductive model *can* be applied to the field of human actions, it is only accomplished through a transformation of the meaning of the action. (ibid)

Here we see positivist inquiry is guided more by its conception of what is to count as valid knowledge of human action – subsuming any action under general, explanatory laws – than by any attempt to understand the actual meaning to the participant(s) of the action. The result is vacuousness and triviality. In similar vein, Louch (1966) illustrates the redundancy of positivist explanation (in this case, behaviourism) in psychology:

Skinner's plan seems to be to replace the normal human and animal environment with laboratory conditions. He conceives of psychology as a piece of human engineering. He wishes to demonstrate that, with adequate controls, any desired kind of behaviour can be produced in a subject. We all know this in a general way, and Skinner is the first to admit that his views are built on quite ordinary conceptions of the function of reinforcement in everyday life. In ordinary life, however, we take these principles of teaching and, if you will, conditioning as techniques that might do the job desired, not as laws that explain the manifold behaviour of human or animal populations. (p. 35)

Here again (as Merleau-Ponty has shown with empiricism) the overriding concern with 'correct form' – the experimental method, the search for general laws of behaviour, the hypothetico-deductive model of theorizing – means that the phenomena under study, whether human or animal behaviour, have to be interpreted in the light of what positivism accepts as valid knowledge.

There is a further consequence of positivism, which follows from its concern to maintain a rigid separation between description and evaluation (a separation which is brought into question in chapter 5). Since adequate speech is thought of by the positivist as purely factual and descriptive, a kind of copy of the world, it must be impersonal, that is, the speech of anyone. Hence theorizing for positivism becomes *un-reflective*:[1] the theorist has no interest in the grounds of his own theorizing, in the process of theorizing itself in so far as it serves to disclose something about the theorist and the kind of world he lives in. Positivism is not concerned with how a theory is generated, but only with how it is empirically validated, and worthy to be considered as valid knowledge. The positivist theorizer is

79

debarred from exploring the phenomenological roots of his own theorizing.

One danger of un-reflective theorizing can be illustrated by looking at Durkheim's (1952) study of suicide. In this study, often cited as a classic of 'scientific' sociology, Durkheim treated suicide rates as social 'things', existing independently of the will of individuals. He wanted to rule out completely the 'subjective' meaning suicide might have to any given individuals. Instead he took suicide rates – as defined by collections of statistics – as objective social facts which could be causally explained by other objective social facts. The cause of the suicide rate in a given society or group was, for Durkheim, the degree of what he called egoism, altruism or anomie exhibited by the individuals of that society or group, which in turn was the result of the degree of social integration of those individuals. However, as has been pointed out (Filmer *et al.*, 1972, pp. 43–5):

> despite the claim by Durkheim that subjective meanings are to be ruled out of his account of suicide, it becomes clear that his analysis is permeated at every level by meanings supplied to make sense of the data. Moreover, these meanings are not, themselves, part of the data under investigation (which would be a requirement of his methodological rationale) but are, rather, drawn from his own common sense understanding of everyday social experiences. (p. 43)

Durkheim is forced to introduce his own common-sense knowledge into his analysis because, having rejected the meaning or significance suicide might have to the members of society or groups, he is faced with the problem of explaining the causal relation between the unchanging norms of society, which tend towards social integration, and fluctuating rates of suicide for different groups (notably Catholics and Protestants). In other words, he has to demonstrate the degree of egoism, altruism or anomie of a given group without any reference to what the individuals concerned might understand by egoism, altruism or anomie. Now to make sense of these terms and apply them successfully he must use some common-sense knowledge. But his reliance on his own unexplicated common-sense knowledge is also brought in – in a way more potentially damaging – when he attempts, for example, to demonstrate a relation between education and the suicide rate, arguing that a high degree of education is associated with a high suicide rate. The problem is that this does not fit the Jews, who have a high degree of education but a low suicide rate. So Durkheim is forced to account for this discrepancy in terms of the different significance of education for the Jews. Now, not only does this hypothetical significance of education for the Jews belie Durkheim's claim that he is not interested in the social meanings of phenomena but only objective social facts – it also raises the interesting question of where Durkheim gets his hypothesis from. The supposed different significance of education for the Jews is not part of his data – however one would go about assembling such data under positivist auspices – and so must come from Durkheim's own common-sense understanding. In similar vein Durhneim advances the argument that common morality reproves suicide, yet offers no evidence from his data to support it. Once again he relies on his own common-sense knowledge (he cannot argue that it is part of the meaning of the word 'suicide' that it is to be reproved, because that would be admitting that a descriptive word can also be normative). The problem is that he never treats the social meanings of phenomena as subjects of investigation, but merely takes them for granted by substituting his own common-sense meanings to plug up the gaps in his explanations.

The question of meaning

As the case of Durkheim reveals, the crucial difficulty in living with positivism as a theory of the social world is its inability to handle the concept of meaning. This is not to say that the concept of meaning finds no place in positivist social science – it would be exceedingly difficult to talk about man or society without bringing in the idea of meaning (although the behaviourists have had a good try). But the trouble with meaning for positivism is that it is not easily susceptible to 'empirical verification', and so the notion of meaning is assimilated into their other concepts, concepts that fit better with the methodological demands of their programme.

This is illustrated in Rudner's book, *Philosophy of Social Science* (1966), which openly advocates a positivist methodology for social science. Early in his book Rudner makes a distinction which enables him to assimilate 'problems' of meaning into his conceptual framework. This distinction is between the *context of discovery* and the *context of validation*, the former concerned with how hypotheses come to be formulated, the latter concerned with how hypotheses are validated or tested. Now Rudner argues that the claim that social science must be 'scientific', in the same way as the natural sciences, is a claim relating not to the context of discovery but to the context of validation, since the validity of 'scientific' knowledge is a function of how it is tested (1966, pp. 5–7).

Having made this distinction, Rudner can turn to 'problems' which might arise, and in particular issues concerned with meaning. For example, in a long section dealing with arguments that might be raised against the scientific status of sociology, Rudner deals with one such 'issue', that of *Verstehen*, which he defines as 'empathetic

81

understanding'. Two points should be noted right away. First, Rudner only deals with the 'issue' of *Verstehen* in a section listing possible objections to sociology's scientific status. In other words, *Verstehen*, or the meaningfulness of social phenomena, is of concern to Rudner only in so far as it might be seen to threaten his methodological claims, rather than as a phenomenon itself, or as a crucial part of his subject of study (society). Second, it is interesting that Rudner defines *Verstehen* as 'empathetic understanding', as a kind of method for imagining oneself into the psychological state of the individual(s) we wish to understand (1966, p. 72). Now this may be part of what Weber and his associates had in mind when they advocated *Verstehen* as an indispensable method for sociology. But they also wanted *Verstehen* to refer to something far more important, namely the fact that social phenomena are intrinsically meaningful, and it is this meaningfulness that sociologists must come to terms with in order to understand social phenomena (cf. Leat, 1972).

Having brought up the 'issue' of *Verstehen*, Rudner is able quickly to dispose of it by fitting it into his positivist framework, and in particular his distinction between the contexts of discovery and validation:

> The issue is not whether achieving empathetic understanding of some subject of inquiry . . . is a helpful, fruitful, or indispensable technique for *discovering* hypotheses. . . . What is at issue is whether empathetic understanding constitutes an indispensable method for the *validation* of hypotheses about social phenomena. (1966, p. 72, italics added)

Hence the 'issue' of *Verstehen* is resolved by pointing out that it can have no place in the context of validation – the crucial context for deciding the indispensability of any feature of positivist sociology. *Verstehen* has no place in the context of validation for the simple reason that there is no way of empirically checking the truth or falsehood of the empathetic understanding of the sociologist (1966, p. 73).

In short, Rudner re-defines the issue of meaning out of existence. Since meanings are not susceptible to empirical investigation or validation, but overt behaviour is, then meanings can be introduced which *are* empirically testable only by tying them to manifestations of overt behaviour: 'All that is required for scientific validation of the relevant hypothesis is that *some* observable state of affairs be a *likely concomitant* of the value phenomenon in question . . .' (1966, p. 80).

The problem for positivism seems to come down to the relation between meaning and cause. Because the positivist methodology demands that explanation must be causal, the meaningfulness of social phenomena must be compatible, for the positivist, with the concept of causality. Now causal explanation, in its strict Humean sense, has three crucial aspects: (1) it establishes a contingent and external relation between two discrete entities or events; (2) the cause must be temporally prior to the effect; (3) there must be a constant conjunction between cause and effect, that is, the relation must be of the form: if A, then B. Now this model of explanation is valid for explaining natural phenomena, such as lighting by electricity, or the actions of billiard balls. But it becomes fundamentally problematic when applied to human behaviour.

The feature that is most frequently taken by positivists to be a cause of human action is its motive, understood as a physiological or psychological state existing independently of, and temporally prior to the action of which it is held to be cause. Now, in a loose sense, this seems to concur with common usage: we say, for example, that he killed his wife because he was jealous, or he drives a big car because he likes to impress the girls. Yet the relationship between motive and action is not contingent and external, but is meaningful, that is conceptual and logical. In other words, it is part of the *meaning* of being jealous that one is liable to kill one's wife, or that one way of impressing girls is driving a big car (whereas having a big mother is unlikely to count). Hence the motive and action are not discrete, separate phenomena, since the motive is an interpretation of the action, or a specification of what the action in fact is (a manifestation of jealousy, a way of impressing girls).

It also makes no sense to argue that motives are temporally prior to actions. We do not ask: when did he start being jealous? Two days before he killed his wife? Five minutes before? During the killing? Did he stop being jealous after the killing? This is because motives – understood sociologically – are not states belonging to people, though they might well be correlated with psychological or physiological processes, but methods for making actions intelligible (Blum *et al.*, 1974, chapter 2). The link between a motive and an action is meaningful, not causal.

Finally the constant conjunction aspect of causal explanation does not fit the explanation of actions in the common-sense world. If I ask 'Why were you late?' and you reply 'Because I wanted to finish watching the movie on TV', this formulation of your *reason* for being late is not of the causal form: if A (being late), then B (watching a movie) since, obviously, there are a host of different reasons for being late on different occasions. The giving of reasons, purposes or intentions for actions in the common-sense world involves specifying the context or sense of an action, not its cause. Furthermore, the assertion that the relation between action (being late) and motive or reason (watching a movie) is causal implies that there is some kind of compulsion on the part of the actor in committing the action if he 'has' the given motive. Yet this is totally unwarranted, since, in normal circumstances, people *decide* if they want to finish watching a movie on TV before going round to see someone (whether that decision is reflective or not, it is not causal).

Now, as I have said, we do use in normal discourse a kind of common-sense version of causality, for example 'Why did you hit that man?' – 'Because I was angry', although here the demand is for a reason or intention, not a Humean cause. Sociologists can use such a common-sense, watered down version of causality, or some variant of causal explanation such as 'sufficient or necessary condition', if they wish, for example, to investigate the 'causes' of suicide or divorce. But, apart from this major transformation in the meaning of 'cause' and its greatly reduced precision, and leaving aside the conceptual difficulties of such inquiries (for example, the difference between causes of divorce and reasons for getting a divorce, what is to count as a valid cause, etc.), the sociologist seems in no better position than a member in deciding what are the relevant causal factors. The matter is, if you like, up for grabs. The 'data' of the positivist, whatever its 'reliability', can always yield competing interpretations, and his 'causal sequences' can usually be found to be either trivial, or dressed up versions of common-sense theorizing.

It is true that social theorists today are beginning to recognize more and more the bankruptcy of positivism in the social sciences. The problem is that the form of life of positivism, its world view, basic assumptions and fund of concepts, are so deeply ingrained, since they are to some extent bound up with the natural attitude, that many social theorists seeking alternatives unwittingly rely on concepts and assumptions of the very form of life they are trying to escape from. Or else vague and rhetorical proposals are put forward for a more 'humanistic' or 'reflexive' approach by social scientists, without specifying the ontological or epistemological bases for such projects (for example, Gouldner, 1971). A viable alternative to positivism can only come about by positing a radically different form of life for theorizing.

Phenomenology and social science

The most important consequence of positivism – in its designating as metaphysical any theorizing that does not meet its requirements of adequate knowledge, and in its treatment of meaning as an epiphenomenon – is that it cuts the social sciences adrift from philosophy. This segregation, as Merleau-Ponty points out, has very serious consequences, for in refusing philosophy and social science any meeting-point, and hence any cross-fertilization of ideas and concepts, they become mutually incomprehensible, placing culture 'in a situation of permanent crisis' (S 98). It is not so much that artists and scientists no longer talk to each other. It is rather that they can no longer understand each other and, even more importantly, no longer understand themselves, since their knowledge is cut off from a philosophical understanding of the relation between knowing and being. Positivism cuts knowledge off from its roots in pre-reflective experience, in common-sense knowledge, and in the life and commitments of the theorist.

Hence the first task of a phenomenological philosophy which aims to challenge positivism is to remind philosophy and social science of their common ground in the intentionality of consciousness. Phenomenological philosophy 'is not a particular body of knowledge; it is the vigilance which does not let us forget the source of all knowledge' (S 110). It is not in rivalry with the social sciences except when they isolate themselves from philosophy. It aims to make the social sciences comprehensible. 'Like sociology, it only speaks about the world, men, and mind. It is distinguished by a certain *mode* of consciousness we have of others, of nature and of ourselves' (S 110).

This philosophic mode of consciousness concerns itself, first, with the phenomenological origin of sociality and social experience. As we have seen (pp. 40–2) there is a core of intersubjectivity and sociality in all human experience. Experience is at the same time particular and general. It is particular or unique because no two experiences are ever exactly the same. It is general, typical or universal because all experiences open onto other experiences, they share common styles, themes or significances, and so can be seen as part of wider experiential *Gestalten*. Furthermore, in our investigation of speech, or the 'lived-spoken', we find an immanent intersubjectivity disclosed (see pp. 00–0). In short phenomenology shows that sociality is at the heart of individuality; or, to put it another way, 'the generality and individuality of the subject . . . are not two conceptions of the subject between which philosophy has to choose, but two stages of a unique structure which is the concrete subject' (PP 450–1).

Society, then, is not a collection of monadic individuals in the classical liberal sense. The social is, rather, a fundamental structure of experience, it is a permanent field and ever-present horizon to all subjectivity and all action, in the same way as the world is the permanent horizon to all perception.

> We therefore recognize, around our initiatives and around that strictly individual project which is oneself, a zone of generalized existence and of projects already formed, significances which trail between ourselves and things and which confer upon us the quality of man, bourgeois or worker. (PP 450)

In fact, even this formulation is too dualistic – it is doubtful if there is 'that strictly individual project which is oneself' *around* which (and therefore, to some extent, separate from) lies the social. Rather individuality and sociality are implicated in each other. From the moment I am born I live in a world of speech, customs, institutions and cultural objects that together form my actions and thoughts in a way that still allows my own individuality to develop. 'My relation to myself is already generality' (PW 138).

Society as intersubjective reality

Phenomenologically, society is intersubjectivity. All action is under-stood as a dialectic between subjective intentions (in the ordinary sense) and their intersubjective consequences or results, so that the actual meaning or significance of an action will emerge from this interplay.[2] Hence we have to recognize 'an average and statistical significance' to our projects (PP 450), a significance not conferred on them by ourselves.[3] So there exists a facticity, an objectivity of society which is evident in this weight of intersubjective and institu-tional meanings, in its forces of social control, the existence of laws, norms and sanctions, and the omnipresence of social roles to be filled. Such features go into what most sociologists refer to as the 'social structure'. Yet a phenomenological approach to society never lets us forget that this *objectivity* of society is really an *intersub-jectivity*, that the facticity of the social structure does not exist over and beyond individuals and their praxis, in some mythical heaven, but is constituted by, and realized in, social interrelations and social praxis.

This is well illustrated in the account by Berger and Luckmann (1966) of the origins of institutionalization, an account which is fully compatible with Merleau-Ponty's phenomenological approach. Berger and Luckmann are concerned, not with the historical origins of institutionalization, but with the phenomenological origins (although it is possible that the two might coincide). Their argument (see pp. 70–85) is that all human action is subject to habitualization (or sedimentation), which implies that the same action will be performed in the future with the same economical effort, thus leaving parts of man's energy free for deliberation and innovation. Now institutionalization occurs 'whenever there is a reciprocal typification of habitualized actions by types of actors. Put differently, any such typification is an institution' (p. 72). That is actions, since they become habitual, also become typified and so are seen as *routines*. Individuals who carry out these habitual and routinized actions are seen as role-players or *actors*. This routinization becomes *reciprocal* if carried out by at least two persons, since each typifies the other's actions and so is able to predict what the other will do. In other words, we find the phenomenological origins of institutionalization in the process of sedimentation or habitualization which attends all experience.

Institutions imply control and historicity. Institutions, by the very fact of their existence, control human conduct by setting up pre-defined patterns of action and expected ways of behaviour. This controlling character is inherent in institutionalization as such, quite apart from any mechanisms of sanctions. Institutions are historical in that typifications of actions and actors occur over time, over the period of a shared history – it takes time for actions to be seen as habitual or routine. Furthermore institutions are intergenerational. The 'reciprocal typification of habitualized actions' by our two theoretical actors takes on a new dimension when the next generation appears, for now this pattern of routines becomes sedimented and objectified. The institution crystallizes, and is experienced by the succeeding generation as existing over and beyond the individuals who, at that moment in time, embody that institution. Whereas the two original actors were there at the birth of the institution, and had the power to deliberately intervene to change its structure, this possibility is far less available to their children and for each succeeding generation, who will be born into a world already institutionalized.

Hence the positivist motto 'treat social facts as things', needs modification to something like 'treat social facts as accomplishments' (Garfinkel, 1967). All sociological constructs such as 'social structure', 'social process', 'social stratification', 'institution', etc., are reifications unless they can be translated into social experience and inter-subjective praxis. Society is not a subjective reality, it is not even an objective reality; it is an intersubjective reality.

The concept of situation

Man in society is understood, in existential phenomenology, in terms of his situation. The term 'role' has been traditionally employed in sociology to indicate the point of insertion of the individual in the 'social structure'. Or, to be more accurate, there was no place for individuals, for concrete men, in the models of social structure in sociology, but only role-players or actors, stripped of any power of innovation or creativity, and who acted in conformity to normative or expected patterns of behaviour, as laid down by the social structure. Even where this rather rigid definition of role was challenged, and the emphasis taken away from the typical or normative aspects of role onto actual role performances, we find the concrete individual still dissolved into a multiplicity of roles.[4] The concept of role leaves no place for concrete, living individuals (Wrong, 1961). The term 'situation', on the other hand, is designed to take into account both the generality and individuality of concrete men, the fact that much of their behaviour can be understood in terms of role-playing, and yet all behaviour manifests that ever-present potential for transcendence, for going beyond the given and transforming the meaning of what one is offered. As Sartre puts it, the situation is the meeting-point of man's facticity and his freedom (1969a, p. 488).

The situatedness of man is simply an extension into the social field of the fact of man's embodiment. There are not men, but men-in-situations. The concept of situation allows us to speak of an individual in relation to other individuals, and in general terms of social groupings in so far as they exist in the common experience and praxis of individuals. We can speak, then, of the situation of the Jews, of the bourgeoisie, of the Negroes in America, etc. By doing so, we specify the context or frame in terms of which any individual Jew, bourgeois or Negro can be understood, so giving a meaning or social significance to his behaviour and experience (which is not the only meaning or significance to his behaviour or experience). So, for example, to write a book about women involves specifying the lived situation of women:

> Woman is a female to the extent that she feels herself as such. There are biologically essential features that are not part of her real, experienced situation: thus the structure of the egg is not reflected in it, but on the contrary an organ of no great biological importance, like the clitoris, plays in it a part of the first rank. It is not nature that defines woman; it is she who defines herself by dealing with nature on her own account and in her emotional life. (de Beauvoir, 1972, p. 69)

Woman defines herself, not in the splendid isolation of pure consciousness, but in terms of her lived, concrete situation. This will consist of a complex interplay between such factors as: the economical and political status of women in society, her own experience as a woman, how other women and men see her, how she sees herself, how she thinks other men and woman see her, which institutional definitions or feminine roles are offered to her, etc. This is not to say that all women are the same, only that, as women, they have a common situation, and so a number of available definitions and meanings. Which of these are taken up, and how they are taken up, will depend on each individual, concrete woman.

The concept of situation makes us aware of the *ambiguity* of social phenomena. This is so, because what is to count as a person's situation is philosophically problematic. There is, first, the important point that *a person is part of his own situation*. One does not step into a pre-given situation like a suit of armour. For a situation consists of the praxis and interrelations of an individual or group and so is, in a sense, achieved through people's own actions and experience. There are also situations that are openly lived and taken up, and those that lie latent or are passively submitted to. The situation – or 'existential project', as Merleau-Ponty often calls it – of the proletariat is different depending on how class conscious they are and how far they live their class exploitation (PP 442–8). Finally, the meaning of a situation changes over time, since man is oriented towards the future and so reinterprets his past life in terms of his present or future projects. What I may take as my present situation, for example being 'comfortably off' on £7,000 a year, I may well see as a situation of extravagance if I later become a religious convert, or go bankrupt.

So what do I take as my situation? My past life, my family, my profession, my bank balance, my race, my sex, my emotional make-up, or, if some combination of these, what combination? The theorist, like the member, if he wants to understand the behaviour and experience of other people and himself, has no choice but to make such elections, to risk imposing his own, perhaps idiosyncratic, view on events. Situations do not exist 'out there' as 'social facts': they are ways of understanding people in society which are open to differing interpretations depending on the assumptions and practical interests of the theorist (lay or professional). Moreover the specification of the situation of a given individual or group serves to assess or evaluate the experience or behaviour of those concerned, since it is the overall context which gives behaviour or experience its meaning. For the phenomenologist, however, unlike the positivist, these are not troubles or nuisances, or things to be swept under the carpet, but an invitation for more radical theorizing, which will take into account, as far as possible, the theorist's own situation, his own assumptions, so that he can attempt to understand his own theorizing and its relation to what he theorizes about.

The concept of structure

Moving to the level of society as a whole, Merleau-Ponty employs the concept of *structure*, in the same way he uses the term to indicate the overall functioning of an individual organism. The search for the structure of a society is an attempt to find the most comprehensive perspective one can take on it, or a 'general system of reference' (S 120) that allows both the point of view of members of the society, the point of view of the theorist, and their interrelation to be taken into account. The structure is an over-arching situation:

the sociologist's equations begin to represent something social only at the moment when the correlations they express are

89

connected to one another and enveloped in a certain unique *view* of the social and of nature which is characteristic of the society under consideration and has come to be institutionalized in it as the hidden principle of all its overt functioning – even though this view may be rather different than the official conceptions which are current in that society. (S 101)

Examples of such structures might be the Marxian models of feudalist, capitalist and socialist societies, the Lévi-Straussian models of primitive and advanced societies, or Foucault's (1970) 'epistemes'.

The structure of a society is the connecting principle, or series of principles, of a large number of social meanings, operating on different levels. There is an articulation between overt and latent meanings, so that an investigation into ideologies or 'myths' (Barthes, 1973) can be carried out. There is also an articulation between the actual existential meaning of social phenomena and other possible meanings. For example, a list of the possible accentuations of the different orifices of the body on the Freudian basis can be drawn up, so that it can be seen which ones are realized by different cultures (S 101).

These options are open to the theorist. But he must remember that these constructions, if they are to be phenomenologically valid, must relate in some way, or at some level, to the social experience of the members of that society. There need not necessarily be an 'actual consciousness' of the structure of the society, but there must at least be a 'potential consciousness' (cf. Goldmann, 1969) among some members. The specification of a structure by the theorist has always something provisional about it. It represents the theorist's most comprehensive understanding to date, but not for all time, and his model is always subject to revision – 'there is no question of substituting the model for the reality' (S 117).

We see, then, a certain paradox in the phenomenological conception of society. On the one hand the phenomenologist is concerned with the roots of sociality in the intentionality of consciousness, in the structure of human experience and its tendency towards sedimentation and generality, so that the processes by which the social world comes to be lived as factual and external can be charted. The phenomenologist can speak, with Berger and Luckmann (1966), of the social construction of reality. The taken-for-grantedness and facticity of the social world is put into brackets; phenomenology is thus 'a break with objectivism and a return from *constructa* to lived experience' (S 112). Yet, on the other hand, the phenomenologist also seeks to understand contemporary society as it is, to found, if you like, a phenomenological sociology. He studies social classes and groups such as anti-Semites, Jews, women, the Communist Party, and historical events such as the Second World War or the Korean War. If he wants to find the existential meaning of such phenomena or the structure that will make them intelligible, he must, to some extent, leave aside the questions raised by the phenomenological reduction and he must, to some extent, take the social world he wishes to understand for granted. He must, for the moment, cease to ask how the objectivity of such social phenomena is achieved, but look instead at how these phenomena articulate with other social phenomena considered relevant. The phenomenological approach to society is characterized by its attempt to balance a transcendental analysis, seeing the ground of the social in consciousness, with a descriptive interest in taking society as it is. It is all a question of being aware of the different levels of analysis, of how the descriptive is founded on the transcendental, yet also that the transcendental is manifested in the descriptive (this dialectic is elucidated in the Conclusion).

4 Marxism

The previous chapter has shown how phenomenology paves the way for a social philosophy or sociology, laying down the essential perspectives and concepts. Nevertheless, as will have been noticed, there is little actual investigation of social or historical phenomena in Merleau-Ponty's early writings. He shows how social and historical experience is possible rather than specifying what forms it takes. It is to Marxism that Merleau-Ponty turns in order to fill in the social, political, historical and economic dimensions of experience, and also in order to gain a perspective on contemporary society and contemporary life.

Marxism, as understood and embraced by Merleau-Ponty, is a kind of phenomenological sociology, aiming at describing and explaining the social rather than revealing its transcendental roots in intentionality and consciousness. So there is undoubtedly a development, or change in emphasis, between Merleau-Ponty's pre-Marxist phenomenology and his Marxist phenomenology (or, more accurately, from when Marxism was an implicit resource or influence to when it became an explicit and fundamental part of phenomenology). The Marxist phenomenologist can no longer be characterized as a 'perpetual beginner', who 'takes for granted nothing that men, learned or otherwise, believe they know' (PP xiv). This is always part of philosophy; but the phenomenologist now looks to Marxism to found some kind of body of knowledge that will enable him to understand the contemporary world. Inevitably, then, parts of the world must be taken for granted. Neither is it clear, as Merleau-Ponty says in the introduction to *Phenomenology of Perception*, that 'it is a matter of describing, not of explaining or analyzing' (PP viii). If explaining means causal explaining and analysing means reductive analysing, then Marxism neither explains nor analyses. But in so far as Marxism seeks to show any society, or social phenomenon, in its historical and economic dimension, and hence to demonstrate how and why it arose and how and why it is maintained, it would seem that the distinction between description and explanation is not easy to maintain in Marxist phenomenology. Finally the reflexivity of existential phenomenology, the continual search for the roots of theorizing, is not so prominent in Marxist phenomenology, where the theorist is more willing to place himself in the world and study what is going on round him rather than look to himself and his own theoretical auspices.

Yet Marxism, that is the Marxism of Marxist phenomenology, is not simply a naïve philosophy of the natural attitude. In the same way that phenomenology reveals the intentional genesis of phenomena, Marxism challenges those assumptions that designate certain social or historical phenomena as 'natural' by disclosing their *historical* dimension and their roots in human praxis. For example, the assumption by the classical economists that private property, the division of labour and the free market economy were 'natural' conditions is exploded by Marx by tracing how these conditions have developed historically, and arguing that they would not exist in a fundamentally different economic system of production and distribution. Similarly, the assumption by classical economists and utilitarians that egoism and competition are 'natural' in man, part of 'human nature', is disputed by Marx, who argues that egoism is the product of a capitalist and competitive economy. Marxism aims to disclose how social and historical phenomena are built out of human praxis and how this becomes alienated under certain historical conditions. Marxism, like existential phenomenology, looks at social and historical life from the perspective of alienation and its transcendence, and so is a philosophy of man's freedom.

Existential phenomenology and Marxism: the charge of incompatibility

Nevertheless it is often maintained that Merleau-Ponty's existential phenomenology (sometimes referred to simply as existentialism) is incompatible with Marxism. Raymond Aron, for example, writes:

> Sartre and Merleau-Ponty, in their pre-political work, belong to the tradition of Kierkegaard and Nietzsche and the revolt against Hegelianism. The individual and his destiny constitute the central theme of their reflection. They disregard that totality whose recognition by the philosopher marks the beginning of wisdom. Unfinished history imposes no truth. Man's freedom is the capacity for self-creation (1969, p. 81)

And hence: 'The Marxists and the existentialists come into conflict at the point where the tradition of Kierkegaard cannot be reconciled with that of Hegel' (1969, p. 86). A more recent formulation of a similar position is found in an article by Schmueli, when he claims (with reference to Merleau-Ponty and Sartre):

> Existentialists, *qua* Marxists, have great difficulties in substituting their own individualistic concepts in describing and explaining actions by Marx's holistic concepts, which seem designed to permit us to talk about collective actions without imputing conscious intentions on the part of individual persons. (1973, p. 141)

Now I want to argue that this view that existentialism (which, for the moment, I will take as synonymous with existential phenomenology, although the latter is a more accurate label for Merleau-Ponty's philosophy) and Marxism are fundamentally incompatible is unconvincing and, moreover, misrepresents both existentialism and Marxism. It misrepresents existentialism (and here I confine myself to Merleau-Ponty, as I consider Sartre less defensible) by making a number of misleading statements about it. For example, Aron claims that Merleau-Ponty belongs to the tradition of Kierkegaard and Nietzsche which is in revolt against Hegel. Now, not only do Kierkegaard and Nietzsche scarcely get a mention in Merleau-Ponty's work, but Merleau-Ponty undoubtedly owes far more to Hegel. Nevertheless, it should be made clear which Hegel Merleau-Ponty is influenced by, since, according to him (SNS chapter 5) there are two Hegels. There is the Hegel of 1827, the Hegel of 'the system', for whom history ends in an hierarchical society accessible only to the philosopher. Certainly Merleau-Ponty – like Kierkegaard and also Marx – is in revolt against this Hegel. But there is also the Hegel of 1807, who attempted a phenomenology of human experience, and who spoke of a genuine reconciliation between man and man. It is from this Hegel that Merleau-Ponty draws inspiration.

Aron also charges Merleau-Ponty with defining freedom as the capacity for self-creation, which would seem to be at odds with Marx's view that it is society that shapes man. Aron, however, appears to confuse *self-creation* with *transcendence*. Human existence for Merleau-Ponty is defined as transcendent, as continually going beyond itself and the given and intentionally instituting a social world. He writes, for example:

> I am the absolute source, my existence does not stem from my antecedents, from my physical and social environment; instead it moves out towards them and sustains them, for I alone bring into being for myself . . . the tradition which I elect to carry on. (PP ix)

But transcendence is not self-creation, because once my existence institutes a situation for me in the world, then, of necessity, I have to inhabit it and reckon with the limits and obligations it imposes on me. I do not choose the tradition that envelops me like I might pick a chocolate from a box, since my incarnation in a given situation obliges me to existentially take up a tradition and culture. The election I make is existential, and is embodied in my praxis and experience. It is not that my tradition or culture defines or determines my existence, but that all existence has a general or social dimension, so that there is no life outside of a tradition.

The crux of the arguments of Aron and Schmueli is that existentialist 'individualism' is incompatible with Marxist holism. Notice that Schmueli writes that existentialists 'have great difficulties in *substituting* their own individualistic concepts . . . by [for?] Marx's holistic concepts' (quoted above, italics added). By writing 'substituting' and not, say, 'fusing' or 'mediating between', Schmueli implies that there are two theoretical positions one can take and two only: *either* individualism (existentialism) *or* holism (Marxism). For Schmueli, to transcend individualism means substituting, putting in its place, holism, and thus cancelling out all reference to individuals or subjectivity, so that holism is to 'talk about collective actions without imputing conscious intentions on the part of individual persons' (1973, p. 141).

This dichotomy, between individualism and holism, is extremely crude. It ignores the fact that the terms 'individual' and 'society' are both abstractions, that they are two poles of an intentional and dialectical relationship that makes of man inherently a social being. The wish to separate the individual from society belongs to classical liberal or utilitarian thought, where it is believed that individual and social actions, conscious intentions and consequences of acts, can be easily distinguished. Merleau-Ponty, however, will have none of this:

> Historical responsibility transcends the categories of liberal thought – intention and act, circumstance and will, objective and subjective. It overwhelms the individual in his acts, mingles the objective and the subjective, imputes circumstances to the will; thus it substitutes for the individual as he feels himself to be a role or phantom in which he cannot recognize himself, but in which he must see himself. . . . (HT 43)

Furthermore the dichotomy between individual and society suggests the relations between the two will be simple: either conformity (the individual swallowed up by society) or non-conformity (society made up of a collection of assertive and independent individuals). In practice, however, there are many subtle interrelations between men and the society they live in, many different kinds of social experience, including rebellion, resignation, dropping out, harmony, anomie, revolution or alienation. Indeed to understand this notion of alienation – absolutely crucial to Marxism and to existentialism – is to understand the mediations between the terms 'individual' and 'society', so that it can be seen how *individual* intentions and actions become swallowed up and distorted in capitalist *society*, so that they are no longer intelligible as the expression of individuals. Alienation involves constant cross-reference between individual and society: a purely 'individualist' or 'holist' analysis could not begin to understand it.

Not only does the Aron–Schmueli position misrepresent Merleau-Ponty's existentialism, but also Marxism. Schmueli, for example, in comparing existentialism with Marxism, writes that 'objective determinism in history is totally incompatible with the existentialist mode of thought' (1973, p. 142). Or again:

> Maurice Merleau-Ponty . . . loosens totally the determinacy of history in Marx. Although he declares himself a Marxist, he states in an entirely un-Marxian manner: 'Thus, the meaning of history is threatened by deviation at each step and is always in need to be reinterpreted.' (p. 143)

Now if this view of Marxism is correct, that it is tied to a doctrine of objective determinism in history, then, to be sure, existentialism must be incompatible with Marxism, since the whole thrust of existential philosophy is anti-deterministic. Determinism, as Sartre says, is an attempt to fill us with things, to make us objects and deny our freedom and capacity for change. However, there exist compelling reasons for doubting that Marxian determinism is the whole story.

There is no doubt, however, that determinism is part of the story. In his preface to the German edition of *Capital*, Marx spoke of the 'natural laws of capitalist production . . . working with iron necessity towards inevitable results', and in his famous formulation of historical materialism he wrote that 'The mode of production of material life determines the general character of the social, political and spiritual processes of life' (quoted in Bottomore and Rubel, 1963, p. 67). But there is another side to Marxism at odds with determinism. The same Marx also wrote about the role of human subjectivity and activity in the creation of history. For example:

> The chief defect of all previous materialism (including that of Feuerbach) is that things (*Gegenstand*), reality, the sensible world, are conceived only in the form of *objects* (*Objekt*) of *observation*, but not as *human sense activity*, not as *practical activity*, not subjectively. (quoted in Bottomore and Rubel, 1963, p. 82)

The materialist doctrine concerning the changing of circumstances and education forgets that circumstances are changed by men and that the educator must himself be educated. (ibid., pp. 82–3)

History does *nothing.* . . . It is *men*, real, living men who do all this, who possess things and fight battles. . . . History is *nothing* but the activity of men in pursuit of their ends. (ibid., p. 78)

There is also the central Marxian notion of work or praxis which defines man, or at least is part of the human potential, and which involves an essential element of subjectivity and creativity in shaping the world in man's image and transcending the givenness of a situation. Thus Marx writes in *Capital*:

Labour is, in the first place, a process in which both man and Nature participate, and in which man of his own accord starts, regulates, and controls the material reactions between himself and Nature. . . . By thus acting on the external world and changing it, he at the same time changes his own nature. . . . He not only effects a change of form in the material on which he works, but he also realizes a purpose of his own that gives the law to his *modus operandi*, and to which he must subordinate his will. (ibid., p. 102)

Such a conception of human praxis cannot be compatible with the determinism of man by his environment.

Now how can these apparently contradictory positions of economic determinism and human praxis be allied? In one sense they cannot: as Merleau-Ponty realized, the Marxism of 'scientific socialism' and objective determinism remains strictly incompatible with any form of existential phenomenology (AD 62). But in another sense, it is the fundamental and crucial Marxian concept of *alienation* that can effect their reconciliation. In capitalist society the human capacities for action, praxis and self-determination are distorted and perverted, swallowed up in institutions and objective social processes, so that man becomes a prisoner of what were at one time his own creations. Under capitalism man is reified, he treats both himself and other men as things, because that expresses his actual experience of himself under capitalism. Men experience themselves as the playthings of objective, blind social forces. This is the truth of historical materialism and economic determinism. But it is a truth *of capitalist society only*. The aim of socialism is to create a truly human society where human work, instead of resulting in exploitation, becomes a means for self-expression. In a genuine socialist society economic determinism will no longer apply and men will regain a measure of self-determination, able to apply their energies, not in denying themselves, but in realizing themselves.

In other words the thesis of historical materialism – that the economic base determines the ideological superstructure – must be applied to itself: the thesis or ideology of historical materialism is itself relative to a certain type of social and economic system, namely capitalism, and the advent of a qualitatively different system will need a re-formulation of the relationship between economy and ideology. This interpretation of Marx, first put forward by Lukács, is adopted by Merleau-Ponty, who writes:

A Marxist conception of human society and of economic society in particular cannot subordinate it to permanent laws like those of classical physics, because it sees society heading towards a new arrangement in which the laws of classical economics will no longer apply. (SNS 125)[1]

The continuity between phenomenology and Marxism

Alienation

Instead of viewing existential phenomenology as incompatible with Marxism, we are led to a view of Marxism as a development from, or extension of Merleau-Ponty's phenomenology. There is a basic continuity between the two. This is perhaps most evident when we consider the Marxian concept of alienation.

We have seen how sedimentation is the other side to innovation and creativity in experience and behaviour. All experience manifests a degree of impersonality, generality and anonymity. The weight of my past, the inertia of my physical body, the permanent acquisitions of habits, skills and all the trappings of culture – these are all a kind of dead weight I carry around with me and can never shed. The tending of all existential spatialities towards physical space and existential time towards generalized time imposes rhythms on my existence that do not emanate from my personal acts. Repression in this sense is universal, says Merleau-Ponty; 'my organism, as a prepersonal cleaving to the general form of the world, as an anonymous and general existence, plays, beneath my personal life, the part of an *inborn complex*' (PP 84).

All this constitutes a kind of primary and inescapable alienation. It follows from the fact that incarnation is my lot, that I have to lose myself in the world in order to find myself:

when I move towards a world I bury my perceptual and practical intentions in objects which ultimately appear prior to and external to those intentions, and which nevertheless exist for me only in so far as they arouse in me thoughts or volitions. (PP 82)

It also follows from the fact that man is a social being, that he exists in a network of social relations and cannot help but interact with others (even hermits have parents), so that individual and conscious intentions often fail to correspond to actual consequences. Man has a social face and must view himself as others see him and must understand himself as others understand him. This is dramatically symbolized in the gaze; at the end of someone's look I feel myself stripped of my subjectivity, objectified and defined by the other, and hence alienated from my own potentialities (cf. Sartre, 1969a).

This notion of alienation – or its synonyms – is fundamental to Merleau-Ponty's description of man in the world. The Marxian concept of alienation merely extends such a conception to the sphere of history and society as a whole. Alienation means self-estrangement, a condition in which man no longer recognizes himself as autonomous, so that he cannot express and realize his own projects in his work and life, but finds his existence is dictated to him from outside. His consciousness is split between what he sees as belonging to himself, and what is part of his social self, or his being-for-others, which enables him to live in a society where he must work, not for his own development, but for the profit of others. And hence 'the more the worker externalizes himself in his work, the more powerful becomes the alien, objective world that he creates opposite himself, the poorer he becomes himself in his inner life and the less he can call his own' (Marx, 1971, p. 135). The self-estranged man is not unlike patients such as Schneider, who manifest a basic disturbance in their mode of being-in-the-world. Marx, however, shows that, apart from the primary alienation inherent in being-in-the-world, there exists an *historically* conditioned form of alienation, which is based on exploitation, and started with the division of labour in society. Alienation, for Marx, points to the fact that man himself has created the institutions and social processes which have turned back on their creators and deprived them of their subjectivity and individuality.

The primary alienation involved in being-in-the-world expresses the fact of incarnation, which is the necessary ground for human freedom; it gives, if you like, the materials for freedom to work on. The historical form of alienation which Marx traces, however, is totally antagonistic to human freedom, since man externalizes instead of expresses himself in his work, so has no capacity for realizing his potentialities. But since historical alienation is a result of man's activity, it can also be abolished by man, the institutions which embody and perpetuate it can be dismantled, and a society no longer based on exploitation be set up. Externalization, self-denial and exploitation are perversions of the impersonality and anonymity of experience that are not intrinsic to human existence, but are imposed by certain kinds of social and economic systems.

Totality

The concept of alienation shows how human praxis can be turned into objective determinism through the creation of repressive social institutions. The point, for Marxism and Marxist phenomenology, is to understand this whole movement, to gain a comprehensive perspective, which will recognize how different areas of investigation can be interrelated and seen as mutually implicatory. Modes of economic and social organization, ideologies and systems of laws and morals are all internally related, they have an 'elective affinity' (Weber) and illuminate each other.

> Should the starting-point for the understanding of history be ideology, or politics, or religion, or economics? Should we try to understand a doctrine from its overt content, or from the psychological make-up and the biography of its author? We must seek an understanding from all these angles simultaneously, everything has meaning, and we shall find this same structure of being underlying all relationships. All these views are true provided that they are not isolated, that we delve deeply into history and reach the unique core of existential meaning which emerges in each perspective. (PP xix)

This search for the 'unique core of existential meaning' is a search for the structure (cf. pp. 89–91) that will tie together all these partial perspectives. The goal of phenomenological analysis – whether of socio-historical phenomena, of a philosophical doctrine or a perceptual object – is the elucidation of the 'total intention', the 'unique mode of existing' of the phenomenon under study, or, in the case of whole societies or civilizations, it is a question

> of finding the Idea in the Hegelian sense, that is, not a law of the physico-mathematical type, discoverable by objective thought, but that formula which sums up some unique manner of behaviour towards others, towards Nature, time and death: a certain way of patterning the world which the historian should be capable of seizing upon and making his own. (PP xviii)

All perspectives are true *provided that they are not isolated* (quoted above, italics added). Truth, for Marxism as for phenomenology, is a *totality*.

100

To understand history, then, does not involve re-living the past or penetrating the minds of historical actors. It involves restoring the horizon to events, taking into account not only the probable intentions of the agents, but what we know of the outcome of their decisions, and of the general historical conditions under which they acted and lived. To this end, we need to locate certain structures or totalizations so that we can place events in perspective, such as Weber's 'Protestant Ethic' and 'Spirit of Capitalism', which reveal certain logical structures in the mass of historical evidence. The notion of 'rationalization', for example, can be used to define capitalism, since it explains by tying together the organization of Western art, science, mysticism, thought, etc., with its social and economic system. Each of these elements acquires its historical significance only in interaction with all the other elements. History has often produced one of these elements in isolation – for example, the rationalization of Roman law, or of calculus in India – without resulting in capitalism (AD chapter 1).

Through such structures or totalizations – necessary in any kind of understanding which involves principles of ordering and classification – the Marxist phenomenologist can see how history takes on a definite significance, both for the participants and for the historian. History takes on meaning and direction (*'sens'*) through a process in which *chance* or contingency becomes *pattern* or order:

> When an event is considered at close quarters, at the moment when it is lived through, everything seems subject to chance: one man's ambition, some lucky encounter, some local circumstance or other appears to have been decisive. But chance happenings offset each other, and facts in their multiplicity coalesce and show up a certain way of taking a stand in relation to the human situation, reveal in fact an *event* which has its definite outcome and about which we can talk. (PP xviii–xix)

These events are not pre-ordained, and the meaning of history is not unilateral or closed, since happenings can be combined in different ways to form different events, and events themselves are subject to competing interpretations. History is open-ended, subject to distortions and even periods of apparent chaos, of non-sense. But there are directions and significances which are *probable*, which are more likely than others, as we can say that it is probable, though not certain, that a man afraid of heights will not be able to climb a mountain, or a man with an inferiority complex will not suddenly become self-confident. History has probable meanings; it is only at certain critical periods that these probabilities become as good as certainties:

An existential theory of history is ambiguous, but this ambiguity cannot be made a matter of reproach, for it is inherent in things. Only at the approach of revolution does history follow the lines dictated by economics, and, as in the case of the individual life, sickness subjects a man to the vital rhythm of his body, so in a revolutionary situation such as a general strike, factors governing production come clearly to light, and are specifically seen as decisive. (PP 172)

The thesis of historical materialism can be understood in Marxist phenomenology as an attempt to view social existence as a totality, as the ground on which all other ways of comprehending society must be based. It is not the economic base as an isolated part of society that determines the rest, but economics understood as a system of production and working, which is itself an expression of the form of human relationships and ways of coexisting prevalent in the society under consideration. Ideas are not reduced to economics, but express the structure of the society. 'Solipsism as a philosophical doctrine is not the result of a system of private property; nevertheless, into economic institutions as into conceptions of the world is projected the same existential prejudice of isolation and mistrust' (PP 171).

The primacy of social existence and coexistence is illustrated in the case of class consciousness. According to a determinist interpretation, class consciousness is simply the product of the 'objective' economic position of the class. Idealism (or rationalism), on the other hand, reduces class consciousness to the simple conscious awareness of belonging to a class. But class must be *lived* before it can be *known*. It is not simply the fact that I occupy a certain position within the economic structure of society that will determine my consciousness of being a worker or proletarian; it is rather that gradually my whole mode of living serves to pattern the social world for me in a certain and definite way, and begins to provide me with certain motives which can lead me towards my class consciousness. My mode of being-in-the-world lends itself to particularly favoured ways of interpreting my life and social world, one of which might be to view myself as a worker under an exploitative system. My proletarian class consciousness exists as a *potentiality* which can become real or actual under the right economic and social conditions (PP 442–8).

We see, then, the continuity between phenomenology and Marxism in the notion of totality which is common to both. The concept of totality is accepted by all Marxists, who accuse their opponents of achieving only partial or ideological perspectives. It is also central to Merleau-Ponty's philosophy, which gives the lie to Aron's claim, previously quoted, that existentialists 'disregard that totality whose recognition by the philosopher marks the beginning of wisdom' (see p. 93). Existential phenomenology is explicitly dedicated to structural understanding in all spheres of investigation. Hence Merleau-Ponty can claim:

> We would undoubtedly recover the true sense of the concept of history if we acquired the habit of modeling it on the example of the arts and language. The close connection between each expression and every other within a single order instituted by the first act of expression effects the junction of the individual and the universal. (PW 85)

In short, the claims of Aron and Schmueli that Merleau-Ponty's phenomenology is 'individualistic' is a nonsense.

It should be noted, finally, that the totalities or structures that Marxist phenomenology aims to uncover are not closed or congealed unities. Any structural totality will represent a certain integration of subordinate structures. We have seen this in the relation between body and mind, where their integration into a higher unity is always threatened with breakdown (see pp. 23–5). Merleau-Ponty understands Marx in an analogous way, as seeking to transcend such dichotomies and seeking their interrelation in new structural unities. Marx rejects the old dualism of spirit and matter, according to Merleau-Ponty, and sees their fusion in actual human existence: 'In Marx spirit becomes a thing, while things become saturated with spirit. History's course is a becoming of meanings transformed into forces or institutions' (AD 33). In other words, what start out as ideas or decisions or experiments in social living can, if accepted and put into practice, become institutionalized and gather a momentum of their own, so that the original creators become powerless to act back on their creations. Spirit becomes a thing because man is reified under capitalism, is treated and experiences himself as a thing. Things are saturated with spirit because man's intentions and purposes are written in all the social apparatuses he has formed and in all his transformations of the natural world. Alienation is then comprehensible as a certain relation between spirit and matter: 'Capital', says Marx in a famous passage, 'is not a thing, but a social relationship between persons mediated by things' (AD 33).

A note on relativism and truth

The thesis of historical materialism, the essential Marxist tool for understanding history, leads us to question the notions of relativism and truth. If ideas and thought, which belong to the superstructure, are in some way the product of the economic base, does this not

103

result in relativism and the impossibility of any truth? This is certainly the case on a deterministic interpretation of historical materialism, where all ideas are strictly determined by the economic base. This means that the truth-value of any statement or belief is entirely dependent on the speaker's class position, his place in the economic system, and hence destroys any idea of truth, in the sense of a comprehensive or total understanding of society. Moreover, in order to be consistent, determinism has to apply its own criteria to itself. Hence it must recognize that determinism itself, as a doctrine, is economically determined, the product of a certain social and economic system, and hence is logically debarred from claiming any truth-value for itself. The relativism of determinism is vicious.

Nevertheless, this does show us a way out. Marxist phenomenology does not interpret historical materialism as an economic determinism but as the thesis that all aspects of a society are mutually implicatory and manifest a common structure. Any belief or doctrine, then, must be seen as part of a totality. There is relativism, then, only in the sense that all beliefs and doctrines require a social context in order to be fully understood. There is relativism because there is no universal or absolute context, and hence no eternally valid truths (cf. Louch, 1966, pp. 204–8). This does not result, however, in a vicious relativism, nor in a denial of truth, but only the argument that all truths require a context.

Merleau-Ponty puts this as follows. He argues, after Lukács, that the thesis of historical materialism – the locating of any ideology within its socio-economic context – must be applied to itself. This is designed to get out of a vicious relativism by *going beyond it*: 'Our ideas, our significations, precisely because they are relative to our time, have an intrinsic truth that they will teach us if we succeed in placing them in their proper context, in understanding them rather than merely suffering them' (AD 30). In the same way Marx was not content to merely characterize himself as a bourgeois under capitalism, but sought to understand this fact in terms of a more inclusive *Gestalt*, namely the class struggle and its historical development. Relativism itself must be put back into history, so that we can recover 'an absolute in the relative', a sphere of truth within our socio-historic period. This notion of relativism is what Mannheim (1960) terms 'relationism', the idea of a valid truth within a determinate social framework. This framework or context can be continually enlarged, so that we can better understand and assess our own ideas and ideologies.

> Of course we know that no history contains its entire meaning
> in itself. . . . *But there are perspectives which take into account
> all preceding perspectives*, which attempt to understand them

even if it means putting them in their proper place and
establishing a hierarchy among them. (AD 194, italics added)

Even the idea of a truth between cultures is feasible, precisely because
translation and communication between cultures is possible. What is
required is that the philosopher take into account both the alien
culture and his own culture, and hence arrives at a critical understanding – a truth – valid for each. 'It is a question of constructing a
general system of reference, in which the point of view of the native,
the point of view of the civilized man, and the mistaken views each
has of the other all find a place' (S 120).

This going beyond relativism is always partial, and the truth
gained always provisional, since the most comprehensive perspective
is still a *perspective*, that is, a certain situated view of myself and of
the world. Self-understanding can never be total. This is what
Merleau-Ponty means when he quotes Lukács with approval as saying 'truth is always to come'. Truth never completely arrives because
it can never be absolute and eternal. And so, for phenomenology as
for Marxism, there can only be a truth within a situation:

> Superficially considered, our inherence destroys all truth;
> considered radically, it founds a new idea of truth. As long as I
> cling to the ideal of an absolute spectator, of knowledge with
> no point of view, I can see my situation as nothing but a source
> of error. But if I have once recognized that through it I am
> grafted onto every action and all knowledge which can have a
> meaning for me . . . [it becomes] the point of origin of all truth
> including scientific truth. And since we have an idea of truth,
> since we are in truth and cannot escape it, the only thing left
> for me to do is to define a truth in the situation. (S 109)

Equivocations

Merleau-Ponty's relationship to Marxism, however, is not simple;
there are – characteristically – degrees of ambiguity in it. He equivo-
cates, for example, over how far Marxism should be an explicitly
moral theory, or rest on purely moral principles. In *Humanism and
Terror*, published in 1947, he characterized Marxism as an humanism,
and identified the proletariat as the carrier of true humanity. Only
the proletariat could resolve the contradictions of capitalism and
transcend all national and class conflicts since it was a 'universal
class' (HT 129–30). And hence Merleau-Ponty claimed:

> On close consideration, Marxism is not just any hypothesis that
> might be replaced tomorrow by some other. It is the simple
> statement of those conditions without which there would be

105

> neither any humanism, in the sense of a mutual relation between men, nor any rationality in history. In this sense Marxism is not a philosophy of history, it is *the* philosophy of history and to renounce it is to dig the grave of Reason in history. After that there can be no more dreams or adventures. (HT 153)

This culmination of rationality and humanism is embodied in the proletariat, which is 'a style of coexistence at once fact and value, in which the logic of history joins forces with labour and the authentic experience of human life' (HT 127).

But even in the same work these enthusiastic statements are tempered by more sober reflections. Merleau-Ponty accepts that a Marxist revolution in the West is not likely to be forthcoming, that the class struggle is effectively masked, and that Marxism has found no significant response among the working class. He thus finds himself in the position of arguing that Marxism can never be jettisoned, as it is the only valid statement of humanism, but at the same time we can at present do nothing to bring about a Marxist revolution, but have to wait 'for a fresh historical impulse which may allow us to engage in a popular movement without ambiguity' (HT xxiii).

This equivocation – between seeing Marxism as the only expression of an authentic humanism, and yet advocating a wait-and-see Marxism because of its lack of fit with the contemporary sociopolitical scene – is torn apart in *Adventures of the Dialectic*, published in 1955. Merleau-Ponty's former acceptance of Russia as the true home of Marxism has gone. He now sees Russia's involvement in the Korean War, where Russia failed to stop the war but used it for its own ends, as marking a fundamental change in Russian policy, and thus making his previous attitude of 'sympathy' obsolete. He now views the belief in the proletariat as the realization of history as a myth, as an illegitimate attempt to suppress the dialectical development of meaning in history. 'The illusion was only to precipitate into a historical fact – the proletariat's birth and growth – history's total meaning, to believe that history itself organized its own recovery' (AD 205). Merleau-Ponty now argues that those 'privileged moments', when the proletariat catches fire and explodes the social structure under which it lives, never last, they flicker out, and the revolutionary impulse becomes transformed into a bureaucracy which will stagnate and pervert the aims of the revolution. 'Revolutions are true as movements and false as régimes' (AD 207). He characterizes the young Marx and Lukács – and implicitly himself in *Humanism and Terror* – as ignoring what he calls 'the inertia of the infrastructure, the resistance of economic and even natural things' (AD 64), and forgetting that history has density, that it drags, and that its meaning appears only gradually.

In short, in *Humanism and Terror*, by advocating a wait-and-see Marxism, and by determining to hang onto Marxism come what may, Merleau-Ponty now recognizes that 'we were not on the terrain of history (and of Marxism) but on that of the *a priori* and of morality' (AD 232). This moral Marxism, 'which remains true whatever it does, which does without proofs and verifications' is not a philosophy of history, a philosophy which keeps up with events and can adapt itself to a changing social and political context, but only a 'Marxism of internal life' (ibid.). In view of the failure of all known revolutions, of Russia's estrangement from Marxism, and the failure of Marxism to inspire the proletariat in the West – which constitute the new 'terrain of history' for Merleau-Ponty – he now puts forward a new interpretation of Marxism, which he terms a 'new liberalism'. He advocates, not total revolution and the complete re-writing of history, but less radical change from within the system (AD 207). He retains some Marxist themes: the belief in the class struggle, the necessity of strikes, the legality of the Communist Party, and revolution as a legitimate expression of working-class aims. But he also accepts the need for permanent self-criticism and opposition, and hence defends the retention of a parliament as 'the only known institution that guarantees a minimum of opposition and truth' (AD 226).

Adventures of the Dialectic represents a radical change in Merleau-Ponty's Marxism. In 1945 he argued that Marxism is not compatible with private property and cannot be achieved by parliamentary means, so that 'if one's goal is to liberate the proletariat, it is *historically* ridiculous to try to attain that goal by non-proletarian means, and choosing such means clearly indicates that one is renouncing one's pretended goal' (SNS 116). And yet this is where Merleau-Ponty stands in 1955. In one sense, then, it could be argued that Merleau-Ponty has abandoned Marxism, or that at least his adherence to Marxism is fundamentally equivocal, as his critics charged. It is certainly true that after 1955 he made fewer references to Marxism, and by the end of his life had turned away from the realm of history and politics.

Nevertheless, Merleau-Ponty never regarded Marxism as a dogma, as a creed to be followed to the letter, but as a 'classic', as a 'matrix of intellectual and historical experiences' which retains an expressive power beyond its specific statements and propositions (S 10–11). Marxism, like phenomenology, does not tell us what is to be done, it does not paint everything in black and white, but gives us the frame and the inspiration to make our own decisions and unravel our own situation. Marxism, as a 'classic', must be based on the realities of socio-political life, on real, concrete situations. If certain parts of Marxism are seen as no longer relevant to contemporary society, then they must be changed, and Merleau-Ponty, along with many present-day Marxists, attempts such a revision. Marxism must accord with the facts, with the *probabilities* that an historical understanding throws up ('the probable is another name for the real, it is the modality of what exists', AD 116). Facts or probabilities can change our perspectives, as the Second World War showed. It drove home to Merleau-Ponty, as to Sartre, the reality of power, of history, and of the social and political world. Merleau-Ponty wrote after the war:

> What makes the landscape of 1939 inconceivable to us and puts
> it once and for all beyond our grasp is precisely the fact
> that we were not conscious of it as a landscape. In the world
> in which we lived, Plato was as close to us as Heidegger, the
> Chinese as close as the French – and in reality one was as far
> away as the other. We did not know that this was what it was
> to live in peace, in France, and in a certain world situation.
> (SNS 140)

Before 1945 Merleau-Ponty and his colleagues had not progressed to an historical perspective which would allow them to see the facts of their situation: 'It is no longer comprehensible that certain of us accepted Munich as a chance to test German good will. The reason was that *we were not guided by the facts*' (SNS 139, italics added). Similarly, in his conclusion to *Humanism and Terror*, after having stated his belief in Russia as the true home of Marxism and the revolution, in spite of the Moscow Trials, Merleau-Ponty adds that his faith in Russia would be subject to fundamental revision if the situation changed, if, for example, Russia decided to invade Europe (HT 184–5). By 1955 he saw Russia's actions, in Europe and Korea, as equivalent to this, and hence necessitating a change in attitude. In short, it is this overriding respect for the facts, for the probabilities in history, and for the gradual but cumulative change in social and historical contexts, that makes Merleau-Ponty's ambiguity over Marxism intelligible.

Nevertheless it may be asked whether Merleau-Ponty's revision of Marxism took the right direction, or was radical enough. In the course of his extended critique of Sartre in *Adventures of the Dialectic*, Merleau-Ponty comments: 'In going from personal history or literature to history, Sartre does not for the time being believe that he is meeting a new phenomenon which demands new categories' (AD 188–9). Yet if Merleau-Ponty's Marxism of 1955 is meant to take into account 'the inertia of the infrastructures' and the bureaucratic stagnation of revolutions, we might ask of Merleau-Ponty's own philosophy whether his revision of Marxism demands new categories and a new way of conceptualizing contemporary capitalism. Perhaps he was aware of this. In another context he wrote:

History has exhausted the categories in which conservative
thought confined it, and it has done the same with those of
revolutionary thought. But it is not just that the human world
is illegible, nature itself has become explosive. Technology and
science range before us energies which are no longer *within* the
framework of the world, but are capable of destroying it.
(TL 103)

It would seem that the future of Marxism lies in those attempts to
take this explosion of science and technology directly into account
(see, in particular, Habermas, 1971, chapter 6).

5   Ethics

In the previous chapter we considered some of the basic continuities between phenomenology and Marxism. There is one further continuity which we did not discuss, and that is their view of philosophy as an ethics or therapy as well as an intellectual exploration. The explicit aim of phenomenology and Marxism is to bring about, through philosophy, a liberation of man, the emancipation and development of his potentialities which are suppressed or repressed. 'The supersession of private property', says Marx, 'is [therefore] the complete emancipation of all human senses and qualities' (1971, p. 152). Merleau-Ponty, while accepting the need for social and political liberation, seeks to specify what this emancipation of our human senses entails and how it can be understood.

> We have relearned to feel our body; we have found underneath the objective and detached knowledge of the body that other knowledge which we have of it in virtue of its always being with us and of the fact that we are our body. In the same way we shall need to reawaken our experience of the world as it appears to us in so far as we are in the world through our body, and in so far as we perceive the world with our body. But by thus remaking contact with the body and with the world, we shall also rediscover ourself, since, perceiving as we do with our body, the body is a natural self and, as it were, the subject of perception. (PP 206)

Both philosophies aim at reuniting man with himself, with those parts of his experience which have become cut off from him. Philosophy seeks to heal our self-estrangement, and this is both an intellectual and moral project. 'True philosophy consists in relearning to look at the world . . .' (PP xx).

However before this theme of philosophy as therapy can be explored and an existential ethics dug out of Merleau-Ponty's descriptions of being-in-the-world, there is a preliminary hurdle to be overcome. This hurdle is the positivist view of language, which maintains that there is a crucial distinction between descriptive statements and evaluative or normative statements, and that any adequate scientific or intellectual discourse must rid itself of the latter. This distinction must be investigated and shown to be untenable, or at least seriously misleading, before we can attempt to found an existential ethics from Merleau-Ponty's philosophy.

Description and evaluation

In the discussion of positivism in chapter 3 four rules were identified that served to define a positivist approach to philosophy. These were: the unity of the scientific method, the rules of phenomenalism and nominalism, and, finally, the rule that maintains an essential difference between description and evaluation and refuses to call the latter knowledge (see pp. 76–7). According to this fourth rule, then, adequate speech for the positivist is purely descriptive and factual.

> Experience, positivism argues, contains no such qualities of men, events or things as 'noble', 'good', 'evil', 'beautiful', 'ugly' etc. Nor can any experience oblige us, through any logical operations whatever, to accept statements containing commandments or prohibitions, telling us to do something or not to do it. (Kolakowski, 1972, p. 16)

The logic of this description/evaluation distinction within positivism itself is as follows:

> on the phenomenalist rule we are obliged to reject the assumption of values as characteristics of the world for they are not discoverable in the same way as the only kind of knowledge worthy of the name. At the same time the rule of nominalism obliges us to reject the assumption that beyond the visible world there exists a domain of values 'in themselves' with which our evaluations are correlated in some mysterious way. (ibid., p. 17)

What this description/evaluation distinction amounts to is that, for the positivist, evaluative, emotive or ethical terms are seen as adding nothing to the factual content of descriptions. They are seen as giving us no new information and presenting us with no new facts about the world. All they do is to express the speaker's own subjective, personal opinions or feelings towards an object, person or event. As such they cannot be counted as *empirical* statements, as either true or false, since they have no factual content, and hence cannot be accredited valid knowledge (cf. Ayer, 1946).

This view has an initial plausibility. The statements 'this is a table' or 'this is a big/yellow table' do seem different kinds of statements to 'this is a nice or attractive table'. The first two statements are purely descriptive, the third is an evaluative or appraising statement, having little or no descriptive content, but expressing our reaction to the table. And this is true not only of inanimate objects. Even if we replace tables by human beings there seems to be no difference: to say 'he is 6 feet tall' seems to be logically distinct from saying 'he is unpleasant'.

But this plausibility, even where it seems to hold in these very simple examples, is deceptive. The positivist view that description and evaluation are logically distinct entails that any evaluation will be totally devoid of descriptive content. If this is so, then it would be correct to say: 'X is good/attractive and Y is bad/unattractive, but there is no factual difference between them'. This statement would be correct because, for the positivist, evaluations express mere personal preferences and have no bearing whatever on the object of the evaluation. But this is intuitively – and phenomenologically – false for to say that X is good and Y bad, or that X is attractive and Y unattractive (and I have deliberately chosen the most innocuous epithets) is to say something *about them* rather than about myself (although, of course, I am also indirectly revealing something of myself). It means asserting that there is something *empirically different* between X and Y which, if pressed, I could go on to specify (for example X helps her mother while Y does not, or X has long hair and Y has short).

Consider another example. To say 'this room is cosy' would seem to be a purely evaluative statement, since there are no easily identifiable empirical criteria which correspond to this quality. To say a room is cosy is to express approval of it. Nevertheless although there are no single phenomena that are an unmistakable part of the quality of cosiness, there is a *range* of phenomena that together would be considered to exhibit 'cosiness' by anyone who understood the meaning of the term. A cold, bare, carpetless room would definitely not count, whereas a warm room, with lots of furniture, a big bed, pictures and drapes on the wall and a thick wall-to-wall carpet would be a much more likely contender. In other words the term 'cosy' – like a whole host of other terms, such as comfortable, cramped, etc. – as well as being an *evaluation* is also a *description*; in calling a room cosy I am saying something about the room as well as expressing my attitude towards it.

These are not isolated examples. The positivist distinction between description and evaluation can be destroyed by more formal argument (here I draw on Kovesi (1967), on Louch (1966, especially chapter 4) and on Pitkin (1972, chapter 10)). In the examples I gave where the positivist view seemed to hold, the examples of pure descriptions concerned either inanimate things (tables) or human beings only in so far as they belonged to the physical or animal world ('he is 6 feet tall'). But as soon as we move from the physical or animal world to the *human* world, and introduce descriptions of objects having some reference to men – for example, 'this is a well-built table' – or occupying a place in the human world – for example, 'this is an antique table' – then already our descriptions are inextricably mixed with evaluations, because to describe a table as well-built or antique is, in most cases, to say something approving about it. And when we come to purely human phenomena, such as descriptions of human actions or of the social world, we find that simple 'empirical' descriptions of 'the facts' become entangled with evaluations for the reason that it is now problematic as to what are to count as the *relevant* facts, or, indeed, as 'the facts' at all.

A purely factual – i.e. empirical and hence evaluatively neutral – description of human action is *logically* impossible because to identify a human action entails both subsuming it under a concept and providing it with an intelligible context. I can take a long, slim object between my fingers and make certain marks on a flat, white substance. Assuming we have the concepts 'writing', 'paper' and 'name', the identification of this series of physical movements presents no great problems. And if we understand what a cheque is, then we can understand my whole series of movements as the action of signing a cheque. Here the context of my action is unproblematic and not in dispute. We know, from the meaning of the word 'writing' or 'signing', that the fact that I have a pen between my fingers is a *relevant* fact, and hence part of the context which serves to identify the action, whereas the fact that I am wearing a dark suit is an *irrelevant* fact. To describe an action is always done *from a point of view*, and it is this point of view that enables me to pick out 'the facts'. Moreover the specification of the context is not always unproblematic – there are times when the *same* series of physical movements constitutes a *different* action depending on the context or point of view. Moving my arm and hand in a certain way can either be the action of waving goodbye, if I am walking away from someone, or trying to attract attention, if I am lost and see a figure in the distance. Raising a glass of wine to my lips will be understood as getting drunk, wine-tasting or toasting the queen depending on the context. In other words, there are no 'pure' actions in the human world, but only actions constituted through the specification of the relevant context, as in perception there are only figures against a background. We do not empirically 'see' actions in the way we see tables and chairs, but understand movements as actions in the light of the assigned context.

113

Not only are there no 'pure' descriptions of 'the facts' in the social world, since facts in the social world only emerge from a specified context. There is the further point that in providing an intelligible context for any phenomenon we are at the same time *assessing* it. To give a context is to imply how a phenomenon is to be viewed. Consider the following example. We see a man pointing a rifle at another man and then firing it, so that the second man falls down and lies motionless on the ground. Now this series of events is describable as murder. This description defines the action in terms of its context, namely that his action was intentional (and hence not an accidental killing) and not carried out under compulsion (for example as part of a firing squad, making the action execution rather than murder). Yet my *description* of the action as murder is also an assessment of it, since *it is part of the meaning of the word 'murder' that it is morally wrong*. This is a purely linguistic or logical point: in describing the event as murder, I am not merely expressing my own subjective attitude of disapproval, but the disapproval of anyone, that is of any language user who uses the term 'murder' in the correct way. 'If I did not disapprove of the child's murdering his father I would not understand the notion of parricide' (Kovesi, 1967, p. 72).

In short, we cannot use descriptive terms like lying, cheating, stealing, intelligent, generous, graceful, mature, shy, nosy, efficient, wasteful, greedy, etc., etc., in an evaluatively neutral way, since evaluation is built into the very language we use. Competing descriptions of a series of events – such as fornicating or making love, being inquisitive about someone or being intrusive – are also competing assessments. In fact evaluation and assessment are so ingrained in speech that we normally take them for granted and fail to realize how pre-interpreted and pre-evaluated the social world is. Consider, for example, the simple sentence 'he helped the blind man across the road'. This is a description of an action or series of actions – yet notice how the words we use carry horizons of expectations or obligations. Calling the man 'blind' means that he cannot see; but it also entails that he is a man who needs to be helped across the road and who deserves special treatment, unlike a person who can see normally. The fact that a person is blind is vectorial, it involves adopting a certain attitude towards him. Furthermore saying that I 'helped' him across the road, as well as describing my taking his arm and leading him across the road, is also an implicit commendation of what I did.

The social world is thus also a *moral* world and to speak a language means employing and trading off sets of evaluations and assessments built into that language. Only computers can have an evaluatively neutral attitude towards the world. And the evaluations we make are not merely the expressions of purely personal opinions or feelings, and hence not subject to criteria of truth or appropriateness. On the contrary, descriptions from an evaluative, moral or emotive point of view, like all other kinds of descriptions, need to be backed up by evidence or reasons.

> We are often told that we cannot move from the statement 'the cat is on the mat' to 'the cat ought to be on the mat'. Of course we cannot. But why we cannot move from the one to the other is not because one is a 'descriptive statement' and the other is an 'ought statement', but because the fact that the cat is on the mat is *not a reason* for saying that the cat ought to be on the mat. If there are reasons for saying that the cat ought to be on the mat, they will be a *different set of facts*. (Kovesi, 1967, p. 88, italics added)

Such a different set of relevant facts might be that the cat will be warmer on the mat or that the floor will be free of cat hairs. The point is simply that evaluations, like all descriptions, cannot be arbitrary, but must be seen to be subject to rational (=giving good reasons) criteria.

It can thus be seen that the positivist distinction between description and evaluation, when applied to the human world, is extremely misleading. This is so because although the distinction *can* be made, it is not a useful one which gives us any insight into the workings of our language. Although there are a few terms or statements that can be seen to be more or less purely descriptive or factual, and a few that are more or less purely evaluative or non-empirical, the vast majority of terms or statements fall somewhere between these two extremes – between good and yellow, in Kovesi's phrase. Furthermore the attempt to categorize terms or utterances as either descriptive or evaluative suggests that terms or utterances are somehow intrinsically or naturally one or the other. But what matters is how terms are *used*, for what purposes utterances are made. Words that seem purely descriptive or factual can be used in evaluative ways, such as 'flat' ('she's a flat-chested girl'), 'heavy' ('he's a heavy smoker') or 'seldom' ('you seldom come to see me'). We don't just make 'pure' descriptions, we make them for a purpose, so that to say to someone 'that's a big shirt you've got on' is to suggest that next time he buy a shirt a size smaller.

If ordinary speech and the everyday world as lived in the natural attitude cannot be understood in terms of a distinction between description and evaluation, then the positivist construction of a value-free ideal language in order to produce valid knowledge about the world would seem to be fruitless, because all it could reproduce would be an artificial 'factual' world which no one has ever experienced. It is one thing to ask for *rational* descriptions made from whatever point of view (physical, evaluative, moral, artistic, etc.), that is, a demand for reasons or justifications being available to show how any description is warranted or not. It is quite another to insist that descriptions be totally divorced from evaluations. The positivist goal of value-free descriptions is metaphysical in its own pejorative sense, that is, having no connection with the real (i.e. experienced) human world.

Yet positivism maintains that 'experience . . . contains no such qualities of men, events or things as "noble", "good", "evil", "ugly" etc.' (Kolakowski, 1972, p. 16). We can only conclude that the concept of experience employed by positivists is so emasculated as to bear no resemblance to any person's real experience of the human world. While living naïvely in the world we experience qualities as inhering objectively in things and people, we experience values, not as 'in themselves', nor as metaphysical entities, but as embodied in actions and attitudes. In short we experience the world as inherently *meaningful* and it is this crucial feature that positivism is unable to handle.

Phenomenology: the grounding of values in facts

The fault of positivism is to take a distinction that can be made for certain specific critical and intellectual purposes and use it to characterize the whole of language. In the same way traditional theories of language took one particular area of language or one language-game, where words are used as names to designate objects in the world, to describe the workings of language as a whole. Or again, rationalist theories of perception took operations that came into play only under special circumstances, namely the critical focusing that occurs when one's perceptual field is ambiguous or unclear, and proposed that they were paradigmatic for perception in general. In all these cases phenomenology seeks to view the phenomenon under study as a whole and in terms of its primitive ground.

Phenomenology shows that in the primordial perceptual field there is no distinction between fact and value, between is and ought. Perception reveals a primitive structure or *Gestalt* which gives perceptual objects their originary significance. In naïve perception, perception is affective as well as cognitive, since I apprehend objects, not as neutral husks, but as charged with an affective and vital meaning, as poles of intentionality. In this perceptual field there is no distinction between perceptual objects (facts) and how I perceive them (values); there exist only perceptual objects as perceived by me in the light of my projects at hand. The perceptual field:

is real, because it is resistant, but pre-objective, and it is
precisely the aim of perception to bring objects into it.
Perception will do so in accordance with the dictates of another
'field', which is myself, a historical being with a situation (as
Sartre would say) and certain exigencies. Although, then, there
is a pre-objective reality, objects are in a sense evaluated into
existence. We live, and are content to live, in a world of
'oughts'. . . . Hume's dichotomy, or antinomy, has been
by-passed. (C. Smith, 1964b, p. 111)

This world is affectively and cognitively revealed to us in our
moods and emotions. Understood phenomenologically, emotions
are not purely subjective reactions, but have cognitive content, and
are ways of disclosing the world to us. Sartre puts this well; hatred,
fear, love or sympathy, he says, 'are merely ways of discovering the
world. It is things which abruptly unveil themselves to us as hateful,
sympathetic, horrible, lovable' (1970, p. 5). Phenomenology reminds
us of something we have known all along: 'if we love a woman, it is
because she is lovable' (ibid.). Beauty or loveliness are not just in
the eyes of the beholder, but in the object or person as well. Of
course standards of beauty will vary between persons or cultures,
but then it is not the standards by themselves that change but the
objects as well.

Phenomenology seeks to trace the birth of values and morality in
perceptual experience, which, according to Merleau-Ponty's thesis
of the primacy of perception (see pp. 34–5), is the ground of all
rationality, all description and all values. Morality is possible
because perceptions open me to other people and a common world.

> Just as the perception of a thing opens me up to being, by
> realizing the paradoxical synthesis of an infinite of perceptual
> aspects, in the same way the perception of the other founds
> morality by realizing the paradox of an *alter ego*, of a common
> situation, by placing my perspectives and my incommunicable
> solitude in the visual field of another and of all the others.
> (PM 26)

Moral discourse is possible because of the ambiguity and uncertainty of our actions in the social world, because any behaviour
on my part can have unintended or unforeseen consequences.
Ordinary moral discourse can be seen as one way of lessening the
cost of such actions that are seen to be mismanaged. Prospectively
we use promises and commitments to reduce the risk of actions not
yet performed or completed. Retrospectively we employ forgiveness,
excuses, justifications or pleas for conduct that has been seen to
come to grief (Pitkin, 1972, p. 149). To perceive, to act, then,

involves us in morality and requires us to adopt a point of view. As Merleau-Ponty says, we are condemned to values: 'one cannot do without a perspective and, whether we like it or not, we are condemned to wishes, value judgements and even a philosophy of history' (SNS 167–8).

Philosophy, willy-nilly, implies an ethics, since it is no more than an elucidated perspective. But the ethics thrown up by a phenomenological philosophy will not be distinct from its descriptions, but an integral part of them. It follows that an existential ethics can only concern itself with values-as-facts, or facts-as-values, that is, with values *embodied* in experience and action. Phenomenology is not interested in constructing elaborate and abstract ethical systems, but in specifying those ethics or values that are a consequence of its descriptions, and of its view of the self and the world: 'if [however] one acknowledges . . . an existence of consciousness and of its resistant structures, our knowledge depends upon what we are; moral theory begins with a psychological and sociological critique of oneself' (SB 223).

Both phenomenology and Marxism demand that values be concrete. Values do not exist in themselves, but are part of a general understanding, part of the specification of the correct frame or context in which events are viewed; 'true morality is not concerned with what we think or what we want, but obliges us to take an historical view of ourselves' (HT 103). Hence Merleau-Ponty's distrust of taking Marxism as a purely moral theory, so that, for example, the proletariat is taken as the only saviour of man and everything is judged from its perspective, as in Sartre's *Les Communistes et la paix* and Merleau-Ponty's own *Humanism and Terror*. Such views do not look at the facts in their historical and political contexts, but see only the black and white judgments of morality divorced from a concrete understanding of the situation (AD 154). By embedding its ethics and moral judgments in its comprehensive understanding of the whole situation, Marxist phenomenology hopes to realize philosophy in action. 'Philosophy would be false only in so far as it remained abstract, imprisoning itself in concepts and beings of reason, and masking effective interpersonal relations. Hence Marxism does not mean to turn away from philosophy, but rather to decipher it, translate it, *realize* it' (SNS 132–3). Abstract and over-generalized principles need to be de-mystified and concretized, so that they can be seen to have some bearing on praxis. Everyone fights in the name of the same principles: justice, freedom and democracy. Marxism demands that these values be made concrete, that we specify *who* are to put these values into practice – the proletariat, the bourgeoisie, self-styled moral reformers, the state? – and *how* this will be done – by reform, state legislation or by revolution (S 221-2)? Hence what Marx intended to do 'to create a human community was precisely to find a different base than the always equivocal one of principles' (S 222).[1]

What we are offered is, then, an existential ethics which is debarred from ever being systemized or issuing a series of abstract principles or a moral code to follow. Phenomenology hopes to get away from any moralizing, but wants to describe from a moral point of view. This is a consequence not only of the primitive grounding of values in facts, but also of Merleau-Ponty's characterization of man's existence as a manifestation of *freedom*. Merleau-Ponty's philosophy is a philosophy of human freedom, and one cannot be free by conforming to an external moral code or rule-book.

Freedom

The concept of freedom is the linch-pin of a phenomenological and Marxist description of man in the world, and hence of their ethics:

> Boiled down to its essence, Marxism is not an optimistic philosophy, but simply the idea that another history is possible, that there is no such thing as fate, that man's existence is open-ended. (SNS 119)

> we would be happy is we could inspire a few – or many – to bear their freedom, not to exchange it at a loss; for it is not only their own thing, their secret, their pleasure, their salvation – it involves everyone else. (AD 233)

Now by freedom Merleau-Ponty does not mean the ability to do anything, to be whatever one wants, act completely without constraint or compulsion. When Sartre writes that 'man is nothing else but what he makes of himself' (1956, p. 291), that 'existence comes before essence' (p. 189), and that 'there is no determinism – man is free, man *is* freedom' (p. 295), it is not certain what he means. If he means simply that there is no human nature in man which predetermines the pattern of his life, and that man's life is not the product of physical or social determinism but a dialectic enacted between man and his environment, then Merleau-Ponty would share in this conception of freedom. If, however, Sartre means to advocate an absolute freedom, where consciousness is defined as 'nothingness' and free to make itself into whatever it wants, where man is free to create himself, and where any attempt to identify oneself or objectify oneself as a *something* is doomed to failure as a manifestation of bad faith – and I leave it open whether this is Sartre's position, as Merleau-Ponty alleges, or merely a caricature of it – then Merleau-Ponty's own view of freedom must be carefully distinguished. For the paradoxical result of this conception of total or absolute

119

freedom, of the completely free act, is that in fact it makes action impossible, since consciousness as 'nothingness' and absolute freedom can find no anchor in the world, but soars above it, so that man is condemned to never being anything and hence never doing anything (PP 434–7).

Freedom is not absolute but *embodied* or *incarnated*. There is freedom only in a situation, in a *field*, that is, in a social space not of our own making or choosing, where there exist obstacles, institutions, conventions, in short an opacity or weight which holds us away from our goals, which can prevent us from achieving what we want, or from acting effectively, or indeed at all. Total freedom exists only in our imagination or fantasies where there is nothing to keep us from getting what we want. In reality, freedom is always limited to our capacities, knowledge and situation. Freedom is not antagonistic to the tendency of all experience towards sedimentation, towards the acquisition of skills and habits resulting in a core of impersonality or anonymity to our experience. On the contrary, sedimentation is the necessary ground of freedom:

> it is by giving up part of his spontaneity, by becoming involved in the world through stable organs and pre-established circuits, that man can acquire the mental and practical space which will theoretically free him from his environment and allow him to *see* it. (PP 87)

Existential or incarnated freedom is not to be confused with *free will*. The traditional arguments about freedom were conducted as a debate between determinism – the thesis that every action is caused – and free will – the thesis that actions are not caused but the result of my free, i.e. uncaused, will. However this dichotomy between determinism and free will is unreal because man is neither determined nor does he have free will. This is because actions are neither caused nor uncaused but are *intentional*, they are enacted for reasons or purposes, and are in no sense arbitrary or gratuitous, as the advocates of free will have it (cf. Sartre, 1969a, pp. 436–9). The error of both determinism and free will is to conceive of anarchy or chaos as the only alternative to determinism or causality. There is order and intelligibility in the world, however, not because everything is determined or predestined, but because man intentionally structures his world, and through his concerted actions in the world he institutes social rules and patterns, and canons of intelligibility. Freedom is not an unconstrained act of the will, in fact it has nothing to do with the will (whatever the will is), but is a quality of all action, whether actively realized or not (cf. PP 435–6). Freedom is not opposed to determinism but, in Merleau-Ponty's formulation, co-extensive with it:

There is [therefore] never determinism and never absolute choice. I am never a thing and never bare consciousness. In fact, even our own pieces of initiative, even the situation which we have chosen, bear us on. . . . The generality of the 'role' and of the situation comes to the aid of decision, and in this exchange between the situation and the person who takes it up, it is impossible to determine precisely the 'share contributed by the situation' and the 'share contributed by freedom'. (PP 453)

Freedom, in a word, is *determinate*. This is because existence is determinate (not determined): 'I am a general refusal to be anything, accompanied surreptitiously by a continual acceptance of such and such a qualified form of being' (PP 452).

So far we have been rather negative. We have said that freedom is not absolute, it is not the capacity for unlimited or unconstrained choice, and neither is it to be confused with 'free will'. More positively, we have implied that it involves a capacity for determinate and existential choice, for creativity enacted on the ground of sedimentation. We can now try to be more specific. Freedom is synonymous with *transcendence*. 'What defines man', says Merleau-Ponty, 'is . . . the capacity of going beyond created structures in order to create others' (SB 175). Freedom is freedom *to* create, innovate and act, rather than purely freedom *from* external compulsion. In other words freedom is praxis, the ability of man to work on and shape his world. But this work is not just physical or practical. The most profound meaning to existential freedom is that man can change his situation, and change his existence, *by changing its significance*. Freedom is 'appropriating a *de facto* situation by endowing it with a figurative meaning beyond its real one' (PP 172). This endowment of a figurative meaning is not carried out by a legislative act of consciousness, but by living and relating to other men in such a way that the real (i.e. effective) meaning of the situation in which one participates is challenged. 'Thus Marx, not content to *be* the son of a lawyer and student of philosophy, *conceives* his own situation as that of a "lower middle class intellectual" in the new perspective of the class struggle' (PP 172). This challenge may be very gradual and take years to effect. Nevertheless a change in meaning, in man's consciousness of himself, means a change in man.

If man is the being who is not content to coincide with himself like a thing but represents himself to himself, sees himself, imagines himself, and gives himself rigorous or fanciful symbols of himself, it is quite clear that in return every change in our representation of man translates a change in man himself. (S 225)

Freedom as the ability to endow new significances does not just entail challenging accepted definitions. It also involves living to the full what I am now, taking up what my situation can offer me. 'It is by being unrestrictedly and unreservedly what I am at present that I have a chance of moving forward' (PP 455–6). So El Greco was not content to merely suffer his visual anomaly as a crippling disability, but integrated it into his personality by employing it to express his own conception of the world (see pp. 24–5). And Cézanne's schizoid temperament becomes a theme in his work, revealing a 'metaphysical sense' (i.e. another layer of meaning) to the disease: a way of seeing the world reduced to a series of frozen and congealed appearances. Cézanne's illness 'ceases to be an absurd fact and a fate and becomes a general possibility of human existence' (SNS 20). Freedom is not an abstract or magical force which works miracles and transforms existence in one go. It is the potentiality in all being-in-the-world to intend a world which can allow human self-expression. Freedom becomes a consequence of intentionality, which builds us a world in which we can live, and yet which, once constructed, we are not free to tear down and start again.

> Two things are certain about freedom: that we are never determined, and yet that we can never change, since, looking back on what we were, we can always find hints of what we have become. It is up to us to understand both these things simultaneously. (SNS 21)

Freedom understood concretely is then a 'creative repetition' (SNS 25).

Once again, in attempting to describe being-in-the-world, we come face to face with the phenomenon of ambiguity, an inter-mixing of levels of meaning and understanding, so that our concepts cannot be clearly defined but shade gradually into their apparent opposites. It is this ambiguity that allows for the possibilities of freedom and innovation, and yet prevents us from ever looking our freedom in the face. Even in situations of extreme social and political oppression, where our actual free space shrinks almost to zero, the potentiality of freedom or transcendence can never be extinguished, since it is co-extensive with ex-istence. 'The world is already constituted, but never completely constituted' (PP 453). Freedom is a rooted creativity.

Freedom and responsibility

In this exchange between innovation and sedimentation that defines freedom, it becomes impossible to generalize about how far human freedom extends. This can also be seen in the case of ideas regarded as a necessary concomitant of freedom, namely the notions of commitment and responsibility. It can be seen that in choosing or acting with existential freedom I am displaying myself as the agent my choice or action, and hence as responsible for what I choose or do (cf. Wild, 1967). Nevertheless, because of the ambiguity of freedom, it is not clear how far this responsibility extends, or, indeed, how far I can hold myself responsible for my own existence. All we can do is dismiss those answers that are too simplistic. Sartre, typically, holds no such reservations on this point. He argues, with characteristic *élan*:

> If [however] it is true that existence is prior to essence, man is responsible for what he is. . . . And, when we say that man is responsible for himself, we do not mean that he is responsible only for his own individuality, but that he is responsible for all men . . . in choosing for himself he chooses for all men. For in effect, of all the actions a man may take in order to create himself as he wills to be, there is not one which is not creative, at the same time, of an image of man such as he believes he ought to be. To choose between this or that is at the same time to affirm the value of that which is chosen; for we are unable ever to choose the worse. What we choose is always the better; and nothing can be better for us unless it is better for all. (1956, pp. 291–2)

By this argument Sartre is able to effect a dramatic switch from individualism to universalism. For example if I decide to marry, whatever the reasons I may have for such a course of action, I thereby commit humanity as a whole to the practice of monogamy (ibid.).

If, however, my subjective choice becomes *immediately* universal, so that in choosing for myself I choose for everyone, and all other men are presumably doing the same, then how do we know that these choices will be communicable or intelligible, or indeed compatible, with each other? Suppose I don't accept what someone else chooses, and so challenge his image of man. In fact, he is not so much creating an image of man as a picture of himself *in his own situation*. In choosing for myself I am not simply choosing for everyone else as well. Individuals are not equatable because they inhabit different situations. My marriage does not commit the whole human race to monogamy because other people do not share the same financial, cultural, sexual and emotional position as I do. In Sartre we have a plurality of individual choices, but no intersubjectivity. There is an immediate transformation of individuality into universalism, but no social mediation. In short, Sartre ignores what Merleau-Ponty calls an 'interworld':

The question is to know whether, as Sartre says, there are only *men* and *things* or whether there is also the interworld, which we call history, symbolism, truth-to-be-made. If one sticks to the dichotomy, men, as the place where all meaning arises, are condemned to an incredible tension. Each man, in literature as well as in politics, must assume all that happens instant by instant to all others; he must be immediately universal. If, on the contrary, one acknowledges a mediation of personal relations through the world of human symbols, it is true that one renounces being instantly justified in the eyes of everyone and holding oneself responsible for all that is done at each moment. (AD 200)

All that can be said is that in any given situation we are both responsible and not responsible (cf. SNS 36). We are responsible because without our presence and our action the situation would be different, and because we have some measure of freedom in what we do. We are not responsible because we are also the product of our situation, which means the following: (1) what we are and what we do is to a large extent the result of our interaction with other people, since any action we commit will have been motivated by a prior action from someone else, or will fit into some interpersonal configuration of behaviour. (2) All our actions are over-determined in that they admit of more than one explanation, and so have a certain opaqueness for us. (3) Our conscious intentions are always to some extent different from the consequences of what we do, since we are never in complete control of any situation, and since the meaning we ascribe to our actions will not necessarily match the meanings other people ascribe to them. All these points illustrate the mediation of the personal through the social and the rootedness of all freedom, so that there is no 'pure' responsibility. Who is responsible for what is a question that can only be raised in the light of the practical concerns of the questioner.

Freedom and moral rules

In advocating an ethics of human freedom, existentialism is often charged with promoting an individualistic and iconoclastic view of morality at the expense of any recognition of social morality, of that morality embodied in rules and conventions.[2] But, as has been argued before, there is no necessary conflict between freedom, that is innovation or creativity, and rules, for freedom requires some form of sedimentation or habitualization on which to work. A non-conventional morality can only emerge against a ground of con-ventional moral rules. Nevertheless an existential ethics cannot consist of conformity to a set of moral rules.

True morality does not consist in following exterior rules or in respecting objective values: there are no ways to *be* just or to *be* saved . . . the value . . . consists of actively being what we are by chance, of establishing that communication with others and with ourselves for which our temporal structure gives us the opportunity and of which our liberty is only the rough outline. (SNS 40)

An existential ethics does not recognize objective values because it sees that all values are context-dependent. The opposite of objectivity in this sense is not subjectivity but rather *embodiment*, 'actively being what we are by chance'. Values do not exist as objects (and therefore as objective) but as expressed or embodied in action. It is not even clear what sense can be given to the notion of 'exterior rules', because, as ethnomethodology has shown (see chapter 2), rules derive their sense in terms of their embodiment in action. Moral rules or principles seem to be methods we use in order to understand or assess actions or beliefs, rather than existing 'in our heads' and in conformity with which we normally act. There might be cases where we act consciously in accordance with social rules, but this is characteristic of rigid or even compulsive behaviour. And even where we might be consciously aware of certain moral demands, these always have to be interpreted in the light of our concrete situation. In other words, to say 'there are no ways to *be* just or to to *be* saved' means that there can be no 'teach yourself books' for morality, there are no sets of instructions for being just or free, for a just or free action can only be identified in context, whereas any set of instructions must to some extent be context-free.

What matters, then, is not the moral principles we claim to live by, which really have the status of rationalizations rather than anything else. It is rather *how* we live and what we actually do that counts. Morality cannot be guaranteed in advance, it has to be worked for, our communication with others has actually to be established, even though our common language makes it possible.

Authenticity

If true morality for Merleau-Ponty is embodied morality, existential freedom becomes synonymous with embodiment, or its cognate, authenticity. How, phenomenologically, are we to understand these notions? We have already been given the conceptual tools for such a task in Merleau-Ponty's implicit distinction between *centre* and *periphery*. Freedom, we have seen, presupposes incarnation, the acquisition and sedimentation of quasi-automatic habits and skills, giving a certain weight to consciousness in the world. Now these bodily processes and habitual ways of behaving affect only the

125

periphery of our being, we are practically unaware of them. They are a permanent background to our more conscious or our more innovative thoughts and actions, to those that involve our attention and energy and so affect us at the centre of our being. It is this dialectic between centre and periphery that makes intelligible the concept of authenticity.

Merleau-Ponty's most extensive discussion of this concept concerns the difference between true (authentic) and false (inauthentic) feelings (PP 377–83). He takes the example of true and false (or illusory) love. The distinction is valid because 'everything felt by us as within ourselves is not *ipso facto* placed on a single footing of existence or true in the same way, and [that] there are degrees of reality within us' (PP 378). False love is not unreal, but it is not centred, it affects me only at the periphery of my existence. False love concerns only a part of me or when I play a certain role (for example, a seducer, a child searching for a mother-figure or a traveller seeking exotic adventures). There are large areas of my being left untouched by my supposed love, whereas true love involves my whole being. False love is more of a projection of my feelings on the loved person, so that my love will disappear when I change. True love, on the other hand, is genuinely intentional, so that my emotion discloses the object of my love to me. The pseudo-intentionality of false love means that I love only qualities of the person (for example the way she smiles, or her youthfulness) whereas in true love it is her whole manner of being, the person she is, that I love.[3]

False or inauthentic love represents a breakdown in my communication with myself: feelings which should concern my whole being take place on the periphery of my existence, making them literally superficial. Inauthentic emotions or feelings are those we adopt on the periphery like conventions and habits. In an important passage Merleau-Ponty terms these inauthentic emotions 'situational values':

> Illusory or imaginary feelings are genuinely experienced, but experienced, so to speak, on the outer fringes of ourselves. Children and many grown people are under the sway of 'situational values', which conceal from them their actual feelings – they are pleased because they have been given a present, sad because they are at a funeral, gay or sad according to the countryside around them, and, on the hither side of any such emotions, indifferent and neutral. . . . Our natural attitude is not to experience our own feelings or to adhere to our own pleasures, but to live in accordance with the emotional categories of the environment. (PP 379–80)

Inauthentic emotions are disembodied, they affect areas of myself not in touch with the rest of myself. Inauthenticity is thus a species of repression. It bears witness to 'the possibility of a fragmented life of consciousness which does not possess a unique significance at all times' (SB 178).

Nevertheless repression, habitualization, sedimentation are all essential parts of being-in-the-world. Hence all authenticity, all integration, is threatened by the breakdown between subordinate structures or between centre and periphery. Inauthenticity is a permanent threat to authenticity. There is then no 'pure' authenticity, as there is no 'pure' freedom, but only degrees of authentic being achieved on the ground of inauthenticity or incarnation.

Self-revelation and self-deception

Authenticity is an ambiguous phenomenon, because it never occurs in an unmixed state. There is a further reason for its essential ambiguity and that is the precariousness of self-knowledge. Now in some sense self-knowledge is a prerequisite of authenticity, because if we do not know what is happening at the centre or periphery of our existence, then we cannot be aware of our true feelings, and hence act authentically. However we can only know ourselves in an ambiguous way for the following reasons: (1) consciousness can never be crystal clear to itself because its essential thrust is to be a transcendence, to lose itself in things, in its perception and involvement with the world, and it can only reflect on itself and attempt to know itself by withdrawing from the world and turning back onto itself. Hence it cannot at the same time reflect on itself and be totally immersed in the world – at best it can only catch fleeting glimpses of itself as it is involved in the world. (2) Self-knowledge is also indirect, since in the world I know myself through the mediation of other people, who have the ability to define me and show me 'what I am'. (3) Furthermore, self-knowledge can only occur in time, so that I can only attempt to know myself after the event. But after the event I am, in a sense, a different person, and my perspective on myself must be different to what it was before, so that while I am living through an event, while I am immersed in a situation, I can never be transparent to myself. (4) Finally we must note that language can sometimes serve to hide our feelings from ourselves; 'I can experience more things than I can represent to myself . . . there are feelings in me which I do not name' (PP 296). This is so because we sometimes have only highly conventionalized words or phrases with which to express what we feel, so that we cannot do justice to the complexity of our feelings or to the fact that we can experience different things on different levels at the same time.

In fact rather than self-knowledge, we should perhaps speak of *self-revelation*,[4] of those experiences when we pull ourselves together and overcome the dispersion that threatens all existence. In self-revelation we catch an intimation of what we are, or grasp the sense of what we are doing. But because self-revelation can only be achieved at a distance, or indirectly, we find *self-deception* as its permanent bedfellow.

The relationship between the terms 'authenticity', 'inauthenticity' and 'self-deception' is extremely complex, involving, as they do, different kinds and different degrees of self-revelation. We can perhaps get an idea of the demarcation between them by considering a few examples. Take the case of a man at the funeral of his father. Three different attitudes seem open to him (at least for the purposes of this example).

(1) There is first an inauthentic attitude, where his sadness and mourning are intelligible as the simple response to his situation, and hence as superficial. There is no exploration of any deeper or perhaps socially inappropriate feelings, such as relief or even joy at his father's death. Here we find a characteristic of inauthentic feelings in their being *totally* explicable in terms of their environment or their motivation. Thus a child's pleasure can be seen as totally explicable because he has been given a present, or an untalented man's decision to become an artist is totally explicable as a compensation for his failure to earn any other kind of living. If an action is completely intelligible in terms of outside pressures or is transparently motivated, it suggests that it did not spring from a spontaneous or authentic impulse of the actor's, but is an expression of a situational value, affecting only the periphery of the man's being.

(2) A second possibility is an authentic response in which the possible contradiction between a man's actual and expected feelings is recognized and faced. This does not necessarily mean that he will express or make public what he really feels. The point is simply that whatever he does, he will act *rationally*, that is, as an expression of his whole personality rather than as a function of isolated structures. Rationality, we may recall, means a concern with grounds, and authentic action is grounded in the whole being of a person.

(3) There is, finally, a response which is a certain mixture of (1) and (2), where the man is in a sense aware of the possible contradiction between his actual and expected feelings, but represses this knowledge, refuses to recognize it, and adopts a forced attitude of sadness and mourning. It is this attitude which we may call one of self-deception, where the possibility of authenticity is recognized on one level, and then denied on another (cf. Fingarette, 1969). As in the case of the phantom limb (see pp. 15–16), self-deception manifests

an ambivalent knowledge, one that takes away with one hand what it offers with the other.

Self-deception illustrates in striking form those cases where we both know something and yet are ignorant of it, where our existence is dramatically split. We can look at two more examples of this paradoxical state of affairs. There is Freud's case of a man who had left a book, which was intended as a present for his wife, in a drawer, and which he then completely forgot about until his wife and he were reconciled after a quarrel, when he suddenly rediscovered it. He had not 'really' lost the book; but neither did he 'know' where it was.

> Everything connected with his wife had ceased to exist for him, he had shut it out from his life, and, at one stroke, broken the circuit of all actions relating to her, and thus placed himself on the hither side of all knowledge and ignorance, assertion and negation, in so far as these were voluntary. (PP 162)

Or there is Sartre's famous example of a woman in bad faith. Out on her first date with a man, she wants to relate to him in two different ways at the same time: as a free and active personality, and as a sexual object. She is unable to balance or fuse these two attitudes and the crunch comes when her partner takes her hand. In order not to have to make a decision, to leave her hand there or withdraw it, which might upset the uneasy alliance of her two attitudes, 'the young woman leaves her hand there, but she *does not notice* that she is leaving it' (1969a, pp. 55–6). This is the crucial point: she lets her hand lie there, in the hands of her partner, like a thing, because she manages to 'forget' that it is there. She practises a kind of selective inattention, and this is what is characteristic of self-deception. The person who deceives himself sees only what he wants to see.

It can be seen that self-deception and inauthenticity are very closely allied since both involve a failure of self-revelation and embodiment. But they are not quite identical. If we change Sartre's example slightly, so that instead of having a rather sensitive young woman who wishes to balance the two sides of her personality, being an active subjectivity or a sexual object, we have a woman who experiences herself purely as a sexual object, then there is no conflict in her attitude, no need for any mechanisms of selective inattention, and hence no self-deception. Such a woman would be inauthentic in not being aware of any feelings deeper than ones of simple sexual desire or submission. She is inauthentic in failing to acknowledge a potentiality of being-in-the-world, namely of acting as a subject. Self-deception would then seem to indicate a more intricate and ambivalent form of inauthenticity (Sartre's 'bad faith' would seem to cover both inauthenticity and self-deception).

Spontaneity

If authenticity is always mixed with inauthenticity and our self-knowledge precarious, having self-deception always present on the horizon, how can we prevent a permanent doubt creeping over all our beliefs and actions? Is not the logical consequence of Merleau-Ponty's philosophy of ambiguity an attitude of passivity or quietism? This is not Merleau-Ponty's conclusion; on the contrary:

> It is true neither that my existence is in full possession of itself, nor that it is entirely estranged from itself, because it is action or doing, and because action is, by definition, the violent transition from what I have to what I aim to have, from what I am to what I intend to be. I can effect the cogito and be assured of genuinely willing, loving or believing, provided that in the first place I do actually will, love or believe, and thus fulfil my own existence. If this were not so, an ineradicable doubt would spread over the world, and equally over my own thoughts. (PP 382)

Existence for Merleau-Ponty is transcendence and this means acting in the world, which is how authenticity can be realized. Now he calls acting 'the *violent* transition from what I have to what I aim to have' (quoted above) and claims that the way to sincerity is through 'a *blind* plunge into doing' (ibid., italics added). This stress on the dramaticality of the action envisaged is perhaps unfortunate because it smacks of the '*acte gratuite*', of action for its own sake, which is not what Merleau-Ponty means. He wants to oppose his conception of action to those acts that are engaged in after much deliberation and soul-searching, to those actions that become a self-conscious seeking after authenticity. The point here is that to make sincerity or authenticity into one's highest value, and to self-consciously try to achieve it in one's actions, is, paradoxically, already to be tainted with inauthenticity, because it turns sincerity or authenticity into an attitude, or a pose, rather than an unreserved commitment to action. I am turned inwards to myself as I try to make myself sincere, instead of outwards to the world, which is the only terrain of authenticity. Merleau-Ponty's stress on the violence and blindness of action is a reaction – perhaps an overreaction – to this conception of 'sincere acting'.

Authentic or embodied action is not self-consciously sincere but *spontaneous*. Spontaneity, that most un-English of qualities distrusted by Anglo-Saxon moralists,[5] is the cash-value of authenticity.

> In morality as in art there is no solution for the man who will not make a move without knowing where he is going and who wants to be accurate and in control at every moment. Our only

resort is the spontaneous movement which binds us to others for good or ill, out of selfishness or generosity. (SNS 4)

Spontaneity is the opposite of control, that conscious and deliberate grip on oneself where one attempts to act only in conformity with what has been carefully thought out beforehand. The controlled person takes no risks, and so his actions tend to be rigid and conservative. He never lives dangerously (Nietzsche). Nevertheless, some of the most basic human activities, such as giving birth, urination and defecation, sleeping, floating on the water, and sexual surrender, require spontaneity, the ability to let go and relax, to have, in Maslow's (1971) phrase, trust in the world and in oneself.

Spontaneity involves integration and authenticity, the intercommunication of centre and periphery. It also implies passion and generosity.[6] It is most often manifested in those graceful and free-flowing movements of children, and it is no surprise that Merleau-Ponty's philosophy harks back to the world of children. In a late text Merleau-Ponty writes that:

there are two ways of being young, which are not easily comprehensible to one another. Some are fascinated by their childhood; it possesses them, holding them enchanted in a realm of privileged possibilities. Others, it casts out toward adult life; they believe that they have no past and are equally near to all possibilities. (S 25)

He meant Sartre to fit into this second category; the first he intended for Nizan, a contemporary of both Sartre and himself, but it is not difficult to see that it fits Merleau-Ponty as well. That would certainly be Sartre's judgment, who wrote:

One day in 1947 Merleau told me that he had never recovered from an incomparable childhood. He had known that private world of happiness from which only age drives us. . . . It established his preferences – choosing, at the same time, the traditions which recalled the rituals of childhood, and the 'spontaneity' which evoked childhood's superintended liberty. (1965b, p. 157)

Nevertheless Merleau-Ponty adds significantly, after the passage I have quoted above, that those who prolonged their childhood 'had to learn that one does not go beyond what one preserves, that nothing could give them the wholeness that they were nostalgic for' (S 25). One can never re-live one's childhood, even if it is never left behind.

This spontaneity, while being child-like, is not *childish*. It does not amount to a refusal or incapacity to take stock of what one does or

131

act without responsibility and with no attempt at self-understanding. Spontaneity is only the consequence of *embodiment*, of a co-ordination between the structures that make up human existence. Spontaneity is possible because it presupposes the embodiment of mind, of thought in speech and of project in action.

Embodiment

Spontaneous behaviour is not unthinking, 'purely instinctual' (whatever that may mean) or mindless, as some moralists are apt to imply. Merleau-Ponty is quite specific in his rejection of such a view.

> To obey with one's eyes closed is the beginning of panic, and to choose contrary to one's understanding is the beginning of scepticism. It is necessary to be able to stand back in order to be capable of a true commitment, which is also always a commitment towards the truth. (EP 70, my translation)

In fact these two processes of standing back in order to grasp the sense of what one is doing, and then committing oneself, can be separated only for the purposes of discussion, for they are both part of the same movement by which man transcends himself in spontaneous action. Committed or embodied action has its own '*sens*', and hence is also 'a commitment towards the truth' as truth, understood phenomenologically, involves the realization of meaning or *Gestalt*.

Consider how this applies to the field of literature. In an essay called 'Studies in the literary use of language' (in TL) Merleau-Ponty refers to what he calls Stendhal's problem. Stendhal found that he either surrendered himself to life, to his feelings, but was then struck dumb and was unable to write anything about it; or, if he acted self-consciously, as if role-playing, in order to be continually aware of what he was doing, he was rightly accused of not 'penetrating' or living in what he wrote about. Stendhal is in the same dilemma as Roquentin, the hero of *Nausea*. 'Man is always a teller of tales,' says Roquentin, 'he tries to live his life as if he were recounting it' (Sartre, 1965a, p. 61). By doing so he must give his story a beginning and an end, and thus breaks up the lived flow of events which, instead of opening onto an indefinite future, are made to lead on intelligibly to the next point in the story. Life, says Roquentin, is lived forwards, but is told backwards. And so: 'you have to choose: to live or to recount' (ibid.).

But these dilemmas, although carrying a grain of existential truth, belong to a mode of living that is not a peace with itself, which lacks embodiment. Stendhal's problem is based on a 'self-misunderstanding':

132

Once he had given up the promotion of his literary and
amatory projects and had opened himself and his writing to
the revery he had at first resisted, he suddenly found himself
capable of improvisation, conviction, creation. He realized
that there is no conflict between truth and fiction, solitude
and love, living and writing. (TL 17)

And on the social and political plane we find the same. 'There is a
way of thinking, in contact with the event, which seeks its concrete
structure. A revolution which is really moving with the march of
history can be thought as well as lived' (PP 363, n. 1). It is those
revolutions that become dissociated from the ideas that nourished
them that tend to turn into repressive régimes.

Truly embodied or spontaneous action presupposes *insight*, the
ability to fuse theory and praxis (Heaton, 1972b). Clear-sightedness
by itself is not enough; Roquentin's unremitting lucidity does not
free him from his alienation. Self-awareness has to be accompanied
by a change in the way one relates to oneself and the world, it has to
herald a change in the meaning of one's existence. Hysterical
symptoms are not cured by understanding their significance or origin.
It is the relationship between patient and doctor which establishes
that change of existence necessary for a real cure to be effected (PP
163). This is true of philosophy as of everything else. The book that
one puts back on the shelf, everything having remained the same,
cannot be true in Merleau-Ponty's sense of the term.

The embodied person acts 'thoughtfully', in harmony with his
reason, and 'with feeling', in tune with his emotions. At its highest
expression, embodiment gives rise to 'peak experiences' (Maslow,
1971), moments of harmony with oneself and between men, when
events respond to one's will. 'Sometimes there is that flash of fire,
that streak of lightning, that moment of victory, or, as Hemingway's
Maria says, that *gloria* which in its brilliance blots out everything
else' (SNS 186). It is such experiences that enable us to make sense
of Merleau-Ponty's almost mystical statements about human
existence realizing a fusion between inner and outer. 'Taken concretely', he affirms, 'freedom is always a meeting of the inner and the
outer' (PP 454). Or again: 'inside and outside are inseparable. The
world is wholly inside and I am wholly outside myself' (PP 407).
Such a total expression of the primitive intentionality on which the
'self' is founded occurs only at rare moments, when man, in his
actions, finds himself in the midst of the world, and *in things*.

Saint-Exupéry plunges into his mission because it is an intimate
part of himself, the consequence of his thoughts, wishes and
decisions, because he would be nothing if he were to back
out.... Over Arras ... he feels invulnerable because he is *in*

things at last; he has left his inner nothingness behind, and death, if it comes, will reach him right in the thick of the world. (SNS 185)

Yet, as we know, all embodiment fails and all integration breaks down, and so the realization of an existential ethics is always provisional:

man is not assured ahead of time of possessing a source of morality; consciousness of self is not given in man by right; it is acquired only by the elucidation of his concrete being and is verified only by the active integration of isolated dialectics – body and soul – between which it is initially broken up. (SB 223)

Merleau-Ponty's humanism

In view of his concern with freedom, Merleau-Ponty is not adverse to calling himself a humanist. Nevertheless, since there is no guarantee of morality or self-understanding, we can see that his humanism – as a philosophy of man – is not an effete admiration of all things human. Humanism – as Merleau-Ponty argues in an essay on Machiavelli – is rather something to be achieved:

If by humanism we mean a philosophy of the inner man which finds no difficulty in principle in his relations with others, no opacity whatever in the functioning of society, and which replaces political cultivation by moral exhortation, Machiavelli is not a humanist. But if by humanism we mean a philosophy which confronts the relation of man to man and the constitution of a common situation and a common history as a problem, then we have to say that Machiavelli formulated some of the conditions of any serious humanism. (S 223)

In defending Machiavelli from those armchair moralists who call themselves humanists, Merleau-Ponty considers that, on the contrary, it is Machiavelli who is the serious humanist in attempting to found his morality on an appraisal of the concrete situation. All of us who at some time are not resigned to passivity or submission are faced with a situation which, by its very logic, demands some violence on our part, the only question being what form of violence – physical, psychological, moral, symbolic – or violence against whom. Merleau-Ponty's humanism dissociates itself from all moralizing, from those attitudes which involve sitting back and passing judgment without dirtying one's hands or soiling one's good conscience. There is indeed a streak of hard pragmatism in Merleau-Ponty's brand of humanism. 'We have unlearned "pure morality" and learned a kind of vulgar immoralism, which is healthy' (SNS 147).

134

An existential ethics will not avoid conflict or even injustice, since there are no guarantees or certainties in action, and because nothing is won without cost. But the existentialist, unlike the 'pure moralist', will not disavow such actions, but instead will seek to learn from them, his aim being one of 're-discovering a system of morals . . . through contact with the conflicts revealed by immoralism' (SNS 4). Nothing in man is pure. If it is true that 'hell is other people' (Sartre), it is no less true that they are also our salvation.

With this balance of apparent opposites – humanism and terror, morality and immorality, hell and salvation, sense and non-sense – we are at the heart of Merleau-Ponty's philosophy and his ethics. We find here the most profound sense of that term that is used, by himself and by others, to sum up his philosophy, namely 'ambiguity'. It is this concept which we must now elucidate. As well as being essentially ambiguous, there is also something tragic about Merleau-Ponty's ethics. This is not surprising, however, since the terms 'ambiguity' and 'tragedy' are intimately connected, and we can begin to understand the one in terms of the other.

> the true nature of tragedy appears once *the same man* has understood both that he cannot disavow the objective pattern of his actions, that he is for others in the context of history, and yet that the motive of his actions constitutes a man's worth as he himself experiences it. In this case we no longer have a series of alternatives between the inward and the external, subjective and objective, or judgement and its means but a dialectic relation, that is to say, a contradiction founded in truth, in which the same man tries to realize himself on the two levels. (HT 62–3)

Ambiguity and dialectic

Ambiguity, like tragedy, is a phenomenon of levels or contexts. Now Merleau-Ponty's philosophy is a philosophy of ambiguity because ambiguity is in things. In perception we find objects charged with a potential ambiguity in the ever-present possibility of a shift in perspective, or horizon or even perceptual field, which is motivated by a change in our projects or interests at hand, and results in new perceptual configurations. The figure/ground structure of perception makes any perceptual object dependent on its context, so that all perceptual meaning is a dialectic between figure and context. The phenomenon of speech and the society introduce us to the flexibility of levels of meaning that defines human experience and allows objects to be invested with figurative or symbolic significances beyond their perceptual value. Furthermore speech illustrates how linguistic meanings emerge from a dialectic between innovation and sedimentation, or between signs within an overall structure, so that speech can be seen as signifying allusively or indirectly. Ambiguity refers to these facts: that meaning is *structural* or *contextual*, and that meaning is a phenomenon of *levels*.

Merleau-Ponty's philosophy is ambiguous because it tries to render intelligible this ambiguity of being-in-the-world. The ambiguity of philosophy is a recognition that it constitutes one perspective among others, a perspective, however, which attempts to be comprehensive, and so must take into account as many other perspectives as possible. Ambiguity is, then, for Merleau-Ponty a positive phenomenon, a description of being-in-the-world. It has to be carefully distinguished from concepts with which, in common discourse, it is normally associated, but which have a different sense. Three such concepts will be considered, ambivalence, equivocation and mystification, in order to show how they differ from ambiguity in Merleau-Ponty's sense.

The most important distinction is between ambiguity and *ambivalence*. Ambivalence is a characteristic of non-integrated thought which thinks in terms of rigid and exclusive categories and refuses to see connections between them. 'Ambivalence consists in having two alternative images of the same object, the same person, without making any effort to connect them or to notice that in reality they relate to the same object and the same person' (PM 102–3). So, for example, a man might view his mother as either totally good or totally bad. If he views her as totally good, then whatever might threaten that image has to be repressed and concealed from himself so as not to tarnish his image of total goodness. All cases of self-deception are based on ambivalence, an inability to recognize areas of experience, or, if they are recognized, to find a viable synthesis between them. Ambivalence often results in a Manicheistic view of the world, and so is characteristic of prejudiced or psychologically rigid people.

A rich source of examples of ambivalent thinking is the work of the cartoonist Feiffer who contributes to *The Observer*. He succeeds well in capturing the peculiar flavour of an ambivalent conception of the self and of the world. Two cartoons, Figures 1 and 2 (reproduced by permission), must suffice. In the first cartoon we have an ambivalence between friendship and love, where each is experienced as antagonistic to the other, and where the protagonist can only vacillate helplessly from the one to the other. In the second cartoon there is an apparent progression, from ambivalence between the categories love = pain and absence of love = loneliness, to a solution in despair. Yet the solution manages to suppress the whole system. The final category, despair, is not a synthesis or mediation between the previous two categories, but a rejection of them, and in fact is the establishment of a new system. This is not to say that the young woman's solution is false or unreal – it is very real, but it is an example of ambivalent rather than ambiguous thought.

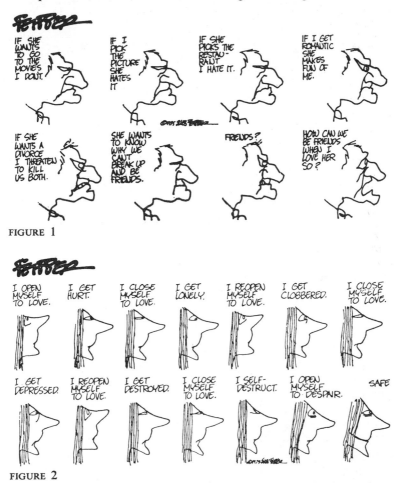

FIGURE 1

FIGURE 2

Ambivalence, then, is not ambiguity; in fact it is a *refusal of ambiguity*, a failure to recognize interplay, shading and transition between concepts or phenomena. Ambiguity is not a manifestation of rigidity but rather of flexibility and maturity. 'It consists in simply admitting that the same being who is good and generous can also be annoying and imperfect. *Ambiguity is ambivalence that one dares to look at face to face*' (PM 103, italics added).

Ambiguity is also to be distinguished from *equivocation* in the sense of refusing to choose or act because nothing is certain or fixed.

Merleau-Ponty's conception of philosophy is not that of the hero of *Either* who delivers this 'ecstatic lecture' on philosophy:

> If you marry, you will regret it; if you do not marry, you will also regret it; if you marry or do not marry, you will regret both; whether you marry or do not marry, you will regret both. . . . Hang yourself, you will regret it; do not hang yourself, you will regret that; hang yourself or do not hang yourself, you will regret both; whether you hang yourself or do not hang yourself, you will regret both. This, gentlemen, is the sum and substance of all philosophy. (Kierkegaard, 1959, p. 37)

Ambiguity does not leave us castrated, unable to utter or do anything of consequence. It does, however, restrict the kind of statements we can make. Such general judgments as 'all is well', or 'all is evil', or even 'all is vain' do not belong to philosophy. Philosophy is *ironic* rather than equivocal. Allusion, implication, suggestion, even word-plays belong to the philosopher's style because he recognizes that one says nothing without inviting ambiguity.

Finally we can consider a class of statements which might be termed *mystifying* or paradoxical and which manifest a kind of masked ambiguity. Take a simple semantic paradox, that of a man who says 'I am lying'. The paradox is that the utterance is true only if it is not true. In other words, if the man is telling the truth (i.e. 'I am lying'), then he cannot be telling the truth, because he must be lying. But the paradox can be made intelligible by making a distinction between two levels of language: the object-level, which is the simple statement 'I am lying', and the meta-level, which is a statement about the object-level, so that when the man says 'I am lying' he implies that his own statement (on the object-level) is not true. This distinction between object- and meta-level is crucial for understanding the difference, for example, between the statements 'London is the capital of Britain' and ' "London" has six letters'. In our example, the paradox arises because it is not clear whether we are to understand the statement 'I am lying' as being on the object-level, meta-level or both at the same time.

This paradox would seem to be a cause of ambiguity, an interplay between two different levels of language. Nevertheless the aim here is to confuse, since the operation of the two language levels is hidden or masked. Merleau-Ponty uses ambiguity in an attempt to gain a comprehensive understanding, and hence to enlighten. Here the intent seems more akin to mystification.

This mystification is more evident in certain paradoxes that occur in everyday interaction often termed 'double binds' or 'knots' (Beavin *et al.*, 1968). A paradigm case would be that of an injunction demanding specific behaviour to be carried out which, by its very

138

nature, can only be spontaneous. Take an order to 'Be spontaneous!' The victim here is in an untenable position, because to comply with the order is to be spontaneous within a frame or context of non-spontaneity. Variations on this form of mystification would be:

(1) 'You ought to dominate me.'
(2) 'I want you to dominate me' (for example, request of a wife to a passive husband).
(3) 'You should enjoy playing with the children.'
(4) 'Don't be so obedient.'

The mystification would be total if the victim is unaware that he is in a paradoxical situation. Laing is particularly adept at revealing such situations. He notes, for example (Laing, 1969), that the best way to get someone to *be* something is not to give him an order, that is tell him what to be, but to attribute qualities to him, that is tell him what he is. Now such attributions are rich in possible mystifications. A common case is where a child does X, when his parents tell him to do Y, but indicate that he is X. Examples of this are:

(1) 'I'm always trying to get him to make more friends, but he is so self-conscious. Isn't that right, dear?'
(2) 'He's so naughty. He never does what I tell him. Do you?'
(3) 'I keep telling him to be more careful, but he's so careless, aren't you?'

It is significant that these mystifications can to some extent be dissolved, or at least made intelligible as behavioural ploys, by commenting on them and pointing out that they rest on a masked confusion between different levels or frames. The mystifications depend on the victim *not* being capable of ambiguous or dialectical thought, so that his perspective will be constricted and he will be unable to view the total context and hence make sense of the paradox in which he is trapped.[7]

The ambiguity of Merleau-Ponty's philosophy is not meant to confuse or to trap, but to make the reader aware of the multiplicity of frames and levels of his analysis. The sense of ambiguity is expressed in the notion of *dialectic*. The dialectic in Merleau-Ponty's usage is never completed or overcome, making the popular formula, thesis – antithesis – synthesis, not a characterization of the dialectic but a misuse of it, an illegitimate attempt to abolish it in a tacit re-establishment of positive, i.e. non-dialectical, thinking. Nevertheless although the dialectic does not terminate in a completed synthesis, neither is it truncated or castrated. Merleau-Ponty's dialectic does not do away with the idea of synthesis, it only recognizes that any dialectical synthesis is always open and incomplete:

What we reject or deny is not the idea of a surpassing that
reassembles, it is the idea that it results in a new positive, a
new position. In thought and in history as in life, the only
surpassings we know are concrete, partial, encumbered with
survivals, saddled with deficits. (VI 99)

It is these partial and provisional syntheses that Merleau-Ponty
designates 'truth'. The dialectic is, then, a 'contradiction founded in
truth' (see p. 135), a provisional synthesis of perspectives that are
inconsistent or contradictory, and yet also coalesce if put into a
certain context which illuminates their interconnections. This new
context can, in its turn, be broken up and re-established in terms of a
level or context which is even more comprehensive. Dialectical truth
is neither equivocal nor absolute, it is simply provisional.

An existential ethics

Ambiguity and dialectic presuppose mediation and communication
between apparent opposites. And this is what an existential ethics
really amounts to: that there is a potential in being-in-the-world for
integration, and this potential is both a description and the foundation
of an ethics. The whole constellation of concepts that go to make up
an existential ethics – freedom, authenticity, spontaneity, embodiment, commitment, insight – all point to the possibility of an integrated existence. Philosophy can tell us what this involves – it cannot
tell us how it can be achieved. For some, this is a fatal weakness:

in spite of its pre-occupation with ethics, existentialism
completely fails to give any concrete advice on what to do.
The command 'Be authentic' gives no help on what course of
action to commit oneself to; it seems to demand a choice
without giving any useful criteria for making that choice.
(Manser, 1963, pp. 24–5)

It is interesting that this criticism of existentialism presents it as
essentially paradoxical, for how can we be *commanded* to be authentic,
when authenticity is a feature of spontaneous action. That, indeed,
is the point. No useful criteria for ethical choices can be given, for
authentic choice is existential choice which arises out of a person's
concrete situation. Neither is philosophy in the business of giving
advice. All it can do is suggest frames or perspectives by which
existence can be described and, at the same time, assessed. What a
person should do in a given situation can only be decided by himself alone. We can suggest how he view his situation, but we cannot
tell him what to do. Indeed, as Sartre says, we always have some

idea of what advice we will receive from a given person, so that in asking advice of that person we usually know in advance what will be offered.

It is often claimed that an existential ethics can deal only with 'extraordinary situations' (Kovesi, 1967, p. 111), or with situations that fall outside the domain of conventional morality (MacIntyre, 1971, p. 107), whereas British moral philosophy has traditionally assumed an established, ordered moral universe and has gone about articulating principles and concepts which it assumes its readers are familiar with and will unhesitatingly accept (cf. Olafson, 1971, pp. 121–4). But this dichotomy between existentialism and British moral philosophy is too stark. Even if a moral consensus is presumed, *how* it is actually employed or embodied is always context-specific. Nevertheless, it is true that Merleau-Ponty writes in a different climate to that of most British moral philosophers. He writes, for example, that 'it is a fact that, in our present situation, there is not one term in the moral vocabulary which has not become ambiguous, not one traditional value which has not become contaminated' (SNS 118). This was written at a time when Fascism had just been defeated and the promise of Marxism was beginning to turn sour in Russia. But as well as this contemporary uncertainty and ambiguity, Merleau-Ponty means to indicate the essential opacity of being-in-the-world which renders any ethics essentially ambiguous. There can be no assumption of a social world crystallized into patterns of conventional beliefs and behaviours, a world with no surprises. This is a fiction of certain social scientists or philosophers. Where are these supposed conventional beliefs or this supposed conventional morality, which is apparently accepted and practised by men and women, old and young, working-class and middle-class, white and black, rich and poor? The notion of an ordinary man has no basis in reality, it is an idealization used for specific intellectual purposes. But Merleau-Ponty is interested in concrete men, each of whom is capable of inhabiting his own extraordinary situation:

> Human life is not played upon a single scale. There are echoes and exchanges between one scale and another; but a given man who has never confronted passions faces up to history, another who thinks in an ordinary way is free with *mores*, and another who lives to all appearances like everybody else has thoughts which uproot all things. (S 310)

We can choose to study men in order to see what is conventional in them, or in order to reveal what is singular, profound or significant about them. Merleau-Ponty seeks to unite both perspectives, since it is a constant theme of his philosophy that creativity is enacted only on the ground of the habitual.

Our final impression of an existential ethics is of a certain kind of a-morality. It is a-moral in the sense that there is no human nature on which we can rely (cf. SNS 28), no pre-given and established moral code we can stick to, so that in a sense, as one of Dostoevsky's characters put it, if there is no God then everything is permitted. It is also a-moral in that Merleau-Ponty exhibits a distrust of any kind of moralizing, of making bland moral judgments. It is true that he writes that 'the lowliest student, ever since Nietzsche, would flatly reject philosophy if it did not teach how to live fully' (PM 161). But to live fully is not something we learn from textbooks. Life might be nourished by philosophy, but philosophy can only realize itself in life.[8]

> Whether it is a question of things or of historical situations, philosophy has no function other than to teach us once more to see them clearly, and it is true to say that it comes into being by destroying itself as separate philosophy. But what is required here is silence, for only the hero lives out his relation to men and the world. (PP 456)

6 Philosophy

The reflective and the pre-reflective

We concluded the previous chapter by trying to put some flesh on the notion of ambiguity which so well defines Merleau-Ponty's philosophy. When we turn to Merleau-Ponty's view of philosophy itself, we will not be surprised to find that it is charged with paradox. Philosophy deals with the relation between thought and life, the reflective and the pre-reflective. Now the essential paradox of philosophy is that it is a mode of reflection whose fundamental aim is to reveal and clarify the pre-reflective, which, by definition, operates below the level of reflection. It is this paradox which some commentators have found unpalatable. Zaner, for instance, interprets Merleau-Ponty as denying the value of any kind of philosophic reflection:

> It is only by *experiencing* my body-proper that *I can*
> *apprehend it as experienced by me.* In short, it would appear
> that a genuine reflective withdrawal is for Merleau-Ponty
> intrinsically unable to grasp my body-as-lived . . . I *know* my
> body-proper only by *living* it . . . and apparently in no other
> manner. (1971, p. 138)

Hence, on Zaner's view, Merleau-Ponty is open to 'the charge of irrationalism' (p. 139, n. 3). Kullman and Taylor take a similar view, arguing that Merleau-Ponty's programme of describing the pre-objective world is in fact nonsensical:

> At first hand it seems as senseless to ask us to return to the
> 'pre-objective world' as it is to ask a man to remember his
> birth. For if he could remember his birth, what happened
> before and what after, we could not call it his 'birth'. Likewise
> what is describable or described in language whose logic is
> predicative, is no longer correctly described as the pre-predicative.

The very attempt to describe the pre-predicative seems to destroy it. (1958, p. 113)

Even de Waehlens, a very sympathetic and knowledgeable commentator, has this to say:

> Expressed in other terms, and it is necessary to note this, the fundamental thesis of Merleau-Ponty's philosophy: all knowledge is rooted in perception, is itself ambiguous. If it signifies that all human knowledge originates in the concrete and follows the explication of it, everything said in his work seems to be established. If on the contrary one understands by that thesis that in no way whatsoever can we ever leave the immediate and that to render this immediate explicit means simply to live it, one cannot doubt that the enterprise of philosophy becomes forthwith contradictory. Now that's an opinion to which the author seems at times to make concessions. (1970, p. 386; translation by Zaner, 1971, p. 139)

In this chapter I want to defend Merleau-Ponty against these charges, or at least make Merleau-Ponty's position intelligible, so that the critiques made of him can be put into perspective. I will argue that his phenomenological programme does not signal the total failure of philosophic reflection, nor the destruction of the pre-reflective when apprehended by reflection, nor indeed the impossibility of grasping immediate experience except by living it. The paradox of philosophy – apprehending the pre-reflective through reflection – is not for him a fatal contradiction, but rather an occasion to consider how this paradox can engender a more radical mode of reflection.

> It will perhaps be maintained that a philosophy cannot be centred round a contradiction, and that all our descriptions, since they ultimately defy thought, are quite meaningless. The objection would be valid if we were content to lay bare, under the term phenomenon or phenomenal field, a layer of prelogical or magical experiences. For in that case we should have to choose between believing the descriptions and abandoning thought, or knowing what we are talking about and abandoning our descriptions. These descriptions need to provide us with an opportunity of defining a variety of comprehension and reflection altogether more radical than objective thought. To phenomenology understood as direct description needs to be added a phenomenology of phenomenology. (PP 365)

Our task is to make intelligible what this phenomenology of phenomenology or radical reflection is.

The critique of introspection

Phenomenological or radical reflection is to be distinguished from those forms of reflection – variously referred to by Merleau-Ponty as Cartesian, idealist, rationalist or intellectualist, or simply as philosophies of reflection – whose aim is to objectify, that is fix in clear and precise concepts, the contents of consciousness. Such forms of reflection are *introspective*. That is, reflection is conceived as the simple antithesis of the empiricist thesis that the relation between the self and the world is external. This purely external relation is replaced by a wholly internal or immanent relation between consciousness and the world. The world is held to be the simple product of consciousness, and the 'facts' of consciousness can be read off by introspective reflection in the same way that the 'facts' of the external world are read off by external observation.

Introspection, then, is a form of internal perception, which makes of knowledge an act of coinciding with what is 'in' consciousness. One's gaze is turned inwards in order to observe the 'psychic facts' of one's inner life. But this enterprise is beset by problems. Not the least of its difficulties is that it is not clear *what* introspection actually reveals. 'If I try to study love or hate purely from inner observation, I will find very little to describe: a few pangs, a few heart-throbs – in short, trite agitations which do not reveal the essence of love or hate' (SNS 52). In order to apprehend what I am meant to be observing, I will need to conceptualize the results of my observation, which means I can no longer be coinciding with what I see. In ordinary perception there are no difficulties here: if I perceive a table, there is no question about what I am perceiving. But consciousness is not peopled by little objects or little men, so there is really nothing to internally perceive.

There is also the problem of imparting my intuitions to others. Since introspection is only meant to bring me the contents of *my* mind, how can I begin to communicate my findings to other people, without making the unwarranted assumption that the contents of their minds will be similar to mine? The philosopher will find himself reduced to 'a sort of incantation designed to induce in them experiences comparable to the philosopher's' (PP 57). Introspection, as a mode of objective thought, leads us into that blind alley where we can only be certain of the contents of our own mind. Introspection bows before the immediate, that 'lonely, blind and mute life' (ibid.).

In order to transcend this conception of reflection as introspection, we need a transformation in our understanding of the immediate.

Each time I find something worth saying, it is because I have not been satisfied to coincide with my feeling, because I have succeeded in studying it as a way of behaving, as a modification of my relations with others and with the world, because I have managed to think about it as I would think about the behaviour of another person whom I happened to witness. (SNS 52)

Radical reflection is not a form of coincidence, a version of the reproductive fallacy, but the apprehension of the *meaning* of what is reflected on. We understand, in philosophy as in everyday life, the feelings, gestures, behaviours of ourselves and others through acts of appropriation 'which we all experience when we say that we have "found" the rabbit in the foliage of a puzzle, or that we have "caught" a slight gesture' (PP 57–8). In other words, radical reflection makes of reflection what the sociologists call *Verstehen*, the understanding of a phenomenon by grasping its sense, by placing it within an intelligible context, by revealing its immanent logic within a given setting. Reflection does not result in a collection of 'psychic facts' – whatever they might be – but is a means of comprehending the style of human existence.

Philosophy as radical reflection

If we return to the criticisms levelled at Merleau-Ponty, we find that, in their view, Merleau-Ponty is arguing that we have to choose between living and knowing: *either* we live the unreflective, but then are unable to reflect on it; *or* we withdraw from the unreflective, reflect on it, but then cannot apprehend its real structure. However this charge of ambivalence is true only of introspection. Introspective reflection vacillates between reflection as coincidence, as living the unreflective, but where there is no understanding, no grasping of the sense of the observed and no communication of one's findings; and reflection as an objective attitude, the fixing in determinate concepts of the 'contents' of consciousness, the noting of 'psychic facts'. But now, in the objective attitude, the unreflective is truly destroyed, for I can accept as factual only what my objective mode of reflection will allow. For example, trying to be 'objective' or impartial in determining 'what I am' involves taking an outside perspective, the point of view of another person, on myself, making me an object. That is, introspection can only apprehend my being-for-others.[1]

Radical reflection, however, is not an endless sliding between a mute unreflective and a fully explicit and objective reflective, but is a mode of reflection which recognizes that the unreflective it apprehends is not the unreflective as lived, but the unreflective as apprehended by reflection. In other words, radical reflection acknowledges that reflection results in a *change in structure* in the unreflective. This point, which is crucial for answering the objections of commentators, is reiterated throughout Merleau-Ponty's writings:

> Reflection cannot be thorough-going, or bring a complete elucidation of its object, if it does not arrive at awareness of itself as well as of its results. . . . Reflection is truly reflection . . . only if it knows itself as reflection-on-an-unreflective-experience, and consequently as a change in structure of our existence. (PP 62)

> It is true that we discover the unreflected. But the unreflected we go back to is not that which is prior to philosophy or prior to reflection. It is the unreflected which is understood and conquered by reflection. (PM 19)

Radical reflection – contrary to Zaner's contention (see p. 143) – is a certain kind of withdrawal from the immediate, a reduction or suspension of our naïve vision, feelings, etc., since to reflect is to gain a measured distance from the object of reflection. Reflection is a suspension of brute experience since it makes it pass into the order of the expressed (IV 38). It is indeed this whole movement, the very birth of expression, that radical reflection seeks to render intelligible.

Radical reflection is an attempt to understand both its object and itself in operation. It is thus *reflexive*, since it turns back on itself in its awareness of its own ground in the pre-reflective, making the philosopher a 'perpetual beginner' (PP xiv). Radical reflection is also *comprehensive* in its attempted grasp of the whole relation between the pre-reflective and the reflective. 'It is a question not of putting the perceptual faith in place of reflection, but on the contrary of taking into account the total situation, which involves reference from the one to the other' (IV 35). Thus one part of reflection involves comprehending experience or being-in-the-world in terms of its meaning, which makes reference to ourselves: 'In order to realize what is the meaning of mythical or schizophrenic space, we have no means other than that of resuscitating in ourselves, in our present perception, the relationship of the subject and his world' (PP 291). But this attention to ourselves and our experience must then be situated in our whole philosophic understanding of being-in-the-world, so that the relation between (my) normal space and the space of the schizophrenic or of myths can be comprehended: 'understanding myth is not believing it, and if all myths are true, it is in so far as they can be set in a phenomenology of mind which shows their function in arriving at awareness' (PP 293).

Radical reflection is mediation between the unreflective and the reflective, a mediation that runs in two directions: 'to possess ourselves we must begin by abandoning ourselves; to see the world itself, we must first withdraw from it' (S 157). That is, we must first of all abandon ourselves to the unreflective, attempt to live it, resume contact with our naïve experience. The first movement is from the reflective to the pre-reflective. But then comes a counter-movement, as we withdraw from our experience, gain a perspective on it, and attempt to render it intelligible by finding concepts fluid and agile enough to give it a meaning not too divorced from its lived significance. This second movement is a recovery by reflection of the unreflective, a recovery that must be, paradoxically, a communication with the unreflective and also a break from the unreflective, as it is conceptualized and made intelligible. It follows that unreflective experience must be potentially intelligible, as indeed it is, shot through with a primitive field-structure which makes it already meaningful. 'Experience anticipates a philosophy and philosophy is merely an elucidated experience' (PP 63).

Now Merleau-Ponty calls philosophy an attitude of wonder at the world, a programme of making the world strange in order to catch the genesis of meaning. Philosophy attempts to diagnose or look through what we take for granted, to walk around the obvious (ob-vious = that which stands in the way). But this does not culminate in the total abandonment of concepts or an attitude of speech-less incomprehension. This, indeed, is characteristic of madness, not philosophy:

> The schizophrenic and the philosopher each knocks himself
> against the paradoxes of existence. As a result each consumes
> his energy in amazement and, we may say, fails to recapture
> completely the world. But not to the same extent. The
> schizophrenic is ruled by his failure which expresses itself only
> in a few enigmatic phrases. What we call the philosopher's
> failure leaves behind him a whole furrow of expressive acts
> which enable us to rediscover our situation. (PW 103–4)

This 'furrow of expressive acts' is precisely that mode of speech known as philosophy.

As we saw in chapter 2, speech does not close us up in a semantic world, but brings us the world; it opens onto being. But this opening is not a direct sign-signified relationship, but rather an indirect, allusive contact with the world through speech. Philosophic speech would speak of being using 'the significations of words to express, beyond themselves, our mute contact with the things, when they are not yet things said' (VI 39). Speech signifies metaphorically and allusively:

> The words most charged with philosophy are not necessarily
> those that contain what they say, but rather those that most

energetically open upon Being, because they most closely
convey the life of the whole and make our habitual evidences
vibrate until they disjoin. (VI 102)

Merleau-Ponty's conceptual revision

The problems faced by any phenomenology of lived experience in
its fashioning of a philosophic mode of speech is that it must take
into account the presuppositions embedded in ordinary discourse.
For example, ordinary language (at least in the West) makes sharp
distinctions between mind and body, subject and object, reason and
emotion, real and imaginary. These are so sedimented into our
ordinary discourse and way of thinking that a philosophic attempt to
challenge such distinctions risks ending up by speaking literally non-
sense. It is not just that the terms employed, for example 'mind',
occur in so many locutions ('it's all in the mind', 'mindless vandal-
ism', 'is his mind all right?'), but they also proliferate in other usages
metaphorically linked to their more primitive meaning ('never mind
about losing your job', 'do you mind if... ?', 'will you mind my
child while I'm away?'). Furthermore, in attempting to challenge
these distinctions, the philosopher has to talk about them, and hence
accord them a certain existence. So the philosopher needs to furnish
his own concepts, and we see Merleau-Ponty's phenomenology
based on a fund of operative concepts – intentionality, embodiment,
being-in-the-world, etc. – in an attempt to transcend some of the
dichotomies of the natural attitude.

The philosophic return to lived experience means an attempt to
suspend some of our scientific prejudices and even some of our everyday beliefs. To this end, another look at the words and concepts we
ordinarily and unthinkingly use is in order. 'We believed we knew
what feeling, seeing and hearing were, and now these words raise
problems. We are invited to go back to the experiences to which
they refer in order to redefine them' (PP 10). For example lay and
medical speech considers the senses, and in particular the concepts of
sight and hearing, as univocal and separate, because our body has
sets of visual and auditory apparatus which are anatomically distinct.
But attention to our lived experience uncovers the phenomenon of
synaesthesia, the primitive unity of the senses, where they are not
distinct but interpenetrate (PP 114–15). The concepts we employ must
be grounded in our naïve experience.

Phenomenology involves not only a transcendence of some of the
presuppositions of ordinary thinking, but also some of the concepts
bequeathed to philosophy by empiricism and rationalism, and by all
modes of positivist or objective thought in general. Merleau-Ponty
spells out what this means:

Objective thought, as applied to the universe and not to phenomena, knows only alternative notions; starting from actual experience, it defines pure concepts which are mutually exclusive: the notion of *extension*, which is that of an absolute externality of one part to another, and the notion of *thought* which is that of a being wrapped up in himself; the notion of the vocal *sign* as a physical phenomenon arbitrarily linked to certain thoughts, and that of *meaning* as a thought entirely clear to itself; the notion of *cause* as a determining factor external to its effect, and that of *reason* as a law of intrinsic constitution of the phenomenon. Now, as we have seen, the perception of the body and the perception of external things provide an example of *non-positing* consciousness, that is, of consciousness not in possession of fully determinate objects, that of a *logic lived through* which cannot account for itself, and that of an *immanent meaning* which is not clear to itself and becomes fully aware of itself only through experiencing certain natural signs. (PP 49)

Instead of this dichotomy between wholly external relations (cause/effect) or wholly internal relations (thought and reason), phenomenology seeks interrelations in terms of other concepts: for example, *Fundierung*, showing how phenomena are grounded on more primitive phenomena, or *motivation*, where phenomena are mutually implicated by being expressions of the same intention or meaning. Merleau-Ponty's philosophic programme can indeed be characterized as a demonstration of the interrelation between concepts that are normally opposed, so that an implicit revision in their sense is made. We have come across many examples of this. Consider just two further illustrations:

Nature/culture:
It is impossible to superimpose on man a lower layer of behaviour which one chooses to call 'natural', followed by a manufactured cultural or spiritual world. Everything is both manufactured and natural in man, as it were, in the sense that there is not a word, not a form of behaviour which does not owe something to purely biological being – and which at the same time does not elude the simplicity of animal life, through a sort of *leakage* and through a genius for ambiguity which might serve to define man. (PP 189)

Contingency/necessity:
Everything in man is a necessity. For example, it is no mere coincidence that the rational being is also the one who holds himself upright or has a thumb which can be brought opposite

to the fingers; the same manner of existence is evident in both aspects. On the other hand everything in man is contingency in the sense that this human manner of existence is not guaranteed to every human child through some essence acquired at birth, and in the sense that it must be constantly reforged in him through the hazards encountered by the objective body. . . . Human existence will force us to revise our usual notions of necessity and contingency, because it is the transformation of contingency into necessity by the act of carrying forward. (PP 170)

This transcendence of apparently antagonistic or opposed concepts by showing their intermixing or even their fusion finds its most dramatic expression in Merleau-Ponty's occasional pairing of what are normally contradictory terms. For example, in trying to overcome the dichotomy of defining time as either the product of a constituting and hence eternal consciousness, or as something already constituted and into which consciousness is totally immersed, Merleau-Ponty refers to the relation between consciousness and time as a *passive synthesis* (PP 427). Or again, in avoiding the dualism of freedom or determinism, he calls freedom a *creative repetition* (SNS 25). Such paradoxical usages are the philosopher's method of bringing the reader to question the meaning of the juxtaposed concepts in terms of their suitability for conceptualizing our lived experience of the world.

Another strategy of Merleau-Ponty's phenomenology is to re-define familiar terms so that they are re-rooted in lived experience. For example, on the analogy of Freud's expansion of the term sexuality to include the sexual experiences of children and non-genital eroticism (a usage Merleau-Ponty himself follows), or Marx's expansion of the term 'economics' to designate productive forces and modes of production in general, Merleau-Ponty expands the sense of such terms as:

action or behaviour to designate the whole mode of interaction between organism and environment. Hence there is no simple distinction between means and ends, but rather 'an analysis of the immanent meaning of action and its intentional structure' (SB 173–4).

perception, which is defined as 'the act which makes us know existents' (SB 224), and so includes our relation to objects, people, my own and other people's behaviour.

understanding:
We said . . . that it is the body which 'understands' in the cultivation of habit. This way of putting it will appear absurd, if understanding is subsuming a sense-datum under an idea, and if the body is an object. But the phenomenon of habit is just

what prompts us to revise our notion of 'understand' and our notion of the body. To understand is to experience the harmony between what we aim at and what is given, between the intention and the performance. (PP 144)

experience is not the recording of sense-data or impressions, but is 'the communication of a finite subject with an opaque being from which it emerges but to which it remains committed' (PP 219), or, more simply, 'the opening on to our *de facto* world' (PP 221).

Where there is no actual conceptual revision, explicit or implicit, Merleau-Ponty makes frequent and sometimes dramatic use of metaphor or simile to convey his meaning:

To return to things themselves is to return to that world which precedes knowledge, of which knowledge always *speaks*, and in relation to which every scientific schematization is an abstract and derivative sign-language, as is geography in relation to the country side in which we have learnt beforehand what a forest, a prairie or a river is. (PP ix)

From the part of the body which it especially occupies, sexuality spreads forth like an odour or like a sound. (PP 168)

The Bergsonian dualism of habit-memory and pure recollection does not account for the near-presence of the words I know, they are behind me, like things behind my back, or like the city's horizon round my house. (PP 180)

On passing from double to normal vision. . . . Monocular images float vaguely *in front of* things, having no real place in the world; then suddenly they fall back towards a certain location in the world and are swallowed up in it, as ghosts, at daybreak, repair to the rift in the earth which let them forth. (PP 233)

When a child cannot speak, or cannot yet speak the adult's language, the linguistic ritual which unfolds around him has no hold on him, he is near us in the same way as is a spectator with a poor seat at the theatre; he sees clearly enough that we are laughing and gesticulating, he hears the nasal tune being played, but there is nothing at the end of those gestures or behind those words, nothing *happens* for him. (PP 401)

In place of the language of the novelist who shows or makes transparent what is true without touching it, criticism substitutes another language which claims to possess its object. But critical language is like one of those descriptions of a face in a passport which do not allow us to imagine the face. (PW 91)

This use of metaphor and illustration which permeates Merleau-Ponty's philosophy is not a stylistic quirk, nor a substitute for a more abstract or formal analysis. Metaphor is not a poor relative of formal argument, but the basic way in which language develops and words take on new meanings (see p. 74). Merleau-Ponty's aim is to use metaphor and example so that the reader can relate what is offered to him to what is familiar or known to him, or what his own experience makes accessible, so that he can gradually 'feel his way in' to Merleau-Ponty's philosophic style. Examples and illustrations allow us to 'hook onto' our own experience, and so rediscover for ourselves what he is saying. Merleau-Ponty's operative and allusive concepts are not there for us to acknowledge intellectually or formally, but to 'find' us and, if successful, to set off echoes which vibrate throughout our experience.[2]

Philosophy as re-presentation

Merleau-Ponty writes:

> Our relationship to the world, as it is untiringly enunciated within us, is not a thing which can be any further clarified by analysis; philosophy can only place it once more before our eyes and present it for our ratification. (PP xviii)

We have seen that, in arguing that philosophy cannot further clarify by analysis our relationship to the world, Merleau-Ponty does not mean to abandon reflection or conceptualization. He only wants to argue against those modes of reflection and conceptualization that believe that the ambiguity, paradox and obscurity that defines being-in-the-world is something that needs to be put right or overcome. Philosophy must not impart a false clarity that satisfies some criteria of intellectual adequacy, but in so doing papers over the cracks of lived experience. Philosophy is rather to be conceived as a kind of presentation, or *re-presentation*, since it only re-presents to us what we have known all along, yet have somehow lost contact with:

> Nothing is more difficult than to know precisely *what we see*. There is in natural intuition . . . a dialect whereby perception hides itself from itself. But although it is of the essence of consciousness to forget its own phenomena, thus enabling 'things' to be constituted, this forgetfulness is not mere absence. It is the absence of something which consciousness could bring into its presence. (PP 58)

Philosophy as re-presentation is to be compared much less to academic or formal philosophy, or the enterprise of natural science, which aim at constructing ideal languages whose prime concern is the adequacy of their mode of discourse rather than faithfulness to the phenomena under study – rather it is the practice of art that philosophy

153

can be compared to. Art, like philosophy, is geared to the re-presentation or disclosure of what is covered over (Heidegger) in everyday living. To this end art evolves a certain mode of speech: 'The essence of poetry is not the didactic description of things or the exposition of ideas but the creation of a machine of language which almost without fail puts the reader in a certain poetic state' (SNS 57). This poetic state is, if you like, a state of being in the machine of language that is poetry. Neither art nor philosophy aim to directly evoke feelings or emotions – drugs are more effective for that – but they intend to disclose the world to us through the development of their own mode of discourse. In so doing, poetry will put us in a poetic state, and philosophy in a philosophic state.

> What is irreplaceable in the work of art – what makes it not just a pleasant occasion but a voice of the spirit whose analogue is found in all productive philosophical or political thought – is that it contains, better than ideas, *matrices of ideas*. A work of art provides us with symbols whose meaning we shall never finish developing. (PW 90)

All the techniques associated with art – style, metaphor, drama in the novel, colour and symmetry in painting, tone and rhythm in music, etc. – are part of the artistic machine of language. Even the most abstract of the arts, music, is to be understood as the creation of a certain kind of language whose function, before being to evoke feelings, is to symbolize (Langer, 1948, pp. 162–89). Music is not a series of stimuli or signals that trigger off feelings in us, but is a form of expression that *symbolizes* emotions, in the way our body symbolizes our existence in the world. Music is the formulation and representation of emotions, feelings and ideas. It presents them, not discursively in concepts, but non-discursively, in a form of expression more primitive than speech. This form of expression, although non-discursive, is still communicative and can present us not just with raw feelings but also with insight and understanding in a way that discursive language cannot duplicate. Hence, when Merleau-Ponty writes that 'philosophical expression assumes the same ambiguities as literary expression, if the world is such that it cannot be expressed except in "stories" and, as it were, pointed at' (SNS 28), it is important to remember that this 'pointing at' is not a dumb gesture, but is part of a machine of language rich enough in symbols and allusions to present to us what by its very nature cannot be expressed in full clarity.

Like art, philosophy is defined by its *style*, by its mode of presentation. Its machine of language, its philosophic state, is gained by a certain kind of reflection. This reflection is like perception in that it depends on attaining the right distance so that the object can

PHILOSOPHY

be viewed without distorting it by being too near or too far away. The philosopher is somewhat like a man who, if he adopts a certain position and a certain mode of focusing, is able to make out a woman's face out of the patterns on the wallpaper, but if he shifts his gaze, or focuses in a different way, he will see the face vanish back into the shapes on the wall. The phenomena of the world

> offer themselves [therefore] only to someone who wishes not to have them, but to see them, not to hold them with forceps, or to immobilize them as under the objective of a microscope, but to let them be and to witness their continued being – to someone who therefore limits himself to giving them the hollow, the free space they ask for in return. . . . (VI 101)

Philosophy, however, can never get its subject-matter into full view. 'We never get away from our life. We never see our ideas or our freedom face to face' (SNS 25).

Both the artist and the philosopher are engaged in the same process of being present at the birth of expression: 'the joy of art lies in its showing how something takes on meaning . . . by the temporal or spatial arrangement of elements' (SNS 58). And likewise philosophy, which is 'like art, the act of bringing truth into being' (PP xx). This philosophic or artistic truth is not defined as a copy of the external world, as in a photograph. Truth is something else, as modern art has recognized. Thus modern painters, according to Merleau-Ponty:

> want nothing to do with a truth defined as the resemblance of painting and the world. They would accept the idea of a truth defined as a painting's cohesion with itself, as the presence of a unique principle in it which affects each means of expression with a certain contextual value. . . . The moderns know very well that there is no spectacle in the world – far less a painting – which absolutely imposes itself upon perception, whereas the imperious stroke of the brush can do more to make our look possess the wool or the flesh than the most patient reconstruction of appearances. But the moderns have not put chaos in the place of the mind's inspection of the very texture of things – they have introduced the allusive logic of the world. (PW 65)

A note on truth and adequacy

We should now be able to construct an answer to those all too frequent objections made about phenomenology, that there are no independent ways of checking or testing the truth or falsity of its

155

statements. This objection is, of course, based on a positivist form of life, where truth is identified with empirical verification, so that what cannot be empirically verified cannot be true or valid. The point is, however, that what counts as verification or confirmation depends on the situation, on our projects at hand, or, in Wittgenstein's terms, on the language-game being played. The answer to the question 'Is it true that you have £2 in your pocket?' can be easily checked, and truth can be defined here as agreement with reality. But how does one verify the answer to the question 'Is it true that you need an increase in salary?', since there are no objective or empirical criteria for deciding if someone is in need (for example, are you in need if you cannot afford to run a car? Cf. Wittgenstein, 1968, paragraph 134). Similarly the procedures for verifying the assertion 'my wife likes chocolate cakes' – namely asking her or watching her eat cakes – are not available for testing the assertion 'my wife doesn't love me, although she pretends to', since asking her or watching her might only reveal her pretence at loving me.

What this amounts to is that truth is a procedural affair, and what counts as truth depends on the rules and canons of procedure we employ as relevant to the situation or language-game being played. The truth of a statement is not independent of the conditions of its utterance (cf. McHugh, 1971).

This does not mean, however, that truth is arbitrary or inescapably subjective. It means simply that truth, like rationality, is what is *grounded*. It is only in the sense of showing the grounds or auspices of an utterance or belief within our frame of reference or system of beliefs that we can claim to be verifying or testing for truth. But this truth exists only within our system.

All testing, all confirmation and disconfirmation of a hypothesis takes place already within a system. And this system is not a more or less arbitrary and doubtful point of departure for all our arguments: no, it belongs to the essence of what we call an argument. The system is not so much the point of departure, as the element in which arguments have their life.
(Wittgenstein, 1974, p. 16)

This is the significance of the phenomenological premiss that truth is situational (cf. pp. 103–5). Truth is in a profound sense existential: 'the philosopher is always implicated in the problems he poses, and there is no truth if one does not take into account, in the appraising of every statement, the presence of the philosopher who makes the statement' (VI 90). Truth, like all meaning, arises out of a dialogue between philosopher and reader.

Truth, then, cannot be absolute or eternal, since it is grounded. One important consequence of this should be noted: 'if the true is what is grounded, then the ground is not *true*, nor yet false' (Wittgenstein, 1974, p. 28). We reach a point where assessment, testing, justification can go no further, where it no longer makes any sense to doubt: 'if I have exhausted the justification I have reached bedrock, and my spade is turned' (Wittgenstein, 1968, paragraph 217). I cannot continue without calling into question my whole system of justification so that my certainties, as well as my doubts, will fall and a quest for truth will become literally senseless.

If truth is what is grounded, what is the ground of phenomenological truth? Although phenomenology seeks to interrogate the natural attitude and put assertions arising from it in brackets, it recognizes at the same time that this can, at best, be only partially achieved, since it is the 'primordial faith' or *Urglaube* of the natural attitude which gives us all our certainties of the world.

> We are in the world, which means that things take shape, an immense individual asserts itself, each existence is self-comprehensive and comprehensive of the rest. All that has to be done is to recognize these phenomena which are the ground of all our certainties. (PP 409)

From the ground of lived experience the phenomenologist builds up his philosophy and constellation of operative concepts.

The ultimate court of appeal in phenomenology is always lived experience (cf. PP 23). But there are also other tacit criteria of adequacy: for example, intelligibility, comprehensiveness, consistency and practical realization (cf. Esterson, 1972). Nevertheless these criteria are fluid, since philosophy is above all a dialogue with the reader, and what the reader is not open to, or cannot comprehend, will never be existentially true for him. Furthermore, Merleau-Ponty does not explicitly concern himself with criteria of adequacy or procedures for confirming what he writes. This is because philosophy *creates* truth by showing connections that have not been seen before, or by disclosing structures or configurations that have not been brought to expression until then. Truth and adequacy are not directly and explicitly aimed at; they arise out of the philosopher's meditation, and are, if you like, constructed as he goes along. 'We do not know in advance what our interrogation itself and our method will be. The manner of questioning prescribes a certain kind of response, and to fix it now would be to decide our solution' (VI 158).

Non-thematic knowledge

We have considered the phenomenological modes of philosophic reflection, discourse, conceptualization and style, and its version of truth. This has all been by way of showing how reflection can grasp the unreflective, and so answering the objections raised at the beginning of this chapter. There is one further step to take, and that is to elucidate the phenomenological version of knowledge, since Merleau-Ponty's critics claim that he constructs an unbridgeable gap between living and knowing.

However, since the text of philosophy is lived experience which is pre-predicative and pre-thematic, and yet which we are aware of and which can be recovered by reflection, it follows that there must be a pre-thematic knowledge with which consciousness or the body is endowed. The body 'knows', for example, where all its parts are without being able to see them in objective space. Philosophical knowledge models itself on this pre-thematic knowledge.

> Looking for the world's essence is not looking for what it is
> as an idea once it has been reduced to a theme of discourse;
> it is looking for what it is as a fact for us, before any
> thematization. (PP xv)

Now for one commentator, this whole idea of a non-thematic knowledge is absurd.

> We cannot say, then, that the body 'knows' anything, even in
> the broadest possible sense of the term. For, in the first place,
> if it were a 'knowledge', it would *not* be at the level of non-
> thematizing experience of the world, since '*knowing*' *is precisely*
> *a thematizing*, presupposing an active attending to and explicating
> of the object(s) 'known', a formulation of judgements based
> upon the active attending and the actively attended-to objects.
> And all such activities (grasping, explicating, relating) even at
> the level of sensuous perception, as Husserl has shown, are
> '*Ich-Akte*'. (Zaner, 1971, p. 207)

Before looking to the logic of this charge, we need to tease out what Merleau-Ponty might mean by a non-thematic mode of philosophic knowledge. To this end I have taken a concrete example, Merleau-Ponty's phenomenology of movement, to consider in some detail.

The central point of this example is that any explicit attempt at *thematizing* the experience of movement, which is the technique of objective thought, destroys the very experience it tries to recapture.

> When we try to think of movement, and arrive at a philosophy
> of movement, we immediately place ourselves in a critical or
> verificatory attitude, we ask ourselves what precisely is given to
> us in movement, we make ready to reject appearances in order
> to reach the truth concerning movement, and we remain
> unaware that it is precisely this attitude which reduces the

phenomenon and must prevent us from coming to grips with it, because it introduces . . . assumptions liable to conceal from me the genesis of movement for me. (PP 267–8)

What are these assumptions? First, concerning the appropriate mode of reflection, which involves thematization, and hence a cutting up of our experience in order to explain it. Second, concerning the nature of the objective world, consisting of spatio-temporally individuated objects, so that movement is defined in terms of an objective change in position in the world.

Suppose, says Merleau-Ponty, I throw a stone across the garden. If I want to think objectively or thematically about this stone in motion, I must decompose it. I will argue that the stone itself is not modified by movement, since it remains the same stone throughout its flight. Movement, I will say, is merely an accidental attribute of the moving stone, and can be defined as a change in the relation between the stone and its surroundings.

However the result of this thematization of movement is that the experience of movement is no longer comprehensible to me, since 'to distinguish strictly between movement and the moving object is to say that strictly speaking the "moving body" *does not move*' (PP 268). If the moving stone is identical throughout the phases of its motion, this implies a spatial and temporal position always identifiable in itself, and therefore a stone which always is and never changes. In short, 'in thinking clearly about movement, I do not understand how it can ever begin for me and be given to me as a phenomenon' (PP 269).

And yet I have the experience of motion, of absolute movement. When I walk I experience my body in motion without having to make reference to my surroundings or to some external landmark. Neither does the assumption of an identical object throughout movement accord with experience.

if I watch workmen unloading a lorry and throwing bricks from one to another, I see the man's arm in its initial and then in its final position, yet, although I do not see it in any intermediate position, I have a vivid perception of its movement. (PP 269)

If I quickly move a pencil across a sheet of paper on which I have marked a point, at no time am I aware of the pencil being over that point. I do not see any of its intermediate positions, and yet I am aware of movement. If, however, I slow down the movement of the pencil and do not lose sight of it, at that very moment the impression of motion disappears. In other words 'the movement disappears at the very moment when it conforms most closely with the definition which objective thought gives it' (PP 270). In naïve experience, on the other

159

hand, we have the phenomenon of 'shift' as part of our visual field. Movement is not an external relation between an identical object and its environment, and we can have movement without any fixed mark, as our experience tells us, and as is confirmed by experimental evidence:

> if we project the consecutive image of a movement on to a homogeneous field containing no object and having no outline, the movement takes possession of the whole space, and what is shifting is the whole visual field. .... If we project on to the screen the post-image of a spiral revolving round its centre, in the absence of any fixed framework, space itself vibrates and dilates from the centre to the periphery. (PP 270)

Objective, thematic thought leaves us in the same position as Zeno's paradoxes, in which thinking about movement in terms of relations between fixed points actually destroys the experience of movement. Phenomenology seeks to put us in contact with a level more primitive than that amenable to thematic conceptualization, so that

> we shall have to rediscover, beneath the objective idea of movement, a pre-objective experience from which it borrows its significance, and in which movement, still linked to the person perceiving it, is a variation of the subject's hold on his world. (PP 267)

Phenomenology directs us back to lived experience before it has been thematized, in this case to a movement anterior to the objective world of fixed points which occurs in the *phenomenal* world in which the perceiver is situated, and which is patterned by our perception.

> We do not say that it is irrational or anti-logical. . . . We need to say merely that the phenomenal layer is literally pre-logical and will always remain so. Our image of the world can be made up only in part of actual being, and we must find a place in it for the phenomenal realm which surrounds being on all sides. We are not asking the logician to take into consideration experiences which, in the light of reason, are nonsensical or contradictory, *we merely want to push back the boundaries of what makes sense for us, and re-set the narrow zone of thematic significance within that of non-thematic significance which embraces it*. The thematization of movement ends up with the identical object in motion and with the relativity of movement, which means that it destroys movement. If we want to take the phenomenon of movement seriously, we shall need to conceive a world which is not made up only of things, but which has in it also pure transitions. (PP 275, italics added)

Thus, for example, in naïve experience things in motion are defined by their manner of 'passing'. A bird flying across my garden is, while it is flying, grasped in terms of its motion, as a greyish power of flight, rather than in terms of its stable properties. My perception of this bird in flight, just like my perception of the garden as at rest, is an expression of my body's hold on the world. The phenomenal world, the world of pre-thematic perception, is not a series of objective points and individuated objects, but a world primitively patterned into a figure/ground structure, and into objects perceived as 'at rest' and 'in motion'. This figure/ground, rest/motion distinction is assigned by my vision in terms of the overall articulation of my visual field (see p. 38).

We are now in a better position to attempt to pick out what Merleau-Ponty means by thematic or non-thematic knowledge. From the example of movement, we can say that thematization, as practised by objective thought, means something like: isolating the phenomenon under study from its experiential roots; attempting to fix it in clear and determinate concepts; decomposing the phenomenon in order to make it amenable to this conceptualization. In short, thematization means isolating the phenomenon from its ground in pre-objective experience. But since phenomenology seeks precisely to re-connect the phenomenon with pre-reflective experience it must, as Merleau-Ponty says, push back thematic significance and knowledge towards its foundation in non-thematic significance. This non-thematic significance is evident in many kinds of experience that resist thematic conceptualization. For example:

for the lover whose experience it is, love is nameless; it is not a thing capable of being circumscribed and designated, nor is it the love spoken of in books and newpapers, because it is the way in which he establishes his relations with the world; it is an existential significance. (PP 381)

The same is true of sexuality and dreams:

The 'latent content' and the 'sexual significance' of the dream are undoubtedly present to the dreamer since it is he who dreams his dream. But, precisely because sexuality is the general atmosphere of the dream, these elements are not thematized as sexual, for want of any non-sexual background against which they may stand out. (PP 381)

Now this last phrase is important. We only achieve thematization if it is able to emerge from its ground in the non-thematic. It will appear, then, that for Zaner to identify knowledge with thematization is as one-sided as designating perception as thematization, for both perception and knowledge incorporate the thematic, the pre-thematic and their interrelation. Whether knowledge will be thematic or not depends on the kind of knowledge required, on the context of its use. For example, in terms of Ryle's (1949) distinction, for certain purposes we might need to know *that* such and such is the case, whereas in other situations it will be knowing *how* to ride a bicycle that is required. 'Knowing that' is thematic, 'knowing how' is not. Furthermore there are modes of interpersonal knowledge which are not reducible to express formalization or conceptualization (for example, 'you're the only person who really knows me'). In conclusion, then, whereas thematic or objective knowledge is certainly to be opposed to lived experience, and is incapable of bringing us the unreflective, this is not the case with non-thematic knowledge, which is that of our experience of the body and is what phenomenology seeks to elucidate.

The paradox of philosophy

I referred, at the beginning of this chapter, to the essential paradox of philosophy in that it seeks, by reflection, to apprehend the pre-reflective. This paradox should now be intelligible. We have seen that philosophic reflection is of a certain kind, and that the un-reflective it aims to recover has undergone a change in structure, without however having been emasculated. Nevertheless, while the paradox is now intelligible, it is not completely overcome, and, indeed it serves to remind us of the nature of the philosophic enterprise.

Let us recall how Merleau-Ponty defined radical reflection (see p. 147): 'It is a question not of putting the perceptual faith in place of reflection, but on the contrary of taking into account the total situation, which involves reference from the one to the other' (VI 35). The paradox remains: how *in reflection* can I apprehend the *total situation* of reflection and the pre-reflective (perceptual faith)? How *in reflection* can I refer from reflection to the pre-reflective and encompass their interrelation? The problem is similar to one Wittgenstein was aware of:

> the aim of this book is to draw a limit to thought, or rather – not to thought, but to the expression of thoughts: for in order to be able to draw a limit to thought, we should have to find both sides of the limit thinkable (i.e. we should have to be able to think what cannot be thought). (1961, p. 3)

Merleau-Ponty is also interested in drawing a limit to thought (reflection), although he pushes the limit farther towards its non-reflective ground than more formal philosophers. Nevertheless, however far the limit can be pushed, it is still a limit. We never reach the unreflective as it is actually lived, but the unreflective as expressed, as conquered by reflection. It is in this sense only that the lived and the known, or being and thought, can be seen as opposed. It is true that this would be an admission of defeat for the positivist, who wants language to capture or mirror being. The phenomenologist, on the other hand, acknowledges that there are levels of being not directly amenable to philosophic expression, however well attuned to the vibrations of experience the philosopher might be, and he is content to look to evidence from other sources in order to gain more understanding of his life in particular and of being-in-the-world in general. The fact that his philosophy is built on shifting sands is no reason for him to pack up his tent and go home. It is rather an occasion for striking deeper roots.

7 Conclusion

In my Introduction, I proposed Merleau-Ponty's existential phenomenology as a way of integrating philosophy and social science by providing a unified perspective on human existence and on the general structures of being-in-the-world. Existential phenomenology can, in fact, be characterized as both a philosophical anthropology, concerned with understanding man and his concrete existence, and as an ontological inquiry, in investigating the sense or meaning of being, or being-in-the-world.[1] I have shown how an existential phenomenological perspective can be applied to varieties of lived experience, and to areas usually dealt with by particular social sciences or specialized branches of philosophy. I have also shown how phenomenology is compatible with those insights generated by Marxism, and I could have done the same with psycho-analysis. However, I have not yet made explicit the overall framework within which to view Merleau-Ponty's phenomenology, and in particular its claim to integrate philosophy and social science. This I now turn my attention to, and in so doing I can also compare Merleau-Ponty's phenomenology to other versions of the relation between philosophy and social science, or of the nature of our knowledge of the world in general.

The transcendental and the descriptive

In their book *On the Beginning of Social Inquiry* (1974), the authors, Blum, Foss, McHugh and Raffel, make what they consider to be a crucial distinction between two types of inquiry. The first of these they term *analytic inquiry*, which is concerned not with things, but with the *grounds* or *auspices* that make those things intelligible.

> Analysis . . . is not finding something in the world, or making sense of some puzzling datum, or answering an interesting

question, or locating a phenomenon worthy of study, or resolving a long-standing disagreement or any other essentially empirical procedure. To analyze is, indeed, to address the possibility of *any* finding, puzzle, sense, resolution, answer, interest, location, phenomenon, etcetera, etcetera. Analysis is the concern not with anything said or written but with the grounds of whatever is said – the foundations that make what is said possible, sensible, conceivable. . . . Our interest [is] in what we call the grounds or auspices of phenomena rather than in the phenomena themselves. (pp. 2–3)

The second type of inquiry they call *concrete inquiry*, which means looking at phenomena themselves, where inquiry is conceived as a reproduction or reporting of what appears, a direct application of thought or language to things (as in positivism). Concrete inquiry is simple description or empirical inquiry.

The authors regard concrete inquiry as a 'degenerate' form of inquiry because, in attempting to just describe or report what he sees, the inquirer merely replicates what members in a society do themselves. Concrete inquiry is also inherently non-reflexive in that the inquirer is debarred from understanding his own inquiry and the grounds on which it rests, since he is limited to describing things in the world. On the other hand analysis, which the authors identify with authentic theorizing, is essentially a reflexive mode of inquiry. 'For the analyst any speech, including his own, is of interest not in terms of what it says, but in terms of how what it says is possible, sensible, rational in the first place' (p. 2). In short, analysis, or theorizing, becomes an explication of what Wittgenstein called the 'form of life' of the phenomenon under study, and of the theorist himself.

Since analysis for Blum *et al.* is concerned not with phenomena as such but with the grounds of phenomena, it follows that anything can be taken as a subject for analysis, and hence used as an opportunity for theorizing. The examples the authors in fact choose – motives, bias, evaluation, snubs, travel and art – have the status only of examples, that is, of exemplifications of their method. We can illustrate this briefly looking at some of these examples.

An analysis of the phenomenon of bias does not consist in identifying instances of bias, nor in proposing remedies for eliminating it – rather it seeks to find the form of life which makes intelligible both a charge of bias and the urge to eliminate it. This form of life the authors identify as positivism, which rests on a conception of adequate speech. For positivism adequate speech is conceived as a copy of nature, so that it must be purged of any trace of subjectivity or commitment on the part of the theorist. It is in terms of this form

165

of life that bias, the re-emergence of the theorist in his theorizing, is seen as a trouble.

In the case of snubs, analysis is not concerned with viewing snubs as behaviour that goes on between real people, nor with picking out certain features of snubs, nor even with investigating how snubs are 'done' or recognized. These are concrete concerns; analysis considers instead how snubs are possible. The form of life that supports snubs is the common-sense everyday world. But analysis does not stop here.

> As we use it, the notion of everyday life has the analytic status of an example. Rather than refer to everyday life as the 'rockbottom' certainty to which our descriptions purport to correspond, such a notion of everyday life is itself a construction. We use it as the point of reference for the conventions of speech and usage with which we begin our analysis. . . . Yet, our use of everyday life is distinguished . . . through our conception of this beginning as itself a result or achievement. Thus, everyday life as the example typifies the concerted tendency of analysis to begin with some 'matter' securely in hand. Our analysis then seeks to dissolve what is in hand by treating the security of the example as covering over and concealing its history. (p. 11)

Hence the everyday world is further analysed in terms of a three-fold dialectic between self/other, togetherness/separateness, and unity/ difference, which actual relations between people embody. Thus a snub is analysed as the recognition of *alter*, but a denial of togetherness and the assertion of difference. It is these dialectics (further explicated in chapter 5 of Blum's work) that make intelligible the phenomenon of snubs and its counterpart, greetings, and why they are intrinsic features of the common-sense world.

Finally we can take the case of motives, which are analysed, not as things in the world, i.e. as states belonging to persons, nor as reports of such states, but as observer's methods for generating the idea of a member or of action in the common-sense world. Thus statements like 'he killed his wife because he was jealous' or 'he left the party because he was bored' are observer's methods of interpreting certain events as methodic actions (cf. p. 83 of this book), so that a biography for the actor is constituted. But, as in the case of snubs, analysis can go one stage further back: the question can still be asked, what form of life is presupposed by the very existence of motives in the common-sense world? Blum *et al.* indicate that such a form of life is what they term a causal world, where events are treated as enigmatic, needing to be explained by reference to things outside themselves (unfortunately they do not clarify this idea: see Blum *et al.*, 1974, pp. 44–5).

166

These examples should indicate the essential differences between analysis (or theorizing) and concrete inquiry. Two implications of this distinction should be borne in mind. (1) Analysis, unlike concrete inquiry, fails to treat the phenomena it studies seriously. Phenomena are not looked at in their own right, for their own intrinsic value. They are not treated as real things, but purely as an impetus for theorizing: 'the point of inquiring about anything – about bias, art, or travel – is not to describe bias, art, or travel, but to make reference to our own commitment to inquiry' (p. 12). Snubs, motives, bias, etc., are treated as essentially trivial – it is the form of life that they exemplify, and the theorist's commitment that they allow to be displayed, which are analytically interesting. (2) The second feature, one we have already mentioned, is the *reflexivity* of analysis, in that the analysis of any phenomenon is an occasion for the theorist to display his own form of life, the deep grounds that make his own analysis intelligible. This, indeed, is what theorizing (analysis) is all about. 'Through theorizing the theorist searches for his self, and his achievement in theorizing is a recovering of his self' (Blum, 1971, p. 304).

Now this distinction between analysis and concrete inquiry corresponds, in spirit if not altogether in substance, to a distinction which in phenomenological terms would be between the *transcendental* and the *descriptive*. The notion of analysis fits well with the phenomenological conception of transcendental inquiry (Blum in fact acknowledges a debt to Heidegger). We should note in particular how Blum's version of analysis transcends the concrete descriptions which stop at the common-sense world, and attempts to view this everyday world from a transcendental perspective, that is, in terms of its genesis or form of life. Now this does not entail for Blum *et al.* a study of consciousness, but their concerns are by no means incompatible with such a study. Nevertheless there is one crucial difference between phenomenology and the work of Blum *et al.* Whereas concrete inquiry for Blum is totally divorced from analysis, and is conceived on the positivist model as an attempt to reproduce the world, phenomenological description is always informed by the transcendental impulse of phenomenology. For Blum, as we have seen, analysis is the only valid concern of the theorist, whereas the concrete is considered degenerate. For Merleau-Ponty's phenomenology, on the other hand, there is a constant *dialectic* to be maintained between the transcendental and the descriptive.

Phenomenology as a dialectic between the transcendental and the descriptive

This dialectic between the transcendental and descriptive in Merleau-

Ponty's phenomenology can be elucidated as follows. He writes, for example, about the objects of philosophic reflection:

> In order to indicate both the intimacy of objects to the subject and the presence in them of solid structures which distinguish them from mere appearances, they will be called 'phenomena'; and philosophy, to the extent that it adheres to this theme, becomes a phenomenology, that is, an inventory of consciousness as milieu of the universe. (SB 199)

Phenomenology is thus transcendental, in that phenomena cannot be understood apart from the notion of a subject or of consciousness as milieu of the universe. Hence Merleau-Ponty speaks of the intimacy of objects to the subject in terms of the intentionality of consciousness. But phenomenology is also descriptive, in that solid structures in phenomena are acknowledged, turning phenomenology into an inventory or description of these phenomena. Now, to be sure, phenomenological description is not positivist description, in the sense of recording objects in the world without making reference to the perceiving or recording subject. Since there are not objects in the world independent of consciousness, the task of phenomenology is to describe them in terms of their intimacy to the subject, in terms of their intentional structure. Phenomenological description is not a copy of the world, but a hermeneutics. This means that

> if knowledge, instead of being the presentation to the subject of an inert tableau, is the apprehension of the meaning of this tableau, the distinction between the objective world and subjective appearances is no longer that of two sorts of beings, but of two significations. (SB 199)

It follows that 'the descriptive method can acquire a genuine claim only from the transcendental point of view' (PP 7, n. 1). Nevertheless, in so far as this description is dealing with real phenomena, with solid structures which are not created by consciousness, phenomenology can be characterized as descriptive as well as transcendental.

Consider another quotation about phenomenology:

> It is a transcendental philosophy, which places in abeyance the assertions arising out of the natural attitude, the better to understand them; but it is also a philosophy for which the world is always 'already-there', before reflection begins . . . and all its efforts are concentrated upon re-achieving a direct and primitive contact with the world, and endowing that contact with a philosophic status. (PP vii)

168

The phenomenological reduction – placing in abeyance the assertions arising out of the natural attitude – represents the transcendental impulse of phenomenology, while the 'direct and primitive contact
with the world' is its descriptive impulse. The aim of phenomenology
is always to tie these two concerns together.

Phenomena are never treated as 'trivial' in Blum's sense, as just
providing an occasion to theorize, for phenomenology wants to
describe the structure of the real, experienced world. Hence Merleau-
Ponty's overriding concern with perception, that mode of experience
that puts us directly in contact with the world. Indeed he speaks of
his philosophy as a 'phenomenological positivism, which bases the
possible on the real' (PP xvii), a formulation which is the reverse of
Blum's definition of analysis. At the same time all the concerns of
phenomenological description are viewed through the perspective
of a transcendental inquiry. Phenomena such as self-deception (for
example, exemplified in the phantom limb), or forms of interpersonal
relations, or socio-historical phenomena, are understood in terms of
the kind of being-in-the-world they exemplify, or the existential
meaning or project in terms of which they are intelligible. To put it
another way: the *ontic* concerns of phenomenology, their descriptions of different aspects of concrete existence and in particular their
stress on such features as freedom and choice, do not end up in
psychologism or sociologism, but have an essential *ontological*
dimension in referring to the fundamental structures of consciousness in the world. In the same way, we may say that Sartre's novel
Nausea is not simply the story of a rather neurotic or morbid figure
– which would make it a work of little consequence – but a way of
disclosing certain basic features of being-in-the-world, notably
those connected with experiences of contingency and anguish, and
the quality of human freedom.[2]

The transcendental/descriptive dialectic defines not only the
phenomenological method, but also the ontological structure of the
world, as revealed by phenomenology. Human existence is comprehensible in terms of what Merleau-Ponty terms the *problem or
paradox of transcendence*:

> Whether we are concerned with my body, the natural world,
> the past, birth or death, the question is always *how can I be
> open to phenomena that transcend me, and which nevertheless
> exist only to the extent that I take them up and live them.* (PP 363,
> italics added)

We have seen, in our studies of perception, space and time, for
example, that the world transcends me, it has a solidity with which I
must learn to come to terms – and yet, at the same time, it is consciousness, as intentional, that institutes temporality and spatiality,

that allows for the articulation of figures and grounds, fields and horizons, which enable the objects of our experience to exist as they do. More specifically, we have seen how the paradox of transcendence defines a phenomenological approach to speech and society. Speech is an entity which exists apart from and external to any individual, and yet is activated only by being spoken. Speech has rules and a grammar to which any individual must adapt, and which pre-date his existence, and yet speech becomes the principal means of an individual's self-expression and objectification in the world. Speech as an institution transcends the individual, yet it has no existence apart from the living words uttered in daily conversation.

In the same way society transcends me, in the sense that human praxis and social relationships create, over time, the conventions, laws and institutions which make up the facticity of society, turning society into a thing massively confronting any individual. And yet this facticity of the social depends for its existence on the willingness or collusion of individuals to see it as a facticity, since society can exist only in and through the praxis of individuals working in concert. Hence we can see why freedom is a necessary structure of being-in-the-world, since it is men who have instituted the social world in which we live, and so it is men who have the potentiality of changing or unmaking what has been created.

If this dialectic between the transcendental and the descriptive is accepted as a valid characterization of Merleau-Ponty's existential phenomenology, it can also allow us to consider other allied schools of philosophy or social science in terms of how they imply (or specify) the relationship between the transcendental and descriptive.

Blum: the failure of the descriptive

We have already indicated how Blum's work differs from Merleau-Ponty's. Whereas for Merleau-Ponty the relationship between the transcendental and descriptive is dialectical, for Blum (and his co-authors) the descriptive impulse is swamped under the weight of the transcendental. Phenomena are treated solely as examples, as occasions to theorize and for the theorist to display his own form of life; phenomena are *essentially trivial* (Blum et al., 1974, p. 121). However in equating theorizing with a display of self, there seems to be a danger that the theorist will lose contact with the world outside of his own mind, and will turn theorizing into a kind of intellectual masturbation. In Merleau-Ponty's words: 'the real has to be described, not constructed or formed' (PP x). Furthermore, it is not clear in what sense theorizing is to be taken as a return to the self. Theorizing displays the self in the sense that it is essentially an elucidation of one's own experience. Nevertheless a transcendental perspective, or the phenomenological reduction does not issue in a return to a self isolated from the world or from other people. 'I discover by reflection not only my presence to myself, but also the possibility of an "outside spectator"' (PP xii) and hence my incarnation in a situation.

Schutz and the ethnomethodologists: the failure of the transcendental

Alfred Schutz sought to apply phenomenology to the social sciences, in order to give a philosophical underpinning to its basic concepts which, according to Schutz, had already been put forward by Max Weber. In *The Phenomenology of the Social World* (1967a) he begins by giving what he terms a phenomenological analysis of meaning and action, since he believed that only after a phenomenological study of the fundamental facts of consciousness as revealed in meaning and action could a basis be found for a clarification of the concepts of social science. He argues that the way consciousness endows its stream of experience with meaning is a result of its own 'inner time' process. The act of meaning endowment is a reflective act which consciousness directs towards already elapsed experience, so that meaning is 'a certain way of directing one's gaze at an item of one's own experience' (Schutz, 1967a, p. 42). Meaning is the result of an activity whereby consciousness reverses the process of physical time in order to look back over its own experience. Now whereas meaning involves reference to the past (already elapsed experience), action involves reference to the future as well as the past. Action is possible because consciousness projects the goal or end of the action in the future, so that it is the completed act which is projected in phantasy by consciousness which gives the meaning to the action as a whole.

Having investigated phenomenologically the concepts of meaning and action in terms of the inner-time structure of consciousness, Schutz then abandons this phenomenological perspective and turns to a description of the structure of the social world. 'We shall start out' he says,

> by simply accepting the existence of the social world as it is always accepted in the attitude of the natural standpoint, whether in everyday life or in sociological observation. In so doing, we shall avoid any attempt to deal with the problem from the point of view of transcendental phenomenology. (Schutz, 1967a, p. 97)

He then offers a descriptive account of the nature of intersubjective understanding, and of the structure of social relationships, his basic point being that there is a fundamental distinction to be made

171

between face-to-face relationships, where actors share a community of time and space, and non face-to-face relationships, where actors are separated by time and/or space. Indirect social relationships (non face-to-face ones) cannot rely on the normal process of intersubjective understanding through speech, gesture, observed behaviour, etc., since these are not available. Instead, actors understand each other through *ideal types*. I apprehend my contemporaries (people living in the same society but whom I do not know) in terms of schemes of typifications which impersonalize and anonymize them in terms of their functions or roles. Thus I do not need to know personally the man who connects my telephone calls or the man who delivers my mail, I only know them as types. It is this investigation of types and typical knowledge that Schutz sees as crucial for understanding the structure of the social world.

The last part of *The Phenomenology of the Social World*, and many of his later writings (see Schutz, 1967b, 1964 and 1966), concern the nature of our social scientific knowledge of the social world. Since, according to Schutz, our common-sense knowledge of the social world is, to a large extent, made up of types or constructs, our scientific knowledge will also consist of such types or constructs, but at a higher level of abstraction and formalization. The types or constructs of common-sense knowledge are only relevant for the concrete purpose at hand. According to Schutz, we have a number of 'recipes' (1970b, pp. 98–9), unquestioned habits and platitudes, which structure our knowledge to a degree sufficient for the regular and orderly living in the everyday world. But this degree of abstraction is insufficient for the social scientist, who replaces the practical concerns of the common-sense actor by his own scientific attitude of disinterestedness and the demand for a formalized mode of knowledge of the social world.

> As scientific observers of the social world, we are not practically but only cognitively interested in it. That means we are not acting in it with full responsibility for the consequences, but rather contemplating it with the same detached equanimity as physicists contemplate their experiments. (Schutz, 1970b, p. 94)

And so

> the social sciences replace the thought objects of common-sense thought relative to unique events and occurrences by *constructing a model of a sector of the social world* within which merely those typified events occur that are relevant to the scientist's particular problem under scrutiny. (1967b, p. 36, italics added)

That is, the social scientist constructs a model of the social world peopled only by ideal-typical actors fulfilling their typical roles or

172

functions, and endowed with a typical common-sense knowledge of the general structures of the world in which they live, as far as is relevant for this daily living.

Now this model of the social world must be constructed in accordance with two postulates, in order to be considered valid. The first is the *postulate of logical consistency*, which means that the model of human action and interaction must be constructed in such a way as to be in full compatibility with the principles of formal and scientific logic. The second is the *postulate of adequacy*, which states that

each term in a scientific model of human action must be constructed in such a way that a human act performed within the life-world by an individual actor in the way indicated by the typical construct would be understandable for the actor himself as well as for his fellowmen in terms of a common-sense interpretation of everyday life. (1967b, pp. 43–4)

The aim of these two postulates is to enable the social scientist's model to be both objectively valid, as formalized in accordance with the canons of logic, and subjectively valid, as adequate for and intelligible to a common-sense understanding of the social world.

Schutz's programme for social science has certainly been influential in what is broadly known as phenomenological sociology, and his work represents probably the best known attempt, at least in America, to apply a phenomenological perspective to social science. His discussions of the nature of typification as a crucial part of common-sense knowledge are certainly valuable, and he has made contributions to a general understanding of common-sense knowledge as a whole (see especially his papers 'On multiple realities' in 1967b, and 'The problem of rationality in the social world', 1970b). Nevertheless, his use of phenomenology takes into account its descriptive impulse, its concern to describe general features of the life-world, at the expense of its transcendental impulse. His phenomenological analysis of meaning and action seems to be open to the objections Merleau-Ponty raises against rationalism, namely that it makes meaning the result of explicit acts of reflection, ignoring pre-reflective or non-thematic meaning and significance. Furthermore, in allowing as actions only planned and organized operations, Schutz ignores the countless everyday activities that do not have this planned character (cf. n. 5 to chapter 5 of this book). But, more importantly, these phenomenological analyses serve merely as a kind of introduction, soon to be abandoned, and appear to bear little relation to the rest of Schutz's descriptions of the social world. They could, indeed, be left out for the little they have to contribute, since Schutz explicitly makes his descriptions under the auspices of the natural attitude.

The basic problem with Schutz's phenomenology is that his approach is more accurately described as *positivist*. His programme is avowedly constructivist. Phenomenological social science consists of the construction of ideal types and scientific models of the social world. Now it is first of all not clear how far common-sense knowledge consists of types and constructs. It does to some extent – but an analysis solely in terms of ideal types ignores the situated, contextual and indexical features of much of our common-sense understanding (see chapter 2 and later). Furthermore there is in common-sense knowledge a constant dialectic between apprehending people as individual or as anonymous, a dialectic which Schutz tends to ignore in his over-concentration on ideal-typical knowledge (although this could perhaps be remedied: cf. Natanson, 1974, chapter 9). But the most important point is simply how far a constructivist analysis can allow us to understand our naïve experience of the world. Schutz goes a long way with positivism in seeing social science as the construction of an ideal language for apprehending social reality. He writes, for example, that 'all empirical knowledge involves discovery through processes of controlled inference, and that it must be statable in propositional form and capable of being verified by anyone who is prepared to make the effort to do so through observation' (Schutz, 1970a, p. 4), although he adds that observation does not mean sensory observation, but the application of *Verstehen*. His postulate of adequacy, that social scientific knowledge must in some way be related to common-sense knowledge, has to be stretched very far to be compatible with his positivist methodology.

Schutz presents us with a formalized and abstracted world which accords with his own version of a scientific theory, but bears little relation to our common-sense experience, except in so far as it can be construed as being typical. He aims to describe general features of common-sense experience, but can only describe what his positivist methodology will accept as valid scientific knowledge, namely analysis of types or constructs. His programme of transcendental analysis through phenomenology, with which he started and under whose auspices he claims to be working, grinds swiftly to a halt, since it demands that the common-sense world which Schutz takes as given, and Schutz's own methodology of positivist analysis, become themselves subjects of a transcendental investigation. In other words, theorizing for Schutz is essentially unreflexive: it aims to construct models of sectors of the social world in an attitude of disinterestedness without regard to the grounds or phenomenological genesis of that social world, and of Schutz's own theoretical impulse. It should also be noted that the characterization of social science as disinterested research represents an acceptance of the positivist distinction between description and evaluation. In short, Schutz offers us a highly formalized method of descriptive inquiry, which purports to be phenomenological, but seems to have more in common with positivism.

Turning to *ethnomethodology*, we find an enterprise more sophisticated than that of Schutz in its investigation of social order, and in particular how it is constructed through talk. Ethnomethodological research centres on members' methods or procedures for creating social order through their orderly talk, where these methods or procedures are seen by ethnomethodologists to have invariant properties. Now this is a descriptive enterprise, as ethnomethodologists would probably be the first to maintain. It is true that there is a partial reduction involved in the ethnomethodological notion of the 'occasioned corpus' (or indexicality) of a member's common-sense knowledge:

> By the term *occasioned corpus*, we wish to emphasize that the features of socially organized activities are particular, contingent accomplishments of the production and recognition work of parties to the activity. We underscore the occasioned character of the corpus in contrast to a corpus of member's knowledge, skill and belief standing prior to and independent of any actual occasion in which such knowledge, skill and belief is displayed or recognized. (Zimmerman and Pollner, 1971, p. 94)

Furthermore, 'the chief purpose of the notion of the occasioned corpus is to "reduce" the features of everyday social settings to a family of practices and their properties' (ibid., p. 98). But this partial transcendental impulse is wholly subservient to the description of common features of talk in the common-sense world, which is the programme of ethnomethodology. As Blum noted (see p. 166 of this book), the common-sense world serves as the 'rock-bottom certainty' for the ethnomethodologist, as that to which his descriptions aim to correspond. Ethnomethodology, like Schutzian phenomenology, is a sociology of the natural attitude.

Wittgenstein: an unhappy dialectic

Whereas Blum's programme of inquiry results in a suppression of the descriptive, and the programmes of Schutz and the ethnomethodologists suppress the transcendental, Wittgenstein's later philosophy can be seen as an attempt to establish a dialectic between the two impulses. Nevertheless the dialectic which Wittgenstein tries to maintain is a dialectic that totters and ultimately fails. There is tension and contradiction rather than interplay and mediation between the descriptive and the transcendental.

175

The transcendental component of Wittgenstein's later philosophy is evident in his concept 'form of life', which Blum takes from Wittgenstein and uses to define his analytic (transcendental) approach. Nevertheless the concept 'form of life' lies very latent in Wittgenstein's own philosophy. What plays a more important role in his philosophy, and also steers it towards the transcendental, is his definition of philosophy as concerned with the *grammar* of things rather than with things themselves (as Blum searches for the grounds or auspices of phenomena). For example, paragraph 90 of the *Philosophical Investigations* (1968): 'our investigation is directed not towards phenomena, but, as one might say, towards the "*possibilities*" of phenomena. We remind ourselves, that is to say, of the *kind of statement* that we make about phenomena'. Philosophy is concerned with the frames through which we view phenomena (paragraph 114). And so Wittgenstein argues:

> It was true to say that our considerations could not be scientific ones. It was not of any possible interest to us to find out empirically 'that, contrary to our preconceived ideas, it is possible to think such-and-such' – whatever that may mean . . . the philosophical problems . . . are, of course, not empirical problems; they are solved, rather, by looking into the workings of our language, and that in such a way as to make us recognize these workings. . . . The problems are solved, not by giving new information, but by arranging what we have always known. (paragraph 109)

Yet this grammatic concern with the workings of language can be seen as well to be a purely descriptive inquiry. In the same paragraph, Wittgenstein writes: 'we may not advance any kind of theory. There must not be anything hypothetical in our considerations. We must do away with all *explanation*, and description alone must take its place'. Or again, paragraphs 654–5:

> Our mistake is to look for an explanation . . . where we ought to have said: *this language-game is played*. The question is not one of explaining a language-game by means of our experience, but of noting a language-game.

It is this opposition to any form of explanation, where explanation is taken to mean causal explanation or any form of reduction in which the original phenomenon is no longer left intact, which makes Wittgenstein's later philosophy in many ways comparable to phenomenology (cf. Munson, 1962). However Wittgenstein's opposition to explanation seems not only to involve a rejection of reduction – as in phenomenology – but also a rejection of a general transcendental framework. In other words description for Merleau-Ponty is always from a transcendental perspective, whereas for Wittgenstein it is a-theoretical, disconnected from experience, and consists only in 'noting language-games'. Now it is true that to note a language-game is to look at how language is used, and so involves reference to behaviour and interaction between persons. Nevertheless the prime concern is only with the description of these usages in as simple a way as possible. How his concept 'form of life' is to be fitted in is not clear, since the form of life refers to the grounds of a phenomenon, and the search for grounds is by its very nature hypothetical and theoretical.

Let us consider again Wittgenstein's idea of philosophy as grammar. This conception of grammar can certainly be understood transcendentally by making phenomena intelligible in terms of the language-game of which they are a part. And, as paragraph 8 puts it, 'to imagine a language-game means to imagine a form of life'. Yet if one looks at how a Wittgensteinian philosopher actually does philosophy, his concerns seem exclusively descriptive. Wittgenstein suggests that doing philosophy consists in: assembling reminders or examples for particular purposes, seeing connections between different aspects of language, putting questions about certain usages, comparing different usages, establishing hierarchies in language to make certain language-games explicit – in short, noting different language-games. Now there is a marked leaning towards pure description in the tendency in practice to treat language as a *thing*, as something to be investigated apart from the world or from experience (cf. pp. 72–3 of this book), and so to treat philosophy as a special method for tampering with or repairing the mechanisms of language when it goes wrong. This is perhaps more true of Wittgenstein's followers than Wittgenstein himself, but the tendency and justification is to be found in his own philosophy.

Wittgenstein can be read from a transcendental or a descriptive perspective, but it is difficult to mediate between the two impulses in terms of his own philosophy. Blum considered the transcendental (analytic) superior to all descriptive or concrete inquiries because he equated the transcendental with theorizing, with a promotion of the free play of the intellect. Yet Wittgenstein's actual method of doing philosophy seems more likely to stunt than nurture the impulse to theorize. It seems to me the failure to establish a dialectic between the transcendental and descriptive accounts for his persistent view of philosophy as a sickness, as an impulse to be cured, or, if it breaks out, as something to be held firmly in check:

> It is not our aim to refine or complete the system of rules for the use of words in unheard-of ways. For the clarity that we are aiming at is indeed *complete* clarity. But this simply means that

the philosophical problems should *completely* disappear. The real discovery is the one that makes me capable of stopping doing philosophy when I want to. – The one that gives philosophy peace, so that it is no longer tormented by questions which bring *itself* in question. (paragraph 133)

Compare this with what Merleau-Ponty writes of philosophy:

The world and reason are not problematic. We may say, if we wish, that they are mysterious, but their mystery defines them: there can be no question of dispelling it by some 'solution', it is on the hither side of all solutions. True philosophy consists in re-learning to look at the world. (PP xx)

Philosophy for Merleau-Ponty is a response to the mystery of the world, not in seeking merely intellectual 'solutions' – and here he is in agreement with Wittgenstein – but in 're-learning to look at the world' from the perspective of lived experience. To this end, philosophy is justified in using words in 'unheard-of ways'. The aim is not 'complete clarity' (there is no such thing) or to bring philosophy peace, since philosophy for Merleau-Ponty is not an impulse which must be cured, nor a manifestation of sickness, but is an attitude to life and to the world, an attitude of wonder. Merleau-Ponty is quite happy for philosophy to 'bring itself into question' if this means a continual exploration of the grounds of philosophy in the unreflective and its inability to completely recapture or reproduce lived experience. But this is not a sign of philosophy's infirmity, but rather a mark of the radicality of its approach (radical = of the roots). For Merleau-Ponty the world is not problematic, it does not defy thought if thought is prepared to be radical. But the world is mysterious, the richness of things in the world and of our experience can never be exhausted, nor can the manifold ambiguities of existence ever be fully catalogued. But for Wittgenstein the world is neither problematic nor mysterious. Philosophy for him concerns itself with *complete* clarity, with dispelling *all* philosophic problems. Philosophy for Merleau-Ponty is rooted in an attitude of child-like wonder; for Wittgenstein, philosophy is more akin to the disillusion of old age. For Merleau-Ponty philosophy can bring insight into life. For Wittgenstein, it is wholly negative: it exposes mythologies (1966, pp. 51–2), removes conceptual puzzles that have bewitched us, and knocks over systems of belief that are only houses of cards (1968, paragraph 118). The great service that Wittgenstein performs, and which in some ways puts him in the same camp as Merleau-Ponty, is his relentless exposure and destruction of the system-building and 'scientific' pretensions of much academic philosophy or allied work in social science. But here he stops, and can only counsel, in an attitude of philosophic resignation, piecemeal investigation of the workings of ordinary language as the only valid domain of philosophy.

Sartre: a dialectic without synthesis

Since there have been several references to Sartre throughout this work, and since, from *Phenomenology of Perception* onwards, Merleau-Ponty took pains to point out his divergences from the philosophy of his colleague, it seems fitting to conclude with a few comments on Sartre's philosophy from the perspective of Merleau-Ponty's phenomenology. In particular Merleau-Ponty criticized Sartre's notions of absolute freedom, of consciousness as pure spontaneity, and as choice or action as voluntarist. In Merleau-Ponty's eyes Sartre ignored or underplayed the incarnation of consciousness in the world, the fact of passivity or sedimentation in being-in-the-world, the mediation between men and things in the 'interworld', and so the essential limits on freedom, choice and action as a result of their fundamental ambiguity. Now it is difficult to judge how accurate these charges are. It is true that they are sometimes tempered by Merleau-Ponty, for example when he acknowledges that Sartre's thought is in revolt against some of its own presuppositions, as in his descriptions of the root in *Nausea*, or the situation and viscosity in *Being and Nothingness*. Certainly many impressive quotations from Sartre can be marshalled to demonstrate his awareness of freedom as situated, and of the existence of the 'interworld' (de Beauvoir, 1955). Nevertheless, it is to Sartre's ontology and basic presuppositions, rather than to his often brilliant concrete descriptions, that Merleau-Ponty directs his objections, which find their most coherent and convincing expression in *The Visible and the Invisible* (pp. 52–95).

In an attempt to empty consciousness of those psychic entities that rationalist philosophies often tried to fill it with, Sartre decided to describe consciousness as an immediate openness to being. By doing this, he could argue that there could be 'nothing' between consciousness and the world, so that consciousness must be directly open to being. Hence he defined consciousness as nothingness and the world as positivity (being). Here, very simply, we have the rationale to his ontology of being and nothingness. However, as Merleau-Ponty argues, Sartre's strategy in fact ends up with the same split between consciousness and the world which Sartre had been trying to avoid:

> From the moment that I conceive of myself as negativity
> and the world as positivity, there is no longer any interaction.
> I go with my whole self to meet a massive world; between it and

myself there is neither any point of encounter nor point of reflection, since it is Being and I am nothing. We are and remain strictly opposed and strictly conmingled precisely because we are not of the same order. (VI 52)

Consciousness can only be entangled with being in a 'magical' manner, by not-being-it (Zaner, 1971, p. 72). Consciousness is thus pure immanence – since it is nihilation, void and transparency – and also pure transcendence – since by itself this void is 'nothing' and so depends for its existence on what is outside it. Sartre's philosophy volatilizes between immanence and transcendence, between negativism and positivism, which oppose each other, since they are of a different order, and yet at the same time are identified with each other, since absolute immanence is at the same time transcendence, and absolute negativism turns into positivism.

In short, for Merleau-Ponty Sartre's thought, at least on its ontological level, is ambivalent or non-dialectical. There are two central ambivalences or splits. First, as we have seen, between being and nothing, which are 'not united precisely because they are the same thing in two contradictories – ambivalence' (VI 69, n. 1). Hence Sartre's negativist thought – which relies on the consistent thinking through of the notions of negativity and nothingness – joins forces with all forms of positivism, in that 'whether considering the void of nothingness or the absolute fullness of being, it in every case ignores density, depth, the plurality of planes, the background worlds' (VI 68), in short the essential *perspectivism* of perception and the *incarnation* of consciousness in the world. The second ambivalence in Sartre's philosophy is that in his actual descriptions of being-in-the-world he recognizes that the dualism of his own ontology is transcended in concrete existence, that consciousness and the world are mixed notions, implicate each other, and so allow of 'the transitions, the becomings, the possibilities' (VI 73). In other words, there is a split between Sartre's ontology of being and nothingness and his more phenomenological descriptions, where the *pour soi* is conceived as in a situation, in history, in a body, and hence neither a pure negative nor a pure positive.

Sartre's ontological ambivalence can be illustrated in his conception of the relations between self and other. As Zaner (1971) points out, Sartre describes interpersonal relations in terms of a strict division between subject and object: *either* I am a subject for the other and he is an object for me, *or*, vice versa, he is a subject for me and I am an object for him. Paradigm cases of these are gazing at another (myself as subject, the other as object) or being gazed at (myself as object, the other as subject). Hence there are for Sartre only two paradigmatically authentic emotions: arrogance (myself as subject) or shame (myself as object) (see Sartre, 1969a, p. 290). Now this framework for understanding relations between people can certainly be illuminating for certain emotions or behavioural ploys – but it is sometimes too dualistic and dogmatic. There are, for example, cases where I can experience the other as a subject for me – when I experience him as a centre of orientation for objects around him, or as the agent of his actions – without, as a correlate, experiencing myself as an object for him, which should be impossible if we stick strictly to Sartre's ontology.

In so far as he keeps to his ontology of being and nothingness, Sartre is precluded from giving a phenomenological account of being-in-the-world, since his ontology rules out the notion of intentionality (cf. Zaner, 1971). Consciousness cannot be intentionally related to the world, since it is only *negatively* related. For Sartre, since there can be no *external* relations between consciousness and the world, as consciousness is no-thing, the relation must be wholly *internal*. According to the thesis of intentionality, however, the relation between consciousness and the world is neither negative nor positive, external nor internal, but intentional: consciousness and the world are the two poles of an intentionality that is the defining quality of each.

In short, Sartre's ontology precludes significant contact with the world. The synthesis of consciousness and the world – the 'in-itself-for-itself' – is only a phantom, never attainable in reality. For Merleau-Ponty, on the other hand, this synthesis of in-itself-for-itself is what he describes as sedimentation or objectification, and is the other side of the spontaneity and creativity of consciousness (cf. C. Smith, 1964b).

For the philosophy of being and nothingness consciousness is absolutely free, because it is 'nothingness', and hence without any external limits in principle: 'either man is wholly determined ... or else man is wholly free' (Sartre, 1969a, p. 442). But this is an abstract and formal doctrine, for actual experience gives us an ambiguous freedom, a freedom dependent on incarnation, and hence mixed with determinism. Whereas Sartre starts with freedom, Merleau-Ponty chooses instead the terrain of experience as his starting-point and ultimate court of appeal: 'either experience is nothing, or it must be total' (PP 258). But instead of grounding his philosophy on lived experience, Sartre grounds it in an ontological dualism of doubtful validity. Sartre *constructs* our experience in terms of his ontology of being and nothingness, instead of describing it. His thought is 'high altitude', that of a spectator consciousness which has access both to itself (nothingness) and the world (being). His philosophy of being and nothingness is, in the words of Merleau-Ponty, a 'summary rationalism'.[3]

So our judgment on Sartre's philosophy from the perspective of Merleau-Ponty's is that Sartre's dialectic fails because it remains without synthesis. It is true that the ambivalence and dogmatism of his thought can be taken only as a difference in style between Sartre and Merleau-Ponty, which appears to be how Sartre himself sees it:

> I was the more dogmatic, he the more subtle, but this was a matter of temperament, or as we said, of character. (Sartre, 1965b, p. 168)

> The truth was that we were each recruited according to our aptitudes: Merleau when it was the time of subtleties, and I, when the time of the assassins had come (ibid., p. 204).

But these differences in temperament and style reflect deeper concerns. Sartre's philosophy is marked by its essential ambivalence, its truncated dialectic, and in particular its failure to integrate the transcendental (his ontology of being and nothingness) and the descriptive. Merleau-Ponty's, on the other hand, is through and through dialectical, seeking interconnections, integrating perspectives, and moving between different levels of analysis in its search for meaning and truth. Sartre is a showman, a conjurer with absruse concepts and gripping descriptions. Merleau-Ponty is a craftsman, weaving a variety of different colours and patterns into his philosophic fabric.

Notes

1 The programme of existential phenomenology

1 Merleau-Ponty claims that Kant, who used the notion of intentionality in the simple sense that all consciousness is consciousness of something, only meant intentionality to be used in the first sense, as an intentionality of acts. He also claims there was a tendency for Husserl to do the same, ignoring operative intentionality (although it was Husserl who formulated the distinction). Both of these contentions are challenged by Zaner (1971, especially pp. 208–18).

2 For example Zaner (1971) accuses Merleau-Ponty of identifying mind *tout court* with the body. Yolton (1954, p. 178) objects to the 'easy monism' of Merleau-Ponty in ignoring those cases where some kind of dualism between mind and body is evident. Kwant (1963, p. 239) argues that Merleau-Ponty makes his victory over dualism easy by closing his eyes to those aspects of our experience that support dualism.

3 The notions of phenomenal field, phenomenal body or phenomenal world must not be misunderstood. Coulter (1973) is quite wrong when he argues that phenomenologists 'confuse us when they appear to assert that there is a "phenomenal world" or a "phenomenal field" somehow superimposed over, or co-occurrent with, the external world' (p. 81), or again that phenomenologists often assume 'that because we recognize things in our environment by their look, sound, smell, taste and feel, we begin by describing their phenomenal properties and work outwards to infer their real properties from their phenomenal ones' (p. 99). Coulter appears to be confusing the notion of phenomenal world with something like Kant's noumenon/phenomenon distinction. The phenomenal field or world is not superimposed over the 'external world' like a thin layer of film, but refers simply to the 'external world' as it appears to perceptual experience, that is, endowed with a primitive physiognomic significance and structured through our perception into figure and ground. The world is phenomenal because it is not external in the sense of being alien to us, but is perceived as a series of interlocking visual fields. The world is phenomenal because it is a field. We

do not infer the 'real' from the phenomenal, because *the phenomenal is simply the real as it appears to us*. Phenomenology denies any sense to a conception of a 'real, external world' which is independent of a perceiver.

4 Aldous Huxley's remarkable document *The Doors of Perception* (1959) reveals many parallels between perception under mescalin and Merleau-Ponty's descriptions of pre-objective experience at its primordial level. For example:

> At ordinary times the eye concerns itself with such problems as *where? – how far? – how situated in relation to what?* In the mescalin experience . . . the mind does its experiencing in terms of intensity of experience, profundity of significance, relations within a pattern. . . . Not, of course, that the category of space had been abolished. When I got up and walked around, I could do so quite normally, without misjudging the whereabouts of objects. Space was still there, but it had lost its predominance. The mind was primarily concerned, not with measures and locations, but with being and meaning. (p. 19)

Here we find an illustration of the distinction Merleau-Ponty makes between perception in the natural attitude, which we understand as occurring in objective space (where? how far? etc.), and pre-objective perception, occurring in phenomenal space, and where we witness the birth of perceptual meaning and organization (relations in a pattern).

Or again, exemplifying the impersonality of pre-objective perception, Huxley records his reservations about his mescalin experience in view of the demands and expectations implicit in perception in the natural attitude: 'What about human relations? . . . How could one reconcile this timeless bliss of seeing as one ought to see with the temporal duties of doing what one ought to do and feeling as one ought to feel?' (p. 30).

5 Cf. Sartre's *The Transcendence of the Ego* (1957), which argues a similar case concerning the non-primitive, derived status of the self or 'I' (and to which Merleau-Ponty may be indebted). Sartre writes, for example:

> I pity Peter and go to his assistance. For my consciousness only one thing exists at that moment: Peter-having-to-be-helped. This quality of 'having-to-be-helped' lies in Peter. . . . At this level, the desire is given to consciousness as . . . impersonal. (p. 56)

Yet there is a difference of emphasis between Sartre and Merleau-Ponty. For Sartre, the founded nature of the ego or 'I' reveals the 'monstrous spontaneity', the ceaseless creativity and activity of consciousness. For Merleau-Ponty, on the other hand, consciousness is something 'set in motion', a fund of pre-reflective experiences which are not pure spontaneity, but an openness to the world, a subject–object dialogue as perceptual experience reveals, so that impersonal consciousness is as much a passivity as a spontaneity.

6 This relationship between the private and the intersubjective nature of our experience is not entirely clear. As we have seen, Merleau-Ponty views a large part of our pre-reflective experience as anonymous. Zaner (1971) objects to this, maintaining that while it certainly makes sense to argue that experiences manifest a common style, and hence can be characterized as having a *typicality*, this is not the same as either *anonymity* or *generality* (pp. 221–2), and that therefore Merleau-Ponty fails to distinguish between these terms. It would seem that in fact Merleau-Ponty would characterize pre-reflective experience in terms of all three. Experience is typical in that it manifests a common style or meaning: 'all consciousness of something, as soon as this thing ceases to be an indeterminate existence, as soon as it is identifiable and recognizable, for example *as* "a colour", or even as "this unique red", presupposes some apprehension of a meaning' (SB 200). Experience is anonymous because, as we have seen, pre-objective experience is pre-personal and the self is founded rather than originary. Experience is general because it partakes of general features, for example spatiality, temporality and embodiment, and hence exists in a form that is inter-subjectively available. Merleau-Ponty writes, for example:

> When I begin to perceive this table, I resolutely contact the thickness of duration (Bergson) which has elapsed while I have been looking at it; I emerge from my individual life by apprehending the object as an object for everyone. I therefore bring together in one operation concordant but discrete experiences which occupy several points of time and several temporalities. (PP 40–1)

He goes on to add: 'Philosophy's task is to reinstate it (i.e. my act of perception) in the private field of experience from which it arises and elucidate its origin' (ibid.). This elucidation of the origin of pre-reflective experience is conceived of as a dialectic between individuality and generality (cf. PW 138), and, presumably, also between individuality and typicality, and individuality and anonymity.

7 Zaner (1971) objects that Merleau-Ponty, in denying that consciousness is synthetic, i.e. that the world and the body can be understood in terms of syntheses carried out by acts of consciousness or constituted by consciousness, has illegitimately defined synthesis, and constitution, as *activities* of consciousness carried out reflectively. However, Zaner maintains, in Husserl's use of the terms, synthesis and constitution are not incompatible with the quasi-automatic and sedimented processes of consciousness (p. 210). Zaner also accuses Merleau-Ponty of assimilating consciousness to the body, echoing an objection raised by Aron Gurwitsch (1964), who writes that:

> Problems of constitution arise not only with regard to material things, cultural objects, ideal objects . . . but also as to our body and embodied existence. In accordance with the principles laid down by Husserl, we therefore submit that constitutive problems must be formulated and treated exclusively in terms of consciousness, both positional and pre-positional. (p. 305)

Now it is not true that Merleau-Ponty simply assimilates consciousness to the body, as I demonstrated in the discussion of the relation between mind and body (see pp. 23–5 of this chapter). He writes, for example: 'consciousness projects itself into a physical world and has a body, as it projects itself into a cultural world and has its habits' (PP 137), suggesting that 'having' a body is of the same intentional order as projecting a physical world. But it is true that consciousness for Merleau-Ponty is always embodied, since it would make no sense for him to conceive of consciousness as somehow separate from the body (or from the world). The body, for him, is an already constituted synthesis. The act of perception, he says,

> takes advantage of work already done, of a general synthesis constituted once and for all, and this is what I mean when I say that I perceive with my body or my senses, since my body and my senses are precisely that familiarity with the world born of habit, that implicit or sedimentary body of knowledge. (PP 238)

Zaner and Gurwitsch want to push this a stage further back, and ask how my body as a 'general synthesis, constituted once and for all', is itself constituted by consciousness. For Merleau-Ponty, however, this makes no sense, for consciousness exists only as embodied.

8 Once again (see n. 5 above) Merleau-Ponty's fluid approach to concepts and their interrelations – in this case that of the real and the imaginary – can be compared to the more dogmatic and rigid approach of Sartre. Sartre writes, for example: 'the image and the perception . . . represent the two main irreducible attitudes of consciousness. It follows that they exclude each other' (1972, p. 138). This means that Sartre will find it difficult to account for what Merleau-Ponty wishes to draw attention to, namely that mode of experience known as *phantasy*. Whereas fantasy suggests experience belonging purely to the realm of imagination, phantasy implicates the imaginary with the real. Laing, for example, argues that phantasy is one essential way of relating to the world, and illustrates it as follows (1967, pp. 26–8):

> Two people sit talking. The one (Peter) is making a point to the other (Paul). He puts his point of view in different ways to Paul for some time, but Paul does not understand.
> Let us *imagine* what may be going on, in the sense that I mean by phantasy. Peter is trying to get through to Paul. He feels that Paul is being needlessly closed up against him. It becomes increasingly important to him to soften or get into Paul. But Paul seems hard, impervious and cold. Peter feels he is beating his head against a brick wall. He feels tired, hopeless, progressively more empty as he sees he is failing. Finally he gives up.
> Paul feels, on the other hand, that Peter is pressing too hard. He feels he has to fight him off. He doesn't understand what Peter is saying, but feels that he has to defend himself from an assault.

Of course, in a sense the whole distinction between 'reality' and the imagination is problematic, for it begs the question of *which* reality. Merleau-Ponty has pointed out that consciousness exists on many different levels at the same time, and can intend different worlds or settings in which it can live – the worlds of dreams, myths, primordial perception, art, science, etc. Cf. Alfred Schutz's discussion of multiple realities (1967b).

2 Speech

1 Cf. Heidegger:

> Listening to . . . is Dasein's existential way of Being-open as Being-with for Others. Indeed, hearing constitutes the primary and authentic way in which Dasein is open for its ownmost potentiality-for-Being – as in hearing the voice of the friend whom every Dasein carries with it. Dasein hears, because it understands. (1967, p. 206)

2 Thus Edie, in his foreword to *Consciousness and the Acquisition of Language*:

> The fact of the matter is that, for Saussure, both synchrony and diachrony are aspects of *la langue*, whereas the study of what Merleau-Ponty calls *la parole*, the speech act as such, falls wholly outside the scientific approach to language defined in Saussure's structural linguistics. (pp. xxx–xxxi)

And Ricoeur (1967):

> The ultimate presupposition of any structural linguistics is that language is an object, like other objects, that is, like the subject-matter of the other sciences, where, also, the 'thing' is resolved into a relationship, a system of internal dependencies. For phenomenology, however, language is not an object but a mediation, that is to say, it is that by which and through which we move towards reality (whatever that may be).
> For phenomenology, language consists in saying something about something: it thereby escapes towards what it says; it goes beyond itself and dissolves in its intentional movement of reference. (p. 16)

3 For example, Ricoeur (1967) speaks of

> the point of departure for a new phenomenology of language [which] would take seriously the challenge of semiology. . . . This reanimated phenomenology cannot be content with repeating the old descriptions of speech which do not recognize the theoretical status of linguistics and its first axiom, the primacy of structure over process. . . . It is through and by means of a linguistics of language that a phenomenology of speech is today conceivable. (p. 19)

And Edie, in his foreword to *Consciousness and the Acquisition of Language*, concludes:

187

In short, the question which we are forced to address to Merleau-Ponty is whether his theory of language, which seems to be exclusively concerned with *words* as they occur in concrete acts of usage, does justice to the role of syntax in the production of meaning and, secondly, what the relation of syntax (if it is given a status independent of *la parole*) is to speech acts. (p. xxxii)

4 Cf. Merleau-Ponty:

It is not because two objects resemble each other that they are designated by the same word; on the contrary, it is because they are designated by the same word and thus participate in the same verbal and affective category that they are perceived as similar. (SB 168)

5 At the risk of repetition or of belabouring a point, it might be beneficial to clear up a possible misunderstanding concerning the phenomenological postulate of the intentionality of speech, because it is so frequently misunderstood, especially by linguistic philosophers. Merleau-Ponty writes: 'the meaning of a sentence is its import or intention' (PP 430), or again:

We say that events have a significance when they appear as the achievement of the expression of a single aim. There is significance for us when one of our intentions is fulfilled, or conversely, when a number of facts or signs lend themselves in such a way as to enable us to take them up as an inclusive whole and carry them forward. (PP 428)

Now in tying meaning to intention, Merleau-Ponty does *not* mean intention in its ordinary sense, as what someone intended by saying something, or in asking what a person's intention is (for example, 'is your intention in inviting me up to your room to seduce me?'). This ordinary meaning of intention does not by itself give the whole meaning of an utterance (although it might do in some cases, depending on the language-game being played). I can claim to understand an utterance as an insult, whereas the speaker can claim he intended it as a joke – who is to say what the 'real' meaning of the utterance is? There is no reason for arguing that the speaker must know what he meant, what his intention is, for it frequently happens that he does not know, or deceives himself, or that he changes his mind ('it started off as a joke and turned into an insult'). Wittgenstein has subjected the view that meaning is the result of an intention residing somewhere in the speaker's mind to a devastating critique. Words do not translate discrete mental intentions which are the 'real meaning' behind words:

An intention is embedded in its situation, in human customs and institutions. If the technique of the game of chess did not exist, I could not intend to play a game of chess. In so far as I do intend the construction of a sentence in advance, that is made possible by the fact that I can speak the language in question. (Wittgenstein, 1968, paragraph 337)

If I give anyone an order I feel it to be *quite enough* to give him
signs. And I should never say: this is only words, and I have got
to get behind the words. . . . But if you say: 'How am I to know
what he means, when I see nothing but the signs he gives?' then I
say, 'How is *he* to know what he means, when he has nothing
but the signs either?' (ibid., paragraphs 503 and 504)

These quotations cannot in any way be taken as a critique of a
phenomenological approach to speech, since Merleau-Ponty would be
the first to agree with them. Merleau-Ponty uses the terms 'intention',
'import', 'significance' as examples of *intentionality* in the phenomenological sense, which refers to the directedness and meaningfulness
(*sens*) of human behaviour, the means whereby consciousness
ex-presses itself in the world. Intentionality is praxis which institutes
and maintains the human world. Particular intentions (in the ordinary
sense) a speaker may claim to have are *one aspect* of the meaning of an
utterance. The sedimented, structural or conventional feature of words
is another aspect, and it sometimes happens that meaning consists in a
dialectic between these two aspects.

6 Erving Goffman, although not an ethnomethodologist, has provided
many brilliant accounts of how this is done. Goffman suggests, however,
that this ability of members to 'manage' their social settings is the result
of deliberation or calculation, whereas for ethnomethodology it is a
part of the unreflective skill of any member (Garfinkel, 1967, p. 174).

7 Hence, when I argued that the intersubjectivity of speech can be seen
in its being rule-guided (see p. 53), the notion of rules must be understood in this ethnomethodological sense of being situated and
occasioned phenomena, rather than existing prior to and independent
of linguistic practices. See Cavell (1966, pp. 154–61) on Wittgenstein's
concept of rule-following.

8 See Marcuse (1968, chapter 7), who accuses ordinary language
philosophers, in their idolization of 'ordinary usage', of being ultra
conservative. But he does less than justice to Wittgenstein by interpreting his philosophy as synonymous with ordinary language
philosophy. Pitkin (1972), in defence of Wittgenstein and ordinary
language philosophy, argues that

the attempt to refute a philosophical position with reference from
ordinary usage is always a vulgarization of the ordinary-language
philosophical enterprise. Wittgenstein is not concerned with
refuting metaphysics or ending philosophy, but with understanding
it. (p. 19)

Unfortunately there seem to be many vulgarizers about.

3 Society

1 I am using 'reflexivity' in the phenomenological sense, where it is
similar to the phenomenological concept of rationality, meaning a
search for grounds or auspices. This is not the same, although neither
is it unrelated, to the ethnomethodological usage of reflexivity (see

pp. 65–6), which refers to the capacity of speech for real-izing social settings by making them account-able.

2 This distinction, between intended meaning and its intersubjective significance, is often termed a distinction between 'subjective' and 'objective' meaning. This terminology, however, seems to me confused, since *all* social meanings are intersubjective. That is, if something is meaningful, then it must be (potentially) meaningful to anyone. This is simply because a social phenomenon can only be considered meaningful in terms of a given language, and any language consists of public, shared meanings. Wittgenstein has shown this in his criticism of the idea of a private language. Thus, strictly speaking, the term 'subjective meaning' makes no sense. And the term 'objective meaning' seems to belie the fact that all meanings are intersubjectively instituted and maintained. Meanings are not objects, but intersubjective achievements embodied in praxis. What this distinction between 'subjective' and 'objective' meanings is meant to refer to is that an action can be intended to mean something by the actor, and yet is taken by other people to mean something else. We have here, however, not a conflict between 'subjective' and 'objective' meanings, but a *competition between different intersubjective meanings or levels of meaning*, of which subjective intentions (in the ordinary sense) and actual consequences in other people's eyes are two components or levels.

3 It is remarkable how often phenomenology is criticized for paying attention to only intended meanings and forgetting their intersubjective or objective significance. For example Goldmann writes:

> The weakness of phenomenology seems to us to lie precisely in the fact that it limits itself to a comprehensive description of the facts of consciousness, or, to be more precise, of their 'essence'. The real structure of historical facts permits, however, beyond the *conscious* meaning of those facts in the thoughts and intentions of the actors, the postulation of an *objective* meaning which often differs from the conscious meaning in an important way. (1969, pp. 32–3)

Or, from a different philosophical tradition, Pitkin writes that writers claiming phenomenological roots

> have argued that only empathy, Verstehen, and phenomenology can help us to understand human affairs. We have argued, by contrast, that Wittgenstein suggests a dualistic or even dialectical view, that what characterizes human action is not the impossibility of external observation, but the coexistence of observation and intentionality. (1972, pp. 323–4)

Merleau-Ponty would, of course, find nothing to disagree with in these statements (cf. chapter 2, n. 5).

4 Cf. Goffman (1961), especially the second essay, called 'Role distance'. Even though he introduces this notion of role distance to leave the individual a margin of 'freedom and maneuverability' (p. 117) – and it is no accident that, for Goffman, freedom is made virtually synonymous

with an ability to manoeuvre between roles – Goffman concludes that 'role distance is almost as much subject to role analysis as are the core tasks of role themselves' (p. 134), and so he can safely combat the 'touching tendency to keep a part of the world safe from sociology' (ibid.). One may legitimately ask what this world is which is unable to protect itself from the cynical eye of the sociologist. 'The image that emerges of the individual', says Goffman,

> is that of a juggler and synthesizer, an accommodator and appeaser, who fulfils one function while he is apparently engrossed in another; he stands guard at the door of the tent but lets all his relatives and friends crawl in under the flap. This seems to be the case even in one of our most sacred occupational shows – surgery. (p. 123)

The world which Goffman portrays is one of individuals cunningly and skilfully managing their role demands. There is undoubtedly some truth in such a picture. Yet there is a sense in which one chooses (in a pre-reflective sense, cf. Goffman, p. 21) to live in this Goffmanesque manner or, on the other hand, attempts to transcend such role demands or forge new ones. To live as a role-juggler is an existential choice.

4 Marxism

1 Support for this anti-deterministic interpretation of Marxism can be found in much non-orthodox Marxist literature. For example, Kamenka:

> The materialist conception of history, at least in its emphasis on the historical laws that determine man's development independently of his will, is the law of man's development in the *period of alienation*, in what the later Marx called the prehistory of mankind (1969, p. 20)

Or Marcuse:

> Marxian theory is, then, incompatible with fatalistic determinism. True, historical determinism involves the determinist principle that consciousness is conditioned by social existence. We have attempted to show, however, that the necessary dependence enunciated by this principle applies to the 'pre-historical' life, namely, to the life of class society. (1967, p. 319)

See also Poggi (1972) for a forceful anti-deterministic reading of Marx, and Meszaros (1970) for a convincing demonstration of the centrality of the theory of alienation in Marx in both his early and his late writings. It is also worth remarking that the thesis of objective determinism makes unintelligible Marx's own enterprise, for if all thought is strictly conditioned by the economic base of society, how could Marx have conceived the idea of going beyond capitalism and laying the ground for a radically different mode of social and economic organization?

5 Ethics

1 Cf. Kamenka (1969):

> Marx [thus] attempts to sidestep the whole problem of justification in morals and the conflict between 'ought' and 'is'. Morality is not a question of what 'ought to be done'. The logical dilemma faced by moralists arises from the fact that they are trying to impose external principles of co-operation on societies that are by their nature incapable of producing spontaneous, rational and lasting co-operation, or from the fact that they abstract men and human activities from concrete social situations and lay down rules and requirements that ignore the realities of human life in that situation, ignore what a concrete man needs and can do. (p. 24)

Kamenka, however, then goes on to comment that Marx is implicitly 'trying to justify his passionate and advocative pleading by pretending that his *moral* distinctions are in fact *logical* distinctions' (p. 25, italics added). Marx does this, according to Kamenka, by creating

> an aura of logical necessity by the use of such terms as 'essence' (distinguished from mere 'existence'), 'truly human' (distinguished from 'empirical man'), 'pre-history' (distinguished from 'true history'). It is this conception of a 'true' man, a 'true' history and a 'true' reality which is quite vital to Marx if he is to elevate a certain way of life, or a certain way of behaving, above others. This position rests on the (false) Hegelian idealist view that ordinary, empirical reality can somehow be logically deficient, lacking true or real reality. (ibid.)

But if any description of the social world implies an evaluation of it, then Kamenka's strict separation of morality and logic breaks down. In speaking of a human essence, or of true humanity or true history, Marx is not making purely *moral* claims, nor purely *logical* ones, but rather *ontological* ones, and in ontological terms it makes perfect sense to claim that 'ordinary empirical reality' is somehow deficient in terms of a transcendental viewpoint, which stresses historical activity (Marx) or the activity of consciousness (phenomenology). Marx is quite justified to claim that under capitalism, while men are allowed a *formal* freedom under the law, they are in fact denied any *actual* or *real* freedom because of exploitation and the existence of private property. Men are alienated from themselves and lack their true reality in the sense of not being allowed to develop their full potential, and hence of real-izing themselves.

2 Thus Plant (1970) quotes Dorothy Emmet on the existentialist analysis of morality as follows:

> Are we left then with an antithesis between role behaviour on the one hand with its legal and moral regulations which Sartre says evade the full freedom and responsibility of the individual, and on the other hand a purely personal morality, free, spontaneous, unbound by rules? The trouble with this antithesis is that it hardly

comes to grips with social morality, and whether we like it or not, social morality impinges on our lives most of the time. We had much better recognize and respect the fact that, as Aristotle remarked, he that could live apart from society might be a beast or a God but not a human being.

Plant himself adds that 'existentialism fails because it neither recognizes nor does justice to the facts of our social situation' (pp. 39–40). I leave it open whether or not this is fair comment with regard to Sartre. He certainly has a tendency towards the view of the individual legislating his own ethical standards. But he also stresses the more acceptable sense of the individual component to ethics that any rule has to be interpreted in the light of the specific context in which it is seen to be relevant. In Sartre's own words: 'the context is always concrete, and therefore unpredictable; it has always to be invented' (1956, p. 308). When we come to Merleau-Ponty, I can see no basis for Emmet's or Plant's charge.

3 Merleau-Ponty is here assuming a parallel between how much of myself is given over to my feeling, and how much of the loved one is actually loved by me – so if only part of myself is affected, then only part of the loved one can be loved. Thus genuine or authentic human relations would seem to be characterized for Merleau-Ponty by reciprocity and mutuality of feeling. In the same vein Marx, writing about how money distorts human relations by enabling men to buy the qualities they don't 'really' have (i.e. which are not authentic), argues:

If you suppose man to be man and his relationship to the world to be a human one, then you can only exchange love for love, trust for trust etc. If you wish to appreciate art, then you must be a man with some artistic education; if you wish to exercise an influence on other men, you must be a man who has a really stimulating and encouraging effect on other man. . . . If you love without arousing a reciprocal love, that is, if your love does not as such produce love in return . . . then your love is impotent and a misfortune. (1971, pp. 182–3)

It would seem impossible in authentic relationships, according to Merleau-Ponty, to be *totally* given over to one's love for *one quality* of another person, and impossible, according to Marx, to have a genuine love for a person who was indifferent to you.

4 Cf. Simone de Beauvoir:

Let me repeat that this personal account is not offered in any sense as an 'explanation'. Indeed, one of my main reasons for undertaking it is my realization that self-knowledge is impossible, and the best one can hope for is self-revelation. (1965, p. 368)

5 Take, for example, Hampshire's formulation of freedom: 'A man becomes more and more free and responsible the more he at all times knows what he is doing, in every sense of the phrase, and the more he acts with a definite and clearly formed intention' (1970, p. 177). The free man, for Hampshire, is an unspontaneous man, always aware of

exactly what he is doing and why he is doing it. It seems to me that the paradigm case of such a 'free' action would be something like buying shares on the stock market, or planning a train route from A to B. Hampshire's view of freedom is at the opposite pole to anything smacking of spontaneity or ambiguity. Compare Merleau-Ponty's remark about 'the happy universe of liberalism where one knows what one is doing and where, at least, one always keeps his conscience' (HT xxxvii).

6 Cf. Sartre: passion, in the Christian sense of the word, is 'a freedom which resolutely puts itself into a state of passiveness to obtain a certain transcendent effect by this sacrifice'. And generosity is a feeling 'which has its origin and its end in freedom' (1967, pp. 35 and 36).

7 Such mystifications can be used in a liberating way, in order to lead a person from one conceptual or experiential system to another by demonstrating the bankruptcy of the first system. Such demonstrations might be experienced as totally mystifying until the person is able and ready to see their sense. The point of the mystification is to allow the person to come to his own system in his own way and in his own time. This is a central aim of some forms of psycho-therapy. It is also a method very common in the teaching of Zen. Some of the stories in Alan Watts's book, *The Way of Zen*, illustrate this well. In one example Hui-k'o is seeking the way to enlightenment from his master Bodhidharma (1962, p. 107):

> Hui-k'o again and again asked Bodhidharma for instruction,
> but was always refused. Yet he continued to sit in meditation
> outside the cave, waiting patiently in the snow in the hope that
> Bodhidharma would at last relent. In desperation he finally cut
> off his left arm and presented it to Bodhidharma as a token of his
> agonized sincerity. At this Bodhidharma at last asked Hui-k'o what
> he wanted.
> 'I have no peace of mind', said Hui-k'o. 'Please pacify my
> mind.'
> 'Bring out your mind here before me', replied Bodhidharma,
> 'and I will pacify it!'
> 'But when I seek my own mind', said Hui-k'o, 'I cannot find it.'
> 'There!' snapped Bodhidharma, 'I have pacified your mind!'

8 The philosopher is, in fact, in a similar position to the psycho-therapist. The patient, according to Heaton (1972a, p. 43),

> believes that somehow or other he can be told how to be happy
> and how to love. That the way to these desirable states of being
> can be pointed out in words by the analyst and then be willed by
> the patient if he follows the rules.

The therapist, however, cannot tell the patient how to be happy or to love, since these are not things that can be put into words, or condensed into simple instructions. The therapist can only give the patient a clear view of his situation, without interfering with it, explaining it or deducing it. The analyst does this by doing what Wittgenstein argued philosophy should do. 'It must set limits between what can and cannot be said and thought "by working outwards through what can be thought" [or said] (*Tractatus* 4.114). So the analyst lets the patient say and think everything he can say or think, thereby helping him find the limits of thought and language' (p. 43).

6 Philosophy

1 Cf. Sartre (1969a). The distinction between radical reflection and introspection is very similar to Sartre's distinction between pure and impure reflection. Pure reflection is a sort of 'recognition' or 'recovery' of the pre-reflective, and 'it implies as the original motivation of the recovery a pre-reflective comprehension of what it wishes to recover' (p. 156). Hence, although it recognizes that it cannot coincide with the pre-reflective, pure reflection is not detached from the pre-reflective. Impure reflection, on the other hand, tries to coincide with the pre-reflective by considering consciousness as a series of 'psychic facts' to be collected. Hence impure reflection is in bad faith, since it is 'an abortive effort on the part of the for-itself to *be another* while *remaining itself*' (p. 161). That is, impure reflection creates a split in consciousness between reflection and the reflected-on.

2 Cf. Heidsieck on Merleau-Ponty's philosophy: 'Il ne s'agit pas en effet de savoir, mais de trouver.' 'Il ne s'agit pas de connaissance seulement, mais d'une *co-existence* qui soutient nos comportements, et dont le savoir n'est qu'un sous-produit' (1971, p. 51). See also the articles by Ihde (chapter 2) and Herbenick (chapter 4) in Gillan (1973) for discussions of Merleau-Ponty's conceptual models and their relation to lived experience.

7 Conclusion

1 Hence Gurwitsch's claim needs correcting. He argues that existential philosophers

> do not so much concern themselves with *the world of common experience, the world of daily life*, but rather with *man and his existence, his way of existing in the life-world*. This distinction . . . defines the line of demarcation which separates Husserl's work from that of the existentialists of every persuasion. (1970, p. 37)

According to Gurwitsch, then, existentialism is essentially a philosophical anthropology rather than a phenomenology. This is not, however, Ricoeur's view, who points out that Merleau-Ponty's phenomenology 'is transcendental before being existential; this means that it arises out of a mutation, a change of sign, the reduction whereby every question concerning being becomes a question concerning the *sense* of being' (1967, pp. 9–10). In my view Ricoeur rather than Gurwitsch is correct (at least as regards Merleau-Ponty). Existential phenomenology, as well as being concerned with man and his concrete mode of existence – which issues in those existential concepts of freedom, authenticity, the nature of human choice, politics, history, etc. – also incorporates the methodology and subject matter of classical phenomenology, in its application of the phenomenological reduction, and in its investigation of perception, knowledge, space, time, etc.

2 Cf. Thévanez (1962): 'Heidegger begins where Dostoevsky, Nietzsche, Kierkegaard, Malraux and Camus end. The empirical (ontic) phenomena of "death", "anxiety", etc. interest Heidegger only insofar as they reveal the ontological structure of the *Dasein*, of human experience' (p. 25). And Natanson (1974) on existential categories:

> dread, aloneness, and death are conceptual emblems for the experiential order which existentialism announces. . . . It is *through* such elements of structure that our lives are given placement and value. The emphasis is not *on* dread but on the experience which hides or reveals the world and its possibilities, an experience grounded in an immanent or self-conscious attendance to the threatening and the demonic. (p. 310)

3 This is the same judgment that the later Sartre returns on his earlier work, notably *Being and Nothingness*. My early work was a rationalist philosophy of consciousness . . . a monument to rationality. But in the end it becomes an irrationalism. because it cannot account rationally for those processes which are 'below' consciousness and which are also rational, but lived as irrational. (1969b, p. 50).

Bibliography

Works of Merleau-Ponty cited in the text

AD *Adventures of the Dialectic*, trans. J. Bien, Evanston, North-western University Press, 1973.

CL *Consciousness and the Acquisition of Language*, trans. H. J. Silverman, Evanston, Northwestern University Press, 1973.

EP *Éloge de la Philosophie*, Paris, Gallimard, 1953.

HT *Humanism and Terror*, trans. J. O'Neill, Boston, Beacon Press, 1969.

PM *The Primacy of Perception and Other Essays*, ed. J. M. Edie, Evanston, Northwestern University Press, 1964.

PP *Phenomenology of Perception*, trans. C. Smith, London, Routledge & Kegan Paul, 1962.

PW *The Prose of the World*, trans. J. O'Neill, London, Heinemann, 1974.

S *Signs*, trans. R. C. McCleary, Evanston, Northwestern University Press, 1964.

SB *The Structure of Behaviour*, trans. A. L. Fisher, Boston, Beacon Press, 1963.

SNS *Sense and Non-Sense*, trans. H. L. and P. A. Dreyfus, Evanston, Northwestern University Press, 1964.

TL *Themes from his Lectures*, trans. J. O'Neill, Evanston, Northwestern University Press, 1970.

VI *The Visible and the Invisible*, trans. A. Lingis, Evanston, Northwestern University Press, 1968.

Other works cited in the text

ARON, R. (1969). *Marxism and the Existentialists*, New York, Harper.

AUSTIN, J. L. (1965). *How to do Things with Words*, ed. J. O. Urmson, New York, Oxford University Press.

AYER, A. J. (1946). *Language, Truth and Logic*, Harmondsworth, Penguin.

BARTHES, R. (1973). *Mythologies*, trans. A. Lavers, London, Paladin.

197

BEAUVOIR, S. DE (1955). 'Merleau-Ponty et le pseudo-sartrisme', *Les Temps modernes*, vol. 10.

BEAUVOIR, S. DE (1965). *The Prime of Life*, Harmondsworth, Penguin.

BEAUVOIR, S. DE (1972). *The Second Sex*, Harmondsworth, Penguin.

BEAVIN, J., JACKSON, D., and WATZLAWICK, P. (1968). *Pragmatics of Human Communication*, London, Faber & Faber.

BERGER, P. L., and KELLNER, H. (1964). 'Marriage and the construction of reality', *Diogenes*, vol. 46.

BERGER, P. L., and LUCKMANN, T. (1966). *The Social Construction of Reality*, Harmondsworth, Penguin.

BLUM, A. F. (1971). 'Theorizing', in J. D. Douglas, ed., *Understanding Everyday Life*, London, Routledge & Kegan Paul.

BLUM, A. F., FOSS, D. C., MCHUGH, P., and RAFFEL, S. (1974). *On the Beginning of Social Inquiry*, London, Routledge & Kegan Paul.

BOLLNOW, O. F. (1967). 'Lived space', in N. Lawrence and D. O'Connor, eds, *Readings in Existential Phenomenology*, New Jersey, Prentice-Hall.

BOTTOMORE, T. B., and RUBEL, M., eds (1963). *Karl Marx: Selected Writings in Sociology and Social Philosophy*, Harmondsworth, Penguin.

BRUZINA, R. (1973). 'Merleau-Ponty and Husserl: the idea of science', in G. Gillan, ed., *The Horizons of the Flesh*, Southern Illinois University Press.

CAVELL, S. (1966). 'The availability of Wittgenstein's later philosophy', in G. Pitcher, ed., *Wittgenstein*, London, Macmillan.

COULTER, J. (1973). *Approaches to Insanity*, London, Martin Robertson.

DREYFUS, H. L., and TODES, S. J. (1962). 'The three worlds of Merleau-Ponty', *Philosophy and Phenomenological Research*, vol. 22, no. 4.

DURKHEIM, E. (1952). *Suicide*, London, Routledge & Kegan Paul.

EDIE, J. (1963). 'Expression and metaphor', *Philosophy and Phenomenological Research*, vol. 23, no. 4.

ESTERSON, A. (1972). *The Leaves of Spring*, Harmondsworth, Penguin.

FILMER, P., PHILLIPSON, M., SILVERMAN, D. and WALSH, D. (1972). *New Directions in Sociological Theory*, New York, Collier-Macmillan.

FINGARETTE, H. (1969). *Self-Deception*, London, Routledge & Kegan Paul.

FOUCAULT, M. (1970). *The Order of Things*, London, Tavistock.

GARFINKEL, H. (1967). *Studies in Ethnomethodology*, New Jersey, Prentice-Hall.

GELLNER, E. (1959). *Words and Things*, London, Gollancz.

GILLAN, G. (1973). *The Horizons of the Flesh: Critical Perspectives on the Thought of Merleau-Ponty*, Southern Illinois University Press.

GOFFMAN, E. (1961). *Encounters*, Harmondsworth, Penguin.

GOLDMANN, L. (1969). *The Human Sciences and Philosophy*, London, Cape.

GOULDNER, A. W. (1971). *The Coming Crisis in Western Sociology*, London, Heinemann.

GURWITSCH, A. (1964). *The Field of Consciousness*, Pittsburgh, Duquesne University Press.

GURWITSCH, A. (1970). 'Problems of the life-world', in M. Natanson, ed., *Phenomenology and Social Reality*, The Hague, Martinus Nijhoff.

HABERMAS, J. (1970a). 'On systematically distorted communication', *Inquiry*, vol. 13.

HABERMAS, J. (1970b). 'Knowledge and interest', in D. Emmet and A. MacIntyre, eds, *Sociological Theory and Philosophical Analysis*, London, Macmillan.

HABERMAS, J. (1971). *Towards a Rational Society*, London, Heinemann.

HAMPSHIRE, S. (1970). *Thought and Action*, London, Chatto & Windus.

HEATON, J. M. (1972a). 'Symposium on saying and showing in Heidegger and Wittgenstein', *Journal of the British Society for Phenomenology*, vol. 3, no. 1.

HEATON, J. M. (1972b). 'Insight in phenomenology and psychoanalysis', *Journal of the British Society for Phenomenology*, vol. 3, no. 2.

HEIDEGGER, M. (1967). *Being and Time*, trans. J. Macquarrie and E. Robinson, Oxford, Blackwell.

HEIDSIECK, F. (1971). *L'Ontologie de Merleau-Ponty*, Paris, Presses Universitaires de France.

HUSSERL, E. (1965). *Phenomenology and the Crisis of Philosophy*, trans. Q. Lauer, New York, Harper & Row.

HUXLEY, A. (1959). *The Doors of Perception and Heaven and Hell*, Harmondsworth, Penguin.

IHDE, D. (1973). 'Singing the world: language and perception', in G. Gillan, ed., *The Horizons of the Flesh*, Southern Illinois University Press.

KAMENKA, E. (1969). *Marxism and Ethics*, London, Macmillan.

KIERKEGAARD, S. (1959). *Either/Or* (2 vols), trans. D. F. and L. M. Swenson, New York, Anchor Books, Doubleday.

KOLAKOWSKI, L. (1972). *Positivist Philosophy: from Hume to the Vienna Circle*, Harmondsworth, Penguin.

KOVESI, J. (1967). *Moral Notions*, London, Routledge & Kegan Paul.

KULLMAN, M., and TAYLOR, C. (1958). 'The pre-objective world', *Review of Metaphysics*, vol. 12, no. 1.

KWANT, R. C. (1963). *The Phenomenological Philosophy of Merleau-Ponty*, Pittsburgh, Duquesne University Press.

KWANT, R. C. (1966). *From Phenomenology to Metaphysics, the Later Work of Merleau-Ponty*, Pittsburgh, Duquesne University Press.

LAING, R. D. (1965). *The Divided Self*, Harmondsworth, Penguin.

LAING, R. D. (1967). *The Politics of Experience and The Bird of Paradise*, Harmondsworth, Penguin.

LAING, R. D. (1969). *The Politics of the Family*, New York, CBC Publications.

LANGER, S. K. (1948). *Philosophy in a New Key*, New York, Penguin.

LEAT, D. (1972). 'Misunderstanding Verstehen', *Sociological Review*, vol. 20, no. 1.

LEVI-STRAUSS, C. (1966). *The Savage Mind*, London, Weidenfeld & Nicolson.

LOUCH, A. R. (1966). *Explanation and Human Action*, Oxford, Blackwell.

MCCURDY, J. (1972), 'The sensory media', *Journal of the British Society for Phenomenology*, vol. 3, no. 2.

MCHUGH, P. (1971). 'On the failure of positivism', in J. D. Douglas, ed., *Understanding Everyday Life*, London, Routledge & Kegan Paul.

MacINTYRE, A. (1971). *Against the Self-Images of the Age*, London, Duckworth.

199

MACQUARRIE, J. (1973). *Existentialism*, Harmondsworth, Penguin.

MANNHEIM, K. (1960). *Ideology and Utopia*, London, Routledge & Kegan Paul.

MANSER, A. R. (1963). 'Existence and ethics', *The Aristotelian Society*, supplementary vol. 37.

MARCUSE, H. (1967). *Reason and Revolution*, London, Routledge & Kegan Paul.

MARCUSE, H. (1968). *One Dimensional Man*, London, Sphere Books.

MARX, K. (1971). *Early Texts*, trans. and ed. D. McLellan, Oxford, Blackwell.

MASLOW, A. (1971). *The Farther Reaches of Human Nature*, Harmondsworth, Penguin.

MESZAROS, I. (1970). *Marx's Theory of Alienation*, London, Merlin Press.

MILLS, C. W. (1970). *The Sociological Imagination*, Harmondsworth, Penguin.

MUNSON, T. (1962). 'Wittgenstein's phenomenology', *Philosophy and Phenomenological Research*, vol. 23.

NATANSON, M. (1974). *Phenomenology, Role, and Reason*, Springfield, Illinois, Charles C. Thomas.

OLAFSON, F. A. (1971). 'Authenticity and obligation', in M. Warnock, ed., *Sartre: a Collection of Critical Essays*, New York, Anchor Books, Doubleday.

PARK, Y. (1970). 'An ontological interpretation of the concept of "expression" in the philosophy of Merleau-Ponty', unpublished Ph.D. thesis, University of Southern California (University Microfilms 71-7731).

PITKIN, H. F. (1972). *Wittgenstein and Justice*, London, University of California Press.

PLANT, R. (1970). *Social and Moral Theory in Casework*, London, Routledge & Kegan Paul.

PLANT, R. (1974). *Community and Ideology: an Essay in Applied Social Philosophy*, London, Routledge & Kegan Paul.

POGGI, G. (1972). *Images of Society: Essays on the Sociological Theories of Tocqueville, Marx and Durkheim*, London, Oxford University Press.

POLLNER, M. (1974). 'Sociological and commonsense models of the labelling process', in R. Turner, ed., *Ethnomethodology*, Harmondsworth, Penguin.

RICOEUR, P. (1967). 'New developments in phenomenology in France: the phenomenology of language', *Social Research*, vol. 34.

RUDNER, R. S. (1966). *Philosophy of Social Science*, New Jersey, Prentice-Hall.

RYLE, G. (1949). *The Concept of Mind*, Harmondsworth, Penguin.

SARTRE, J.-P. (1956). 'Existentialism is an humanism', in W. Kaufmann, ed., *Existentialism from Dostoevsky to Sartre*, Cleveland, Meridian Books.

SARTRE, J.-P. (1957). *The Transcendence of the Ego*, trans. F. Williams and R. Kirkpatrick, New York, Noonday Press.

SARTRE, J.-P. (1965a). *Nausea*, Harmondsworth, Penguin.

SARTRE, J.-P. (1965b). 'Merleau-Ponty', in *Situations*, trans. B. Eisler, Greenwich, Conn., Fawcett.

SARTRE, J.-P. (1967). *What is Literature?*, trans. B. Frechtman, London, Methuen.

SARTRE, J.-P. (1968). *Literary and Philosophical Essays*, trans. Annette Michelson, London, Hutchinson.

SARTRE, J.-P. (1969a). *Being and Nothingness*, trans. H. Barnes, London, Methuen.

SARTRE, J.-P. (1969b). 'Itinərary of a thought', interview with J.-P. Sartre, *New Left Review*, no. 58.

SARTRE, J.-P. (1970). 'Intentionality: a fundamental idea of Husserl's phenomenology', *Journal of the British Society for Phenomenology*, vol. 1, no. 2.

SARTRE, J.-P. (1972). *The Psychology of Imagination*, London, Methuen.

SCHMUELI, E. (1973). 'Pragmatic, existentialist and phenomenological interpretations of Marxism', *Journal of the British Society for Phenomenology*, vol. 4, no. 2.

SCHUTZ, A. (1964). *Collected Papers II*, ed. A. Brodersen, The Hague, Martinus Nijhoff.

SCHUTZ, A. (1966). *Collected Papers III*, ed. I. Schutz, The Hague, Martinus Nijhoff.

SCHUTZ, A. (1967a). *The Phenomenology of the Social World*, trans. G. Walsh and F. Lehnert, London, Heinemann.

SCHUTZ, A. (1967b). *Collected Papers I*, ed. M. Natanson, The Hague, Martinus Nijhoff.

SCHUTZ, A. (1970a). 'Concept and theory formation in the social sciences', in D. Emmet and A. MacIntyre, eds, *Sociological Theory and Philosophical Analysis*, London, Macmillan.

SCHUTZ, A. (1970b). 'The problem of rationality in the social world', in D. Emmet and A. MacIntyre, eds, *Sociological Theory and Philosophical Analysis*, London, Macmillan.

SMITH, C. (1964a). *Contemporary French Philosophy*, London, Methuen.

SMITH, C. (1964b). 'The notion of object in the phenomenology of Merleau-Ponty', *Philosophy*, vol. 34.

SMITH, D. (1974). 'K. is mentally ill', unpublished paper.

SPICKER, S. (1973). 'Inner time and lived-through time: Husserl and Merleau-Ponty', *Journal of the British Society for Phenomenology*, vol. 4, no. 3.

SPIEGELBERG, H. (1971). *The Phenomenological Movement: a Historical Introduction* (2 vols), The Hague, Martinus Nijhoff.

THEVANEZ, P. (1962). *What is Phenomenology?*, Chicago, Quadrangle.

TURNER, R. (1974). 'Words, utterances and activities', in R. Turner, ed., *Ethnomethodology*, Harmondsworth, Penguin.

WAEHLENS, A. DE (1970). *Une Philosophie de l'ambiguité: l'existentialisme de Merleau-Ponty*, Bibliothèque Philosophique de Louvain.

WATTS, A. W. (1972). *The Way of Zen*, Harmondsworth, Penguin.

WILD, J. (1967). 'Freedom and responsibility', in N. Lawrence and D. O'Connor, eds, *Readings in Existential Phenomenology*, New Jersey, Prentice-Hall.

WINCH, P. (1958). *The Idea of a Social Science and its Relation to Philosophy*, London, Routledge & Kegan Paul.

BIBLIOGRAPHY

WITTGENSTEIN, L. (1961). *Tractatus Logico-Philosophicus*, trans. D. F. Pears and B. F. McGuinness, London, Routledge & Kegan Paul.

WITTGENSTEIN, L. (1966). *Lectures and Conversations on Aesthetics, Psychology and Religious Belief*, Berkeley and Los Angeles, University of California Press.

WITTGENSTEIN, L. (1968). *Philosophical Investigations*, trans. G. E. M. Anscombe, Oxford, Blackwell.

WITTGENSTEIN, L. (1974). *On Certainty*, trans. G. E. M. Anscombe and G. H. von Wright, Oxford, Blackwell.

WRONG, D. (1961). 'The over-socialized conception of man in modern sociology', *American Sociological Review*, vol. 26.

YOLTON, J. (1954). 'The dualism of mind', *Journal of Philosophy*, vol. LI, no. 6.

ZANER, R. (1971). *The Problem of Embodiment*, The Hague, Martinus Nijhoff.

ZIMMERMAN, D. H., and POLLNER, M. (1971). 'The everyday world as a phenomenon', in J. D. Douglas, ed., *Understanding Everyday Life*, London, Routledge & Kegan Paul.

Note: a comprehensive bibliography of works on Merleau-Ponty can be found in *Journal of the British Society for Phenomenology*, vol. 2, no. 3, October 1971, pp. 99–112, by Francis H. Lapointe.

Index

action, 151, 171, 173
Adventures of the Dialectic, 106, 107, 108
alienation, 96, 97–100, 191
ambiguity, 44, 135–40; and ambivalence, 136–7; and equivocation, 137–8; and freedom, 122; of history, 102; of perception, 38, 135; of self-knowledge, 127; of social phenomena, 88–9; of speech, 66–72
analytic and concrete inquiry, 164–7
Aristotle, 193
Aron, R., 93–6, 102, 103
art, 33, 130; and philosophy, 153–5
Austin, J. L., 65
authenticity, 73–5, 125–30, 193
Ayer, A. J., 111

bad faith, 129
Barthes, R., 90
Beauvoir, S. de, 88, 179, 193
Beavin, J., 138
behaviour, 14, 151; empiricist account of, 10–12
behaviourism, 10, 50, 79, 81
Being, 46–7
being and nothingness, 179–81
Being and Nothingness, 179, 196
being-in-the-world, 14–16
Berger, P. L.: and Kellner, H., 61; and Luckmann, T., 61, 86–7, 90

Bergson, Henri, 152, 185
bias, 165–6
Blum, A. F., 75, 77, 78–9, 83, 164–7, 169, 170–1, 175, 176, 177
body, 21–5; body image, 22; and expression, 45; and intentionality, 19–20, 29; and knowledge, 22, 110, 158; and mind (or consciousness), 23–5, 103, 183–4, 185–6; and movement, 38; and perception, 27–8; phenomenal body, 22, 24, 28, 183; reversibility of, 46; and speech, 56; and understanding, 151–2; and world, 46–7
Bollnow, O. F., 38
Bottomore, T. B., and Rubel, M., 96–7
Bruzina R., 7

Camus, A., 196
Capital, 96, 97
Cavell, S., 189
centre and periphery, 125–6
Cézanne, 33, 46, 122
choice, 18, 123, 191
class consciousness, 89, 102; universal class, 105
Les Communistes et la paix, 118
consciousness: and being, 179–81; and embodiment, 21, 185–6; as expressing, 43–5; and *Gestalt*, 14; and intentionality, 7, 17; and

introspection, 145–6; non-positing, 150; as perceptual, 42–3; and rationalism, 13; as spontaneity or passivity, 184; and time, 42; and world, 10; *see also* reflection
Consciousness and the Acquisition of Language, 187
constancy hypothesis, 25
contexts of discovery and validation, 81–2
contingency and necessity, 150–1
Coulter, J., 183

Darwin, Charles, 51
Descartes, R., 6, 12
description and evaluation, 77, 79, 111–16, 192
dialectic, 139–40
distance, 37–8
The Divided Self, 1
The Doors of Perception, 184
Dostoevsky, F., 142, 196
dreaming, 33, 36, 44, 161
Dreyfus, H. L., and Todes, S. J., 32
Durkheim, É., 76, 80–1

Edie, J., 74, 187
Either/Or, 138
embodiment, 23–4, 27–8, 56–7, 125, 132–4
Emmet, D., 192
emotions (and feelings), 7, 117, 126–7, 154, 180–1
empiricism, 10–12, 13–14, 21, 25–6, 36, 40, 50, 77, 79, 145, 149
Esterson, A., 157
ethnomethodology, 3, 4, 62, 65–6, 67, 68–71, 72, 125, 175, 189, 189–90
existence, 9, 16; and essence, 9; and expression, 44; and spatiality, 37
existential: categories, 196; ethics, 110–11, 118, 119, 124–5, 134, 135, 140–2
existentialism, 4, 9, 93–6, 124, 140, 141, 192–3, 195, 196
experience, 152, 181; empiricist account of, 11–12; individual and

general, 85–6, 185; phenomenological understanding of, 41; positivist account of, 111, 116; social, 85–6, 92, 95–6
expression, 43–5, 50–1, 155
Eye and Mind, 45

Feiffer, J., 136–7
Feuerbach, Ludwig, 96
Filmer, P., 65, 80
Fingarette, H., 128
flesh, 46
form of life, 165, 176, 177
Foucault, M., 90
freedom, 88, 93, 94, 99, 119–25, 133, 151, 170, 179, 181, 190, 192, 193–4; and moral rules, 124–5; and responsibility, 122–4
free will and determinism, 120–1
Freud, S., 4, 44, 90, 129, 151
Fundierung, 34, 150

Garfinkel, H., 65–6, 68, 69–71, 87, 189
gaze, 99, 180
Gellner, E., 72
Gestalt, 14, 23; psychology, 4, 28
Gillan, G., 59, 195
glossing, 68–72
Goffman, E., 189, 190–1
Goldmann, L., 90, 190
Gouldner, A. W., 84
El Greco, 24, 122
Gurwitsch, A., 185–6, 195

Habermas, J., 5, 75, 109
hallucinations, 36, 37
Hampshire, S., 193–4
Heaton, J. M., 4, 133, 194–5
Hegel, F., 4, 6, 93, 94, 100, 192
Heidegger, M., 4, 6, 9, 108, 154, 167, 187, 196
Heidsieck, F., 195
Hemingway, Ernest, 133
Herbenick, Raymond, 195
historical materialism, 96–8, 102, 103–5, 191
history: and Marxism, 93, 96–7; philosophy of, 106; understanding, 100, 101–3, 108–9

humanism, 105–6, 134–5
Humanism and Terror, 105, 106, 107, 108, 118
human nature, 93, 119, 142
Hume, David, 83, 117
Husserl, E., 4, 6–10, 12, 17, 77, 158, 183, 185, 195; and phenomenology, 6–8
Huxley, A., 184

ideal types, 172
Ihde, D., 50, 195
indexicality, 71, 175
insight, 133
institutionalization, origins of, 86–7
integration, 23–4, 39, 140
intentional arc, 20
intentionality, 7, 16–21, 181, 183; and intentions, 17, 188–9; and speech, 53–4
intersubjectivity, 41, 52–3, 85, 86–7
inter-world, 123–4, 179
introspection, 145–6

Kamenka, E., 191, 192
Kant, I., 6, 12, 183
Kierkegaard, S., 4, 93, 138, 196
knowledge: of body, 22, 110, 158; non-thematic, 157–62; positivist, 76–7, 85, 111, 115; social scientific, 172–3
Kolakowski, L., 76, 111, 116
Kovesi, J., 112, 114, 115, 141
Kullman, M., and Taylor, C., 143
Kwant, R. C., 46, 57, 183

Lacan, J., 73
Laing, R. D., 1, 139, 186
Langer, S. K., 45, 154
language: and art, 154; limits of, 195; positivist view of, 77, 115, 174; and self-knowledge, 127; and speech, 58; traditional theories of, 116; *see also* speech
language-game, 63, 176, 177
Leat, D., 82
Lebenswelt, 8–9, 32–3
Lévi-Strauss, C., 53, 90
linguistic philosophy, 2–3; *see also*

ordinary language philosophy; Wittgenstein
Louch, A. R., 79, 104, 112
Lukács, György, 98, 104, 105, 106

McCurdy, J., 36
Machiavelli, N., 134
McHugh, P., 156
MacIntyre, A., 141
Macquarrie, J., 9
Mallarmé, Stéphane, 61
Malraux, André, 196
Mannheim, K., 104
Manser, A. R., 140
Marcuse, H., 189, 191
Marx, K., 4, 90, 93, 94, 95, 96, 97, 98, 99, 103, 104, 106, 110, 119, 121, 151, 191, 192, 193
Marxism, 4, 164; as classic, 107; and determinism, 96–8, 102, 104, 191; and freedom, 119; Merleau-Ponty's relation to, 105–9; and morality, 105–7; and phenomenology, 92–105, 110; and values, 118–19, 192
Maslow, A., 131, 133
meaning, 52, 59, 60, 136, 171, 173; and cause, 82–4; and consciousness, 43–5, 171; and embodiment, 50; and freedom, 121–2; of history, 101, 106; immanent, 150; and intention, 188–9; and positivism, 81–4; social, 80–1, 90, 190; and use, 64
Meszaros, I., 191
Mills, C. W., 77–8
moral discourse, 117
motivational relationship, 150
motives, 83–4, 166
movement, 38, 158–61
Munson, T., 176
music, 154
myth, 36, 44, 90, 147

Natanson, M., 174, 196
natural attitude, 8–9, 33, 37, 69, 157, 184
naturalism, 6–7
nature/culture distinction, 150

Nausea, 132, 169, 179
Nietzsche, F., 93, 94, 131, 142, 196
Nizan, Paul, 131
nominalism, rule of, 76–7, 111

object and world, 30–2
Olafson, F. A., 141
On the Beginning of Social Inquiry, 164
ontology, 46–7, 164, 192; and ontic, 169, 196
ordinary language philosophy, 72, 189; *see also* linguistic philosophy; Wittgenstein
other persons, 40–2; and morality, 117; and self-knowledge, 127

Park, Y., 33, 45, 47
Parsons, T., 78
peak experiences, 133
perception, 25–35, 116, 151, 169–70; ambiguity of, 38, 135; and illusion, 31; and movement, 160; perceptual faith, 31, 147; primacy of, 34–5; and speech, 51–2; three worlds of, 32–4; and time, 28, 38–9; and values, 116–17
performatives, 65
phantasy, 186
phantom limb, 15–16, 169
phenomenal field (or world), 28, 160–1, 183–4
phenomenalism, rule of, 76, 77, 111
phenomenon (in phenomenology), 7, 9, 168
phenomenological reduction, *see* reduction
phenomenology: of Husserl, 6–8; of Merleau-Ponty, 4–5, 8–10; and ontology, 46–7; of phenomenology, 144; and social science, 84–6, 90–1, 171–5; transcendental and descriptive, 7, 91, 167–70
Phenomenology of Perception, 10, 15, 18, 35, 46, 58, 59, 92, 179
Phenomenology of the Social World, 171, 172
Philosophical Investigations, 63–5, 176

philosophy, 5, 49–50, 177–9; and art, 153–5; and conceptual revision, 149–53; and equivocation, 137–8; and ethics, 110–11, 118, 140; and experience, 1, 148; and grammar (in Wittgenstein), 176–7; and life, 142; and madness, 148; paradox of, 143–4, 162–3; and psycho-therapy, 194–5; and reflection, 143–9, 154–5; as representation, 153–5; and social science, 84–5, 164, 171–5; and speech, 148–9, 154–5
Philosophy of Social Science, 81–2
Piaget, Jean, 55
Pitkin, H. F., 64, 112, 117, 189, 190
Plant, R., 3, 192–3
Plato, 108
Poggi, G., 191
Pollner, M., 3
Politzer, 44
positivism, 2, 3–4, 6, 73, 76–85, 111–16, 149, 156, 163, 165, 167, 168, 174, 175
Positivist Philosophy: from Hume to the Vienna Circle, 76
praxis, 17, 97
pre-objective world, 32–4, 143
primordial faith, 31, 157
psycho-analysis, 4, 164

rationalism, 12–14, 21, 25–7, 36, 40–1, 50, 56, 59, 102, 116, 145–6, 149, 173, 179, 196
rationality, 34–5, 66, 116, 128, 189, 196
real and imaginary, 44, 186–7
reason, 7
reduction: eidetic, 8; in ethnomethódology, 175; phenomenological, 7–9, 169
reflection: and introspection, 145–6; philosophical, 143–9, 154–5; and pre-reflective, 143–9, 157–63; radical, 146–9; rationalist, 13, 145–6
reflexivity, 65–6, 79, 93, 147, 165, 167, 174, 189–90
relativism, 103–5

Ricoeur, P., 59, 187, 195
role, 87–8, 190–1
Rudner, R. S., 81–2
rules, 53, 66, 71, 124–5, 189
Ryle, G., 13, 21, 162

St Augustine, 13
Saint-Exupéry, Antoine de, 133
Sartre, J.-P., 5, 9, 12, 44, 52, 75, 88, 93, 94, 99, 108, 117, 118, 119, 120, 123–4, 129, 131, 132, 135, 140, 169, 179–82, 184, 187, 192, 194, 195, 196
Saussure, Ferdinand de, 58, 59, 187
schizophrenia, 1, 20–1, 147, 148
Schmueli, E., 94–6
Schneider, Mr, 19–20, 53–4, 99
Schutz, A., 3, 78, 171–5, 187
scientific world, 32–3
sedimentation, 23, 57–60, 64, 67–8, 86–7, 120, 181
self, 35, 40, 184; -deception, 127–9, 136, 169; -knowledge, 127; -revelation, 127–9, 193; and others (for Sartre), 180–1
sense and signification, 51
sexuality, 18, 42, 151, 152, 161
situation, 87–9, 123–4; and freedom, 121; and truth, 105
Skinner, B. F., 79
Smith, C., 20, 117, 181
Smith, D., 66
snubs, 167
social science, 3–4, 76, 77, 81, 84–6, 90–1, 164, 171–5
society, 85; and the individual, 95–6; as intersubjective reality, 86–7; for positivism, 78; and situation, 87–9; and structure, 89–91; and transcendence, 170
sociology, 76, 78, 81–2, 87, 92, 173, 175
space, 35–7, 47, 169
speech: ambiguity of, 66–72, 135–6; authentic, 73–5; and the body, 56; for ethnomethodology, 65–6; gestural and conceptual levels of, 54–6; and intentionality, 53–4; and intersubjectivity, 52–3; and

language, 58; and perception, 51–2; phenomenology of, 48–52; for positivism, 165; as praxis, 60–2, 64; and reflexivity, 65–6; and sedimentation, 57–60; and silence, 48, 51; and structure, 58–60; and thought, 56–7, 67; and transcendence, 170; for Wittgenstein, 62–5; and the world, 72–3; see also language
Spicker, S., 39
Spiegelberg, H., 6
spontaneity, 130–2, 139
Stendhal, H. B., 132
structure, 64, 89–91, 100–1, 103; and sedimentation, 57–60
Structure of Behaviour, 10, 14
Studies in Ethnomethodology, 65–6
style, 17, 154
subject/object distinction, 28–9, 40, 46, 59, 95, 168, 180–1

tacit cogito, 46, 59
thematization, 158–62
Thévanez, P., 196
thought: limits of, 162, 195; objective, 150, 158–62; and speech, 56–7
time, 38–40, 42, 127, 151, 169
totality, 93, 100–3
Tractatus, 62–4, 77, 195
tragedy, 135
transcendence, 16, 88, 94–5, 121; problem of, 169–70
The Transcendence of the Ego, 184
transcendental and descriptive, 164–82; see also under phenomenology
truth, 35, 100, 132; and adequacy, 155–7; birth of, 155; and dialectic, 140; and relativism, 103–5; in a situation, 105
Turner, R., 65

unconscious, 44
understanding, 151–2

values, 125; and facts, 116–19; situational, 126, 128

Verstehen, 81–2, 146, 174, 190
The Visible and the Invisible, 45, 179

Waehlens, A. de, 24, 144
Watts, A., 194
The Way of ten, 194
Weber, M., 82, 100, 101, 171
Wild, J., 123
will, 18
Winch, P., 53
Wittgenstein, L., 2, 3, 9, 53, 61, 62–5, 66, 72, 75, 77, 156, 157, 162, 165, 175–9, 189, 190, 195
world: and body, 45–7; and consciousness, 10; and intentionality, 20–1; and object, 30–2; and speech, 72–3; three worlds of perception, 32–4
Wrong, D., 87

Yolton, J., 183

Zaner, R., 143, 144, 147, 158, 161, 180, 181, 183, 185–6
Zeno's paradoxes, 160
Zimmerman, D. H., and Pollner, M., 175